EIGHTH
CENTURY
PROPHETS

EIGHTH CENTURY PROPHETS

A Social Analysis

D. N. PREMNATH

CHALICE
PRESS

ST. LOUIS, MISSOURI

Biblical quotations, unless otherwise marked, are author's translation.

Bible quotations marked NRSV are from the *New Revised Standard Version Bible*, copyright 1989, Division of Christian Education of the National Council of the Churches of Christ in the United States of America. Used by permission. All rights reserved.

Those quotations marked RSV are from the *Revised Standard Version of the Bible*, copyright 1952, [2nd edition, 1971] by the Division of Christian Education of the National Council of the Churches of Christ in the United States of America. Used by permission. All rights reserved.

Scripture quotations marked (NEB) are from the *New English Bible*, copyright Oxford University Press and Cambridge University Press 1961, 1970. Reprinted by permission.

Cover art: Christie's Images/Superstock
Cover design: Grady Gunter
Interior design: Hui-chu Wang
Art direction: Elizabeth Wright

This book is printed on acid-free, recycled paper.

Visit Chalice Press on the World Wide Web at
www.chalicepress.com

10 9 8 7 6 5 4 3 2 1   03 04 05 06 07 08

Library of Congress Cataloging–in–Publication Data

Eighth century prophets : a social analysis / D.N. Premnath.– 1st ed.
    p. cm.
Includes bibliographical references and index.
  ISBN 0-8272-0817-0 (alk. paper)
  1. Bible. O.T. Amos–Social scientific criticism.   2. Bible. O.T. Hosea–Social scientific criticism.   3. Bible. O.T. Micah–Social scientific criticism.   4. Bible. O.T. Isaiah–Social scientific criticism.   5. Land tenure–Palestine–History.   6. Land tenure–Biblical teaching. I. Title.
  BS1585.6.L28P74 2003
  224'.067–dc22

                                                    2003014872

Printed in the United States of America

Dedicated
To
My Parents

Easter Rakshanya Das (1918–1997)
and
Saraswathy Das (1924–)

Contents

Preface

The basic groundwork for this book comes from my doctoral dissertation submitted to the Graduate Theological Union, Berkeley, California, in 1984. The passage of time has brought challenges and rewards. It was challenging and at times frustrating to update and revise something that was written so long ago. On a more mundane level, the tedious task of transferring materials composed originally on a typewriter was a significant chore. But thank God for scanners. It made my job a lot easier. Nonetheless, the updating of scholarship was a daunting task. It involved not only biblical and archaeological fields but also social sciences. Fortunately (for me) or unfortunately, the updating with regard to peasant studies was minimal. The study of peasants and peasant societies reached its peak in the 1960s and 1970s. The conceptual discussion has not seen much progress in recent years. In fact, serious questions have been raised in some circles within the field of social sciences about the relevance of continuing to use the category of "peasants." Despite the noblest of intentions, there is always the possibility that one may fail to do full justice to the breadth of scholarship pertinent to this field. The present work may not be an exception to this.

The updating and revision process has been gratifying for many reasons. First, the updating in the area of the social history of eighth-century Israel and Judah, particularly in relation to the archaeological information, has been helpful. I feel that now I have a stronger case to present. Second, over the years I have benefited from the critique and input from colleagues and students both here in the U.S.A. and in India. Using the materials in classroom over the years has helped me to refine my thinking and articulation. The radically revised arrangement and presentation of the textual materials in chapter 4 is clear evidence of that.

Several people have played a role, explicitly or implicitly, in the making of this book. First and foremost, I wish to acknowledge my profound debt of gratitude to my teachers–Norman Gottwald, Marvin Chaney, and Robert Coote among others–for introducing me to the social scientific method of study. Their support and guidance have been a source of encouragement all these years. In particular, those familiar with the research and writings of Marvin Chaney will immediately recognize his influence in these pages. I am deeply grateful for his guidance, not only during the dissertation stages of this project but also his continued interest in and support of my work, and, above all, for simply being a friend. I am also thankful to Walter Brueggemann for his writings on the prophets, which have enabled me to see beyond the social analysis to issues of relevance for contemporary faith and practice. I am indebted to my parents for their wisdom in life and for what I am today. To these and others, I remain in debt. And finally, I am grateful to Jon L. Berquist, senior academic editor at Chalice Press, for believing in this project and providing quality editorial assistance throughout the process.

Introduction

Scope

The object of this study is to examine evidences of, and allusions to, the process of land accumulation (latifundialization) in the oracles that pertain to the eighth century B.C.E. in the books of Amos, Hosea, Isaiah, and Micah, and to explore the significance of the prophetic message and vision in today's context. Latifundialization (derived from the term *latifundia*, meaning large estates) can be generally defined as the process of land accumulation in the hands of a few wealthy elite to the deprivation of the peasantry. In this study, latifundialization will be analyzed in its systemic interrelatedness.

Central to the process of latifundialization is the accumulation of land. However, there are multiple dimensions and causative factors pertinent to this phenomenon. They relate broadly to the systems of production (e.g., factors and nature of production) and distribution (e.g., consumption and systems of exchange and distribution). Changes affecting these areas will be analyzed. Despite attempts to enumerate specifics and nuance details, it should be stated clearly that the net result of the process of land accumulation is the steady worsening of the plight of the peasantry, which is directly related to the loss of easy and secure access to arable land. The peasants' access to cultivable land, particularly with reference to the cost involved, terms under which such access is available, and the security of such an arrangement, are dictated and/or controlled by the system(s) of land tenure. In other words, the bottom line is that land tenure arrangements determine the pattern of how the surplus/income from the agricultural enterprise gets distributed within the society (Dorner 1971:15). The various aspects of the process of land accumulation and factors that contribute to it are dealt with in chapter 1. The purpose of this chapter is not only to provide a general background for

1

understanding the process of latifundialization but also to formulate categories to be used in the construction of a working hypothesis for the social history of eighth-century Israel and Judah.

Chapter 2 offers an overview of Israel's social history leading up to the eighth century, focusing on aspects pertinent to the issue of land.

Chapter 3 proposes a working hypothesis for the social history of eighth-century Israel and Judah at a systemic level, examining the interrelatedness of structures and functions of the various systems of the society in particular reference to the growth of large estates. This chapter serves an important methodological purpose. One of the common tendencies in the study of the prophets is the circular argument of attempting to analyze the prophetic oracles in light of information gathered from the oracles themselves. The hypothetical reconstruction undertaken in this study will draw upon information from the field of archaeology, study of nonprophetic texts in the Hebrew Bible, information from extrabiblical texts, and the use of models and insights from the field of social sciences. In this regard, the current work is indebted to and builds upon some excellent pioneering work done by scholars such as Chaney (1983; 1986; 1989) and Coote (1981). From a methodological point of view, the purpose is to be in constant dialogue with various avenues of information and to move to higher levels of integration. The working hypothesis of the systemic reality of the eighth-century Israelite and Judahite societies will be tested against the information from the prophetic texts.

Chapter 4 is devoted to examining the prophetic oracles themselves from Amos, Hosea, Isaiah, and Micah in relation to the various aspects of the process of latifundialization. Passages are grouped according to each aspect they address in either explicit or implicit terms. This analysis tests extensively the hypothetical reconstruction of the systemic reality of the eighth-century Israel and Judah proposed in chapter 3. The purpose of this analysis is to demonstrate how significant aspects of the oracles not covered by previous exegesis can be explained and/or illumined by the hypothesized process of latifundialization and also to show how this hypothesis has more consistent explanatory power than alternative analyses that have been proposed.

The concluding chapter explores the function and significance of the prophetic message and vision for today's context.

Methodology

A wide variety of approaches parade under the banner "sociological." It is important to clarify what kind of sociological approach is undertaken in this study. The intent of a particular study shapes its methodological emphasis and research strategy. The intent of this study is to gain access to the social world of the eighth-century Israelite and Judahite societies through systemic analysis and to use that as a basis for interpreting the prophetic oracles. The key operative word is "systemic." Systemic analysis focuses on the dynamic interrelatedness of various structures and functions of a society. In this sense, systemic sociology is macrosociological in character. By focusing on the systems in a society, one is able to discern not only a complex of interdependencies among parts, components, and processes that manifest a certain relationship, but also the interdependency between the complex and its surrounding environment. The nature of relationships can be more adequately understood if the whole complex of multiple dependencies is taken into account.

The twin foci of the systemic sociological approach employed in this work can be characterized thus: comparative and historical. The comparative dimension of systemic sociology leads one to look at the society not only in terms of interrelated structures and functions but also to compare it with other societies. The historical dimension of systemic sociology focuses on significant changes that modify the society as a whole. The systems are studied not only in their interdependence at any given time but also in their evolution over a period of time.

Comparative

The present study is dependent on comparative studies of agrarian societies, past and present, from the fields of anthropology and sociology. Comparison is necessitated by the fact that ancient Israel and Judah belong to the genus of agrarian societies. Agrarian societies are defined as those in which the principle means of subsistence is the cultivation of fields using the plow and traction animals, but with no significant access to inanimate sources of energy (Lenski and Lenski 1974:90–91). Peasants or rural cultivators form the majority of the population.

The problem one faces in the study of the process of latifundialization is the lack of a body of theoretical knowledge or a set of agreed-upon categories. What is available is a wide range of specific studies dealing with this subject with reference to different countries/societies. Many of these studies were published as part of the explosion of peasant studies seen in the 1960s and 1970s due to industrial growth coupled with a global awareness and interest in developing countries (Shanin 1987a:1). Not much new scholarship has been generated in the study of this area since the 1970s. In fact, serious questions have been raised concerning the validity of the use of the concept of "peasantry" itself. One has to wade through a plethora of details before distilling a set of conceptual categories to analyze the subject. In addition, it is also true that many of the specific treatments tend to lack a general theoretical framework. What is attempted in this study, in a modest way, is a conscious effort to bridge the gap between the empirical and theoretical aspects.

When a comparative analysis entailing data from present societies is used in the study of societies of antiquity, critics are quick to challenge the appropriateness of using information about modern societies to study ancient societies and societal development. From a methodological point of view, this question needs to be addressed. The comparative analysis can be of immense help in many ways. First of all, the comparative method suggests what kind of information to seek. By establishing a paradigm of categories on the basis of comparative study, one can establish a list of things to examine. Second, it can shed light on particular aspects, thus enabling one to clarify variations and nuance positions. Third, comparisons can help in reinforcing and fortifying conclusions. Wherever information is available, common categories might help to reinforce and verify conclusions. Where there is lack of data, these categories might provide useful clues to examine materials and infer details for a hypothetical reconstruction. Fourth, it provides opportunities to test hypotheses (Lenski 1976:559–60). Fifth, a comparative perspective can lead to asking useful and sometimes new questions. Sixth, at an important level, comparisons can serve as an effective check on explanations and conclusions that may have been taken for granted. Seventh, comparisons can lead to new generalizations (Moore 1966:xiii–xiv). Finally, even if contradictions were to emerge in the course of the analysis, it should help in making a more refined and hence a more realistic assessment of a particular society. On a comparative basis, it is possible to speak in terms of a generic agrarian societal type, focusing on their social and economic organization. In such a characterization, it must be recognized that there may be variations among societies. However, the internal variations within a society may often be greater than those between any two such societies. While emphasizing the importance of applying generic patterns and categories to the study of Israelite and Judahite societies, it is important to acknowledge that historical evidence may demonstrate that these societies differed from the generic type in one or more details.

It must be clarified that the comparative method is only one of the tools employed in this study. Archaeology and information from historical documents concerning the biblical period in question are some of the important tools that provide data on the social and cultural systems of Israel and Judah in the eighth century B.C.E.

Historical

Most historical studies of Israel and Judah can be characterized as particularistic. Historical particularism views history primarily in relation to the part played by important individuals and events. In this type of approach, there is very little interest in a systemic integration. In contrast to this, generic history attempts to study the changes that modify the society as a whole. In the process of social evolution, both specific and systemic changes occur. The latter, however, are less frequent. In the field of social sciences, there is a body of theory dealing with the process of social evolution.[1] This body of theory can provide valuable information for the recognition and explanation of systemic change. The key to understanding

---

[1]Parsons's emphasis (1977) is on the structural-functional analysis as a way of studying how the interrelated and interacting units of a system contribute to the development and maintenance of that system. The theoretical perspective represented by Lenski (Lenski and Lenski: 1974) can be described as a structural-functional-ecological-evolutionary approach, which is sometimes referred to as an ecological-evolutionary approach for convenience. This approach developed in response to the growing awareness that the structural-functional analysis alone cannot explain two crucial aspects of human life: change and conflict. The ecological-evolutionary approach concentrates on three aspects: (1) relationships within and among human societies, (2) relationship between societies and their biophysical environments, and (3) the processes of sociocultural change and development. The distinctness of Marvin Harris's approach is summarized in his phrase "cultural materialism." The aim of cultural materialism is to account for "the origin, maintenance and change of the global inventory of sociocultural differences and similarities" (1979:27; see also 1968). In this sense, Harris focuses on the general evolution on a broad basis, seeking to transcend disciplinary, ethnic, and national boundaries.

systemic change is to isolate the nature and causes of social change. This method of social history provides useful criteria to periodize history in terms of systemic watersheds, which can provide a healthy balance to the particularistic approach. The detailed smaller database of the historical particularist and the broader scheme of the generic comparativist are both integral and important to a sound historiography for the purpose of informing and keeping each other honest.

1

Understanding the Growth of Large Estates

Very often latifundialization is described in terms of the concentration of land holdings in the hands of a few. While it is true that that is the central phenomenon, there are various particulars/causative factors related to it. Instead of reducing it to a single phenomenon or factor, a more useful way of dealing with the subject is to get a fuller picture by focusing on multiple dimensions. Understanding the process of latifundialization entails not only delineating some key conceptual categories to provide a general frame of reference but also developing a catalog of particulars/aspects relevant to the issue. The strategy in this study is to address these concerns in successive stages.

In agrarian societies, land constitutes the primary economic base, and the majority of the population are rural cultivators or peasants. The term "peasants/peasantry," though in frequent use in the social scientific literature, lacks consensus when it comes to defining it. For extensive treatments of this subject the reader is referred to some key relevant works.[1] The difficulty in defining the term is twofold. First, there is a tendency to oversimplify and describe groups as belonging to either one or other category. Groups of human beings are classified

---

[1] For detailed descriptions and diverse treatments of the definition of the term "peasant" or the concept of "peasantry" see Dalton 1972:385–415; Fallers 1961:108–10; Landsberger 1974:7–13; Foster 1967:2–14; Shanin 1987a:1–11; Wolf 1966:2–9.

as being either "in" or "not in" the category. Second, such categorization (either "in" or "not in") is done on the basis of only one criterion or as few as possible (Landsberger 1974:9). For instance, there have been attempts to define peasants in relation to ownership of land or control of the production process or orientation to market. These individual descriptions are true and valid. But, the picture is more complex.

Henry Landsberger proposes a different strategy, which the author finds helpful not only for the definition of peasants but also for the subject under discussion. There are two crucial elements in Landsberger's approach (1974:9–10). In the first place, the focus is on continuing variables instead of either-or categories. The example he cites to illustrate this point is that we tend to characterize people as tall or short. The fact of the matter is that people have a certain height. There may be other positions in society according to which people can be characterized. The second element has to do with recognizing multiple dimensions to characterize a phenomenon. The two key dimensions in the case of the peasantry are economic and political. In analyzing protest movements involving peasants, Landsberger points out that technology and environment are critical variables. This determines what kind of peasantry arises. From a methodological point of view, Landsberger's insight is helpful in that it points out the inadequacy of a single-criterion definition because it cannot focus on the various dimensions of the phenomenon and also the possible causes and effects. For the purposes of this study, however, peasants are understood as small-scale rural cultivators who cultivate the land with access to simple technology for their own livelihood and for the transfer of the agricultural surplus to the dominant ruling class.

The categories used for providing some general background to the issue of latifundialization are brought under two heads: (1) categories relating to production and (2) categories relating to distribution. These categories are by no means mutually exclusive. They interface at several points.

Categories Relating to Production

The production categories are further classified into (a) factors of production and (b) nature of production. The section on factors of production is further subdivided into segments dealing with land, labor, and capital.

Factors of Production

LAND

In agrarian societies the principal means of subsistence is provided by the tillage of fields without access to inanimate sources of energy. Needless to say, land becomes an important factor in this context. The peasants' access to land, with particular reference to the cost involved, terms under which such access is available, and the security of such a privilege, is dictated and/or controlled by the systems of land tenure. Here we are concerned with questions such as: Who owned the land? How was ownership acquired? How was ownership maintained? In pursuing these questions, one might also discover how systems of land tenure determined the distribution of power and privilege in a society. In other words, land tenure relations are social relations. One person's relation to another is determined by the use of land. In this sense, in an agrarian community, land tenure arrangements may actually define the status of individuals socially and economically (K. Parsons 1956:4).

In the process of latifundialization, there is a steady worsening of the plight of the peasantry, which is directly related to the loss of easy and secure access to cultivable land. To express this in terms of land tenure relations, there is a shift from peasant-held small-plot type of domain to a combination of patrimonial, prebendal, and mercantile domains (Wolf 1966:50–57). Patrimonial domain refers to the arrangement where access to land is determined by lineage (Wolf 1966:50). In the prebendal domain, land is given as a grant to members of the bureaucracy in return for their services to the state (Wolf 1966:51). This domain presupposes the existence of a centralized form of governing. In some cases, land acquired under the prebendal domain could become a heritable property. The mercantile domain has to do with conditions that allow the buying and selling of land. Land is viewed as a private property (Wolf 1966:53). These three forms of domain can exist side by side in the same social order. As to the nature of relationship between the three, one cannot place them on an evolutionary scale. The shift toward a combination of the above-mentioned forms involves a change in the direction of large land holdings. The major social consequence of this shift is that the number of people owning land continues to shrink as the expanse of land held by this group increases. The land-owning class becomes smaller and smaller with the growth of large estates. In this process, the peasants are at the losing end with maximum risk and minimum security of tenure. The worsening plight of the peasantry with the growth of latifundia is directly related to the loss of easy and secure access to cultivable land. In a subsistent economy, primary producers control the means of production. However, the control of the means of production may be more decentralized, local, and familial. Was land always vested in kinship groups? Probably. However, as May Diaz points out, in some societies it is possible to conceive of land ownership resting in the village community as a whole (1967:52). This implies that the rights to manage and distribute land are held by the village community. Individual households are assigned plots to which they had right of access. These plots are means of residence and subsistence never to be sold as commodities (Heilbroner and Thurow 1978:46). This form of communal settlement with small plots and freeholding peasants fosters maximum security and minimum risk to their access to land.

With regard to ownership of land, two other aspects are relevant: property relations and pattern of inheritance. As Teodor Shanin points out, the concept of property relations is virtually nonexistent (1971:246). However, there may be a different understanding of land as a property. In a subsistence economy, the major concern of the peasant is to provide for the members of the family by cultivating the land. This leads to a physical or corporeal sense of property. In an economy where market begins to play a vital role, the conception of property also changes. An intangible understanding of property emerges that is related to access to markets (K. Parsons 1956:4). The reason for this is the increase in the value of land depending on the accessibility to markets. In K. H. Parsons's words: "Then there evolves a new form of property rights in land—incorporeal property that rests upon right-duty relationship. Here the right is valuable to the creditor because the payment of debt is a duty of the borrower" (1956:9).

The value of market access creates an asset out of land, which can be pledged for debt.

In the growth of large estates, the pattern of inheritance does play a part. Eric Wolf distinguishes between two patterns of inheritance: partible and impartible. Partible inheritance involves more than one heir. The heritable land is divided among many members so that all members get some land. In contrast, impartible inheritance involves only a single heir (Wolf 1966:73). This creates within the social order the classes of heirs and disinherited. The pattern of impartible inheritance in a society where there are large estates only helps to perpetuate large holdings.

LABOR

Labor or productive human energy is organized in particular productive units. In conjunction with the process of latifundialization, there is a shift from freeholding peasant proprietors to landless day laborers. Before the rise of a market economy, land, labor, and capital are never considered as commodities for sale (Heilbroner and Thurow 1978:46). Labor is considered as a social duty to be performed. In other words, the bonds of kinship govern the economic activities (Nash 1967:5). With the rise of market economy, there is a complete change in the composition and structure of the productive units. Labor, which was once considered as a social obligation, becomes a commodity, an abstract quantity to be offered for sale in the market. With regard to the structure of the productive unit, as Neil Smelser argues, there is "an evolution from a multifunctional role structure to several more specialized structures" (1967:32). Under the subsistence economy, the productive units tend to have multiple purposes. There are many smaller productive units similarly structured, all doing the same thing (Nash 1967:5). The only division of labor to be found is based along the lines of sex and age. With the rise of market economy, economic activities are no longer confined to the family productive units. With the change in the role structure comes an increasing division of labor. The division of labor facilitates specialized structures of productive units, which are geared to the market economy. Under such conditions, agricultural wage labor undermines the family productive unit. Although the shift may be described primarily as a change from freeholding peasant proprietor to landless day laborer, the overall picture is probably more nuanced than that. The net result of this process leads to a stratification of the peasantry. We can classify three types of peasantry. At the higher end of the spectrum, there is a very small group of peasants of some means who produce commercial crops for the market. At the other end of the spectrum, there are the poor peasants who probably constitute the majority of the population. This group, deprived of the land, is forced to sell their labor in the market. In the middle are peasants with small land holdings to produce subsistence only.

Because of its inability to meet the demands of providing sustenance for the family, this group is under constant pressure to sell its labor.

CAPITAL

Even though we cannot talk about capital in relation to the subsistence economy in the modern sense of its usage, in some sense there did exist the idea of capital in antiquity. Robert Heilbroner and Lester Thurow comment, "capital is as old as the first hunting implements or digging sticks" (1978:46). Like land and labor, capital is never considered as a commodity for sale. But with the change in the system of tenure, the factors of production become saleable entities due to the influence of the market process. Rent capitalism becomes an important component of the new domain. Rent capitalism refers to the process of splitting up the means of production into several units to which a monetary value is attached (Wolf 1966:55). The peasants who are tenants in the large estates have not only to pay for the use of the land but also for the various means of production like water, seed, work animals, and human labor. In order to produce, the peasant has to pay rent for these. Needless to say, the cost of production goes up.

The high cost of production coupled with the inability of the peasants to pay for these factors of production force the peasants to borrow, probably at a high rate of interest. The needs of the peasants include such essentials as replacement of livestock, agricultural implements, seed, water, and, above all, food to sustain the family (Lambton 1953:380). Loans are usually obtained on the value and security of the next harvest. If crops fail due to a bad season, the peasant goes into deeper debt. This means that the peasants' capacity to repay is further diminished. The diminishing capacity to repay, together with the increasing demand for loans and the desire on the part of the creditor to capitalize on the misfortunes of the peasants, contribute to driving up the interest rates (Wolf 1966:56). Besides the usuriousness of the terms of the loans, there are other ways the landlords and moneylenders try to squeeze the peasants of their livelihood. The peasants lose money by being forced to sell their crop at the time of the harvest, when the prices are always the lowest (Feder 1971:147). The peasants are also shortchanged through the use of false weights and measures when the crop is divided. This way, they are subject to undue exactions. The ultimate effect of all this is the heavy indebtedness of the peasantry, which eventually leads to foreclosure. Foreclosure through debt instruments becomes a major means of accumulating land. The legal machinery, instead of safeguarding the interests of the poor peasantry, in fact serves as means of rubber-stamping corrupt and unjust practices. The reason for this is the fact that the legal courts have not reached the independence to act and to enforce the law on their own (Feder 1971:165). This is probably because the ruling elite control the court officials.

Nature of Production

In this section, we will be looking at the shift that occurs in the nature of goods produced. The basic shift is from a mixed subsistence type of farming to a single cash crop type of farming. The market orientation brings about a change in the production pattern. The change from a subsistence orientation to a market orientation is probably the best single scale for interpreting the various aspects of an economic system. The production for market brings about a whole set of changes in the structure of economies (K. Parsons 1956:8). First of all, as Smelser argues, the introduction of cash crops "marks a differentiation between the contexts of production and consumption" (1967:34). Under the subsistence economy, the productive as well as the consumptive units are the same. In other words, here, people who are engaged in production produce for their own consumption, and they consume what they produce. But in the market economy, production is geared to the market for an unknown consumer, both locally and outside. In order to be economically profitable, commercial crops require extensive plantations and thus come to occupy large expanses of land in response to market pressures. Commenting on the effect of commercial crop production in the Brazilian context, Shepard Forman writes:

> Agricultural development is a two-part process: the marketing system will lead to a restructuring of the production system when the latter is unable to meet consumer demands. In the Brazilian case, this structuring will result in the consolidation and concentration of landholdings, reinvestment in commercial crop production as in cattle raising and displacement of peasants from the land and proletarianization of rural labor. (1975:115)

Growing cash crops for export and also local consumption adversely affects the production of staples. The production to meet the local subsistence needs is neglected. In this connection, the peasants are the hardest hit. With what little income is at their disposal, they have to spend more for buying staples. The need to buy staples (which they used to produce for themselves) forces them into an unfamiliar market system where the merchants take advantage of them with false measures and rigged scales and weights. Further, the vagaries of rain agriculture affect the yield significantly, forcing them into debt. One other factor contributing to peasant poverty is the cyclical cultivation required by crops such as vines and olives. In the off-season, laborers are left jobless, forcing them to seek more loans, which they likely cannot repay.

Categories Relating to Distribution

Under this heading we are concerned with categories that deal with the disposal of goods produced–the ways in which the products of agricultural labor are distributed within a society. Three aspects become important in this regard: (a) consumption, (b) systems of exchange or distribution, and (c) the nature of distributive systems.

Consumption

In the subsistence economy, the productive unit is also the consumptive unit. It is a subsistent production aimed at providing for the family or kinship unit. But with a shift in the land tenurial system, the composition of the consumptive unit not only changes but also expands. As pointed out earlier, the introduction of cash crops marks a separation between the social context of production and consumption. The peasant cultivator is now producing for an unknown consumer. The production happens in one social context, but the consumption happens in another context. The consumptive unit expands to include royalty, bureaucrats, soldiers, merchants, artisans, and cultic personnel (Diaz 1967:51). The agricultural surplus is no longer distributed within the family or kinship unit. It is transferred to the ruling class, which has control over the economic activity.

In a stratified society, the distribution of goods and services is dictated by the power and status of individuals, whereas, in a less stratified society, the distribution is dependent on need. A stratified society reflects a situation where a dominant class of people controls and dictates the distribution of goods and services. The basic concern for the dominant class is how to extract the maximum surplus from the primary producers. It requires achieving a delicate balance between extracting the maximum surplus, yet allowing just enough for the producing group to survive in order to continue production. This has implications for the structure of the society. When such exploitation embodies and expresses itself in social structure, it has been called class struggle (Ste. Croix 1981:43). Focusing on the class structure helps to delineate the lines of conflict within a society. Failure to note this dimension obscures the nature of agrarian societies.

At the heart of the pattern of exploitation is the extraction of surplus, which may take many forms within two modes: (1) direct and individual, and (2) indirect and collective.

Direct and individual: This refers to the extraction of surplus by individuals such as employers, landlords, and moneylenders. This could take the form of (a) exploitation of wage labor; or (b) exploitation of "unfree" labor like slaves, serfs, and debt bondspeople; or (c) lease of land and house property to tenants in return for money, payment in kind, or services (Ste. Croix 1981:53). The scope of this extraction is limited in comparison with the indirect and collective way. The latter is more effective in acquiring larger portions of surplus for a longer period of time.

Indirect and collective: The agent of this mode of extraction is the state. The state, controlled by the dominant class, may extract large portions of surplus in indirect ways. The extraction of surplus may take the form of internal taxation, imposition of compulsory state services (e.g., corvée or forced labor, military conscription), and a policy of imperialism (Ste. Croix 1981:53). Internal taxation is probably the major and most continuous source of revenue for the state. Taxation becomes an effective instrument of transferring the agricultural surplus from the primary producers to the center. The burden of supporting the state and the privileged class falls on the shoulders of the peasants. In addition to regular taxation, there may be other occasions that may prompt special taxation: for example, payment of tribute during war, particular building projects undertaken by the state, or agricultural operations in a state-owned estate.

Another means of surplus extraction is corvée. This refers to the imposition of compulsory state services on the common population for accomplishing building projects, laying roads, digging canals, and erecting forts. The state can accomplish these projects by using free labor. From the perspective of the peasants, corvée is a means of fulfilling requisitions in kind (Smilianskaya 1966:236). Through the corvée, the state's dominant class provides for its security and luxury. The privileged class's penchant for imposing structures and mammoth buildings requires extensive labor, which creates the need for corvée. These structures become visible symbols of the elite's economic prowess. Peasants provide both the labor and the financial resources for these projects. The members of the upper class disdain physical labor, and therefore they put peasants to work. The establishment of a network of roads allows the growth of trade and commerce, which the crown undertakes and maintains in an agrarian society. The building of military fortifications secures internal political control and also establishes defensive frontiers against foreign powers. The preparation for war involving the provision of defense systems and waterworks necessitates the employment of forced labor.

The state's policy of imperialism determines the role of military conscription in the extraction of surplus. Like the institution of forced labor, military service takes the peasant away from agricultural work to accomplish things that are of interest to the ruling elite. Agricultural production suffers because the peasants expend their energies in military service and forced labor. The production and supply of war materials is a drain on the local economy.

Military conscription is only part of a larger policy of imperialism that may take a more direct or indirect form. Establishing military superiority through territorial conquest is a direct form of imperialism. An indirect form would be a policy of economic imperialism. The distinction, however, is not so clear-cut. Territorial expansion often results in economic gains. Conversely, a policy of economic imperialism may result in the establishment of political control. The fundamental motivation for imperialistic designs is the extraction of surplus. Most often, increasing expenditures and inadequate local resources necessitate this course of action. The elaborate building projects, maintenance of a huge army, state bureaucracy, and the royal paraphernalia are of enormous economic consequences. Thus, the economic surplus from the agricultural periphery flows into the center to support the agriculturally nonproductive personnel and projects. The economic benefits of imperialism are threefold: plunder, tribute, and trade. The predatory policy is a more primitive and short-term form of economic gain. In contrast, the extraction of tribute is a more steady and long-lasting source of revenue. The payment of tribute has dire consequences for the economy of the extracted. Through internal taxation from common people, the crown raises the tribute. Sometimes, rulers have to pay tribute in advance to avoid drastic consequences at the hands of the aggressors. The threat of foreign invasion also accelerates the preparation for war. The military buildup creates economic pressure on the royal coffers.

A strong policy of imperialism is possible only under a strong state. The colonization of new territories promotes active trade under the royal/state hegemony and thereby ensures a steady flow of surplus. The extracted surplus goes primarily to underwrite the elaborate and expensive lifestyle of the elite and also to support those who provide goods and services to the upper class (Wolf 1966:4). Those who provide goods and services to the society are, from an agricultural point of view, nonproductive competitors for the agricultural surplus. In the distribution of goods, a major portion goes for conspicuous consumption by the ruling elite, who not only do not produce but who also plainly scorn physical labor. Abstention from hard labor becomes an expression of "superior pecuniary achievement, respectability and a requisite of decency," to use the words of Thorstein Veblen (1912:43). Their only occupations are government, war, and sports. Two prominent features of the lifestyle of the elite are conspicuous leisure and voluptuous consumption. Veblen defines leisure in this context as the "non-productive consumption of time" (1912:43). This is for two reasons. First, the nonproductive consumption of time comes out of a sense of "the unworthiness of productive work." At the same time, nonproductive consumption is an evidence of one's economic prowess to afford a life of inaction and leisure (1912:43). Conspicuous leisure goes hand in hand with voluptuous consumption. The common element to both is waste. Consumption is no longer a means to stay alive. It becomes a way of life, a status symbol to show off one's wealth. Expensive feasts, entertainment, costly presents, and elaborate attire become the paraphernalia for displaying one's economic strength.

The high propensity to consume is matched by a low propensity to invest. The elite spend their wealth on consumer goods, attire, ornaments, weapons, or in ways quite unrelated to agriculture. In Ernest Feder's words, the propensity for "conspicuous consumption expenditures of the wealthy is paralleled by a penchant for showy structures and the like" (1971:98). This penchant for showy structures affects the agricultural laborers in another way. The laborers expend their energies in cultivation and performing compulsory state services. Needless to say, subsistence agricultural production suffers. Growing cash crops for export and local consumption adversely affects the production of subsistence crops to meet local needs. In this situation the peasants are the hardest hit. With the meager resources at their disposal, they have to buy the staples to survive. The need to buy staples, which they once produced themselves, forces them into unfamiliar market system where the merchants may cheat them with false measures and rigged scales.

Systems of Exchange

In this arena, the shift is from the local exchange arrangements to a wider market. Under the subsistence economy, there is very little exchange outside the family or kinship or village circles. But with the advent of the market condition, the situation changes drastically. Wolf describes some important details in this shift: First, the market system puts an end to the group monopolies on the local level. Second, monetary considerations begin to govern the exchange of goods and services (Wolf 1966:48). Goods and services increasingly become part of the market system. This results in an expanding market. Factors that promote the expansion of local and interregional trade include improvements in farming techniques, increase in production, growth of urban centers, increased use of an effective medium of exchange, colonization of new territories, and an increase in population (Blum 1961:602).

With the expansion of the market network, trade develops in the areas of both exports and imports. Cash crop items serve as effective media of exchange because they are worth more than subsistence items. Improved means of transportation and storage facilities help in the growth of trade. Improved transportation, inland and seaborne, facilitates the easy movement of goods over vast distances. Increased storage facilities enable the storing of goods for a longer period of time.

In discussing the economic history of ancient Mesopotamia, Leo Oppenheim draws attention to a phenomenon that is of interest to any student of the ancient societies. Oppenheim highlights the role of the palace in the economic system in ancient Mesopotamia (1957:31). He argues that the palace functions as the center of economic activity; the palace becomes the channel for storage and distribution of goods.

This gives rise to the evolution of a bureaucracy for bookkeeping and accounting. In this process, political control is reinforced by economic control and vice versa. It is important to keep in mind the fact that regional or interregional trade in agrarian societies of antiquity was initiated, maintained, and monopolized by the state/royal crown.

Nature of Distributive Systems

This section will focus on changes in the dynamics of the distributive systems. According to Gerhard Lenski, two principles dictate the distribution of all products of human labor: need and power (1966:26–27). In simpler societies marked by a subsistence economy, the available goods and services are distributed mainly on the basis of need. But in advanced societies, power is the determining factor. Power determines privilege. In other words, power becomes the determining force in the distributive process. People in power are willing to share the products of human labor only to the extent that it would allow just the survival and continued productivity of those who provide the goods and services. Another observation relevant to this dynamic is that the degree of inequality in a society will tend to vary in relation to the society's surplus. With the surplus comes economic power.

In a subsistence economy, political power is not related to economic power in the same way it is in a more developed economy. In a more developed economy, there is a close relationship between economic and political power (Forde and Douglas 1967:21). In a subsistence economy, the peasant is subject to very little extrinsic economic control. The economic activities are governed by religious, familial, or communal sanctions. But in a situation where market conditions play a vital role, money begins to govern the economic activity. By controlling production, those in power are able to secure political advantages and privileges in consumption (Forde and Douglas 1967:21). K. H. Parsons isolates three dimensions of production that serve as potential sources of economic power: control of land use, markets, and credit (1956:9). By a skillful and/or devious manipulation of land use, market forces, and sources of credit, the ruling class is able to extend its tentacles of power over the powerless majority. The most critical feature of this development is the growth of dependency relationships. Inequalities in land distribution fuel this dependency. Land tenure patterns and production arrangements force the landless workers and smallholders to subject themselves to the hegemony of wealthy landowners. Forman illustrates this from the Brazilian context (1975:48). Political and religious institutions also play a crucial role in the distributive process. In simpler societies, the political and religious institutions, whatever form they take and however simple they might be, serve as important means of redistributing resources and surplus. In a more advanced society, the same institutions serve the purpose of promoting and/or legitimizing inequalities.

The Process of Latifundialization

Thus far in this chapter we have looked at some key categories pertinent to the processes of production and distribution in agrarian societies. This discussion was geared toward understanding the dynamics involving shifts from a subsistence economy to a market economy. In order to sharpen the discussion further, it would be helpful to identify some specific aspects or particulars relating to the process of latifundialization. This will serve a twofold purpose. It will bring further clarity to the discussion by focusing on specific aspects. Second, this catalogue of particulars will be used as a framework for organizing the prophetic oracles in chapter 4.

1. Land Accumulation

Central to the process of latifundialization is the growth of large estates. The small plots of land to which the common peasants have access for residence and cultivation of staples are taken over by the landed elite. The accumulation of land grows in inverse proportion to the number of people owning land. The landowning class gets smaller and smaller, but the land held by this group gets larger and larger. This deprives the common peasants of their right of access to land, which constitutes the main economic base for the society.

2. Growth of Urban Centers

The growth of urban centers is very much related to the growth of a market-oriented economy. A market-oriented economy gives rise to the emergence of privileged social groups such as ruling class, officials of the royal administration, wealthy land owners, merchants, and moneylenders. The whole market economy is geared toward catering to the whims and fancies of these privileged groups. The best of the goods and services flow into a handful of urban centers. The importance of the urban center/city stems from its political (administrative and military), economic, and religious functions. The social groups associated with these various functions have to be supported. Being the productive base, the vast agricultural periphery is the main provider of goods and services to the urban centers. In the initial stages of the development of agrarian societies, this might have been an arrangement of mutual benefit. The primary producers provided goods and services in return for military protection. But with the balance of power tilted in favor of the ruling class, the mutual dependence soon degenerates into outright exploitation. The cities as administrative centers of the state function effectively in extracting the surplus from the rural areas. The urban centers virtually live off the rural areas. One may even compare this to a leech living off a human body draining its blood.

3. Militarization

The dominance of the ruling class over the peasant group is possible because of the military power of the former. There is a concerted effort to ensure that the state has a strong military force at its disposal. The ruling class understands the basic equation that the stronger one's military power, the more powerful one can be politically. The more political power one has, the more social and economic benefits one can derive. The more social and economic benefits one has, the more one can pump into the military. And so goes the vicious cycle.

4. Extraction of Surplus

The systematic extraction of agricultural surplus is accomplished through a careful system of taxation. Two things are critical to the success of the taxation system. First, the highly organized nature of the operations of ruling aristocracy gives them an advantage even though they are a minority. Second, the ruling class can accomplish what it wants because they have the military power, which gives them the political clout.

5. Lifestyle of the Upper Class

The extracted agricultural surplus goes to support a life of leisure and luxury for the elite. The two key words that describe the lifestyle of the upper class are leisure and luxury. Leisure is the nonproductive use of time. This comes from a disdain of physical work and a sense of vanity in being able to afford an idle life (Veblen 1912:43). Luxury is written all over their lifestyle. It applies to where they live, what they consume, what they wear, and what they do in their leisure. One common feature of their leisure and luxury is the element of waste. But from the point of view of an elite, they constitute symbols of prestige and power. First, the erection of palatial mansions and expensive furnishings is one of the ways the economic surplus is used. From an agricultural point of view, these undertakings are not only nonproductive but also a drain on the royal coffers. Second, the ruling class uses the local agricultural specialties (commercial crops) for their conspicuous consumption. The ability to afford a life of decadent consumption becomes a way of showing off one's wealth. In addition to local consumption, these agricultural specialties are also prominent items in the export-import transactions. They are exported to neighboring territories, often in exchange for military and luxury items. The acquisition of military items is a critical piece in ensuring and perpetuating political dominance and control. Third, in keeping with the elite's flair for pomp and glory, personal adornments such as fine clothing, jewelry, perfume, and footwear become a way of exhibiting their wealth and power. Besides, the long hours spent in self-adornment is in character with their life of leisure. Fourth, the favorite pastime of the upper class consists of engaging in activities such as war, sports, music, and partying. Large agricultural surpluses enable a leisurely and luxurious living.

6. Trade and Commerce

One other area with significant impact at many levels is the growth of trade and commerce. This comes with the expansion of the market network. In agrarian monarchies, trade and commerce are initiated, maintained, and monopolized by the royal group. Hence, the beneficiaries of this enterprise are also the same group of people. In fact, interregional and international trade are geared toward procuring items that are of value and interest to this group. In this connection, the systematic development and control of trade routes are vital for the movement of goods as well as generating revenues from trading caravans.

7. Market Condition

This refers to the abuses/corrupt practices in the market situation. With the advent of a wider market orientation, drastic changes occur in the area of production. The demands of market forces promote the cultivation of those crops that can gain maximum economic advantage. This means that more and more lands are converted to producing commercial crops, leaving the staples in short supply. The peasants need these for their survival. Consequently, they are forced to buy in the market the staples that they once produced themselves. The merchants may take advantage of their unfamiliarity with the market conditions and shortchange them through unscrupulous tampering and deceit in the transactions.

8. Indebtedness of the Peasants

Many factors drive peasants into debt. First, the exactions in agricultural produce are heavy, sometimes more than half of the total produce. Prices tend to be the lowest at the time of the harvest. Illegal business practices on the part of the landowners further cut into the returns. Second, the common peasants bear the brunt of much of the taxation to support the programs of the state. The energies of the peasants are expended between fulfilling their agricultural and corvée obligations. Participation in one does not earn them a reprieve in terms of the other. But their performance and productivity suffer in both. Third, when the peasants are dependent primarily upon rain for agriculture, there are serious consequences if rains fail. They are forced to borrow to feed the family. If the rains fail for subsequent seasons, the peasant goes into deeper debt. Often, the peasants may offer either the piece of land they own or an article of value or a member of the family as collateral. Failure to repay mounting loans results in the foreclosure of land and/or being sold into debt slavery. Accumulation of land through debt instruments does become a way of creating large estates.

9. Role of the Creditors

Creditors and moneylenders play a critical role in the impoverishment of the peasantry. In some cases, it is conceivable that the creditors and moneylenders were the landed elite themselves or a separate class within that group who specialized in that operation. There is no doubt, whatsoever, about the drastic result of their operation on the condition of the peasantry.

10. Role of Judicial Courts

Judicial institutions play a critical role in sealing the fate of the peasantry. The only court of appeal for the peasants to seek redress of a situation or arbitration is the juridical institutions. But those chances are dim, because the ruling class controls the courts and its officials. Again, the judicial officials may be either part of the upper class or puppets in the hands of the ruling elite. The venality of the ruling class is in its calculated and concerted effort to manipulate the system to render an air of legality to their evil machinations.

All these aspects/particulars put together illustrate the more comprehensive process of latifundialization. They are systemically interrelated and mutually influential.

This frame of reference will be used to analyze and organize the eighth century prophetic oracles pertaining to Israel and Judah.

2

Land Ownership Patterns prior to the Eighth Century B.C.E.

This chapter traces developments critical to ownership of land in the periods preceding the eighth century B.C.E. in the Hebrew kingdom(s). The systemic reality of the eighth century can be understood better in relation to the developments leading up to that point. An exhaustive treatment of this subject matter is beyond the purview of this work. Since the focus of the study is on land and the process of latifundialization, the historical survey will also be limited to the same. The two entities central to this process are land and peasantry. As is typical of agrarian societies, land is the primary means of subsistence. The peasant cultivators form the majority of the population. In understanding this reality, questions concerning the ownership of land—the manner of acquisition of ownership and the maintenance of it—become critical. In an important way, ownership patterns enable us to understand how people and land are related.

The Late Bronze Canaanite Society

The starting point of our brief historical survey is the Late Bronze Age (1550–1250 B.C.E.) which provides the immediate context for the emergence of premonarchic Israel. In Late Bronze Canaanite society, the ultimate title to all of the cultivable land belonged to the crown. Hence, the crown also had the right to dispose of the land as it deemed fit. Lands were granted to members of the royal

Historical Periods of the Hebrew Kingdom(s)

Early Bronze Age	3000–2100 B.C.E.	
Middle Bronze Age	2100–1550 B.C.E.	Ancestral History
Late Bronze Age	1550–1250 B.C.E.	
Iron Age I	1250–1050 B.C.E.	Premonarchic Israel: Exodus, Wilderness Wanderings, and Formation of Premonarchic Israel
	1050–1025 B.C.E.	Transition: Period of Judges
	1025–1000 B.C.E.	Inauguration of Monarchy
	1000–922 B.C.E.	Monarchic Israel: United Kingdom David and Solomon
	922–900 B.C.E.	Division of the Kingdom
Iron Age II	900–800 B.C.E.	Monarchic Israel: Ninth Century Omrides (North) Jehoshaphat (South)
	800–700 B.C.E.	Monarchic Israel: Eighth Century Jeroboam II (North) Uzziah (South)
	722 B.C.E.	Fall of the Northern Kingdom
	700–600 B.C.E.	Seventh-century Judah Josiah
	597–587 B.C.E.	Judean Deportations/Diaspora

administration in return for civil and military services. These lands eventually tended to become hereditary estates. In Wolf's terminology, we have here a combination of the patrimonial (inherited land) and prebendal (land grants from the crown) systems of land tenure (1966:50–59). In this context, the task of agricultural production was left to the peasants, since the holders of the patrimonial and prebendal domains never applied themselves to it due to their aversion to physical labor. Consequently, lands were leased out to the peasants to be cultivated in return for taxes and/or rent. The immediate titleholders to these lands made sure that there was a steady flow of agricultural surplus into their hands to underwrite their leisured and luxurious lifestyle. The perpetuation of such a practice became embodied in a social structure constituting a highly stratified society. It promoted a socioeconomic structure where the majority of the resources were at the disposal of a small minority of the population. As a result, poverty and misery were the lot of the peasant majority.

Even though the dominant systems of land tenure were patrimonial and prebendal domains, it is quite conceivable that some of the practices and structures of the old communal or tribal subsistence economy did survive in some form. In fact, the survival and persistence of these patterns of communal land tenure may explain the practices under the premonarchic Israel. The movement leading to the formation of premonarchic Israel consciously set about the task of separating itself from the existing Canaanite sociopolitical and economic structures of the Late Bronze period. The very opposition to and rejection of the oppressive Canaanite structures probably stems from the dormant notions of tribalism and communal land tenure (Gottwald 1983:6). They lay buried under the imposing sociopolitical and economic and even religious structures of the society. The official Canaanite religious ideology reflected the human society in that the world of the gods was to a significant extent the projection of the human social pyramid, with the ruling class at the top and the common mass at the bottom. Insofar as religious ideology impinges upon a society, the Canaanite religion legitimized, reinforced, and perpetuated a stratified society and its values. The emergence of the premonarchic Israel can be seen as a conscious revolt against and secession from such oppressive socioeconomic and political systems of the Late Bronze Canaanite society.

Premonarchic Israel

The emergence of premonarchic Israel became a subject of vigorous debate following the publication of Norman Gottwald's *The Tribes of Yahweh: A Sociology of the Religion of Liberated Israel, 1250–1050 B.C.E.* The debate has not only brought a lot of clarity and nuances to the subject but also a lot of questions. The bottom line is that no serious student of this period can afford to neglect the advancement of scholarship in this area. Even though a treatment of this question, lengthy or brief, is outside the scope of this work, how one understands the formation question is of critical importance in understanding not only the nature of the society that emerged in this period but also its importance for the subsequent periods as well.[1]

Two of the prominent models to be generated in the pre-Gottwald era were the Conquest model and the Peaceful Settlement/Gradual Infiltration/Immigration model. The Conquest model interprets the formation of Israel as a result of a total sweeping military campaign by the Israelites under the leadership of Joshua (Albright 1935; 1939; Wright 1946; Lapp 1967). The proponents of this model derive biblical support from Joshua 1–12 and also archaeological information. The Peaceful Settlement model, on the contrary, sees the process as a gradual settlement with very little military confrontation (Alt 1966; Noth 1960; Weippert 1971). The proponents of this model seek biblical support in the early parts of the book of Judges and do not give much credence to the archaeological materials. Neither of these models really addressed the unique nature of the Israelite society that was born. The Peasants' Revolt model was first initiated by George Mendenhall (1962) but systematically developed later by Gottwald (1979) and further nuanced by Chaney (1983). Here the emergence of premonarchic Israel is seen as a result of a revolt against and a geographic withdrawal/secession from the oppressive socioeconomic and political systems of the Canaanite city-states. Even though in recent years Gottwald has opted to use "agrarian social revolution" instead of "Peasants' Revolt," the idea of a social revolution is still applicable. The revolution ushered in some key experiments in political, social, economic, and religious spheres. The most pertinent change for this study relates to the area of land tenure arrangements. In contrast to the combination of patrimonial and prebendal domains of the Late Bronze Canaanite society, we see here a redistributional land tenure. Under this system, land gets apportioned among families as a unit of residence and subsistence. The apportioned land changes hands periodically, probably on an

---

[1]Many works are available that can provide the background to and treatment of areas pertaining to the formation of premonarchic Israel. For the most recent and helpful summary of this subject, the reader is directed to McNutt 1999:33–103. For an excellent analysis of the relative merits and demerits of the Conquest, the Immigration, and the Revolt models, see Chaney 1983:39–90. Other notable discussions include, among others, Lemche 1985, Coote and Whitelam 1987, and P. R. Davies 1995.

annual basis. Here again, Gottwald has moved in favor of "communitarian mode of production" instead of "redistributional." Other scholars have also argued in favor of a communal land tenure (Dybdahl 1981; Hopkins 1985). These two modes need not be seen as mutually exclusive. As Daniel Bates and Amal Rassam point out, the practice of *Musha'a* in the Levant entailed common tenure and redistribution of land. What is of particular interest are the circumstances under which *Musha'a* is found (Bates and Rassam 1983:137–38). *Musha'a* is often found in areas which have minimal rainfall and in areas "occupied recently by tribal communities" (1983:137). Under this arrangement "it was usual to periodically redistribute fields among families according to familial need as well as to equalize access to better plots" (Bates and Rassam 1983:138). This would fit the land tenure practices in premonarchic Israel. Two primary principles governed the land tenure arrangements: Yahweh is the ultimate owner of land, and, therefore, land is inalienable. These are reflected in Leviticus 25:23. Even though the levitical/priestly traditions might have been consolidated/redacted in a much later period, the principles preserved in this text date back to the bold experiments of the premonarchic period.

Emergence of Monarchy in Israel

In most discussions of the emergence of monarchy in ancient Israel, the Philistine threat has been accorded prime importance. But thanks to the pioneering works of scholars such as James Flanagan (1981) and Frank Frick (1985), there has been shift in focus to the internal changes that a society undergoes. Flanagan, using the theoretical framework of Elman Service's work (1975) on societal development, sees premonarchic Israel evolving through the stages of egalitarian/segmented society, to chiefdom, and finally state (1981:47–49). Within this larger context, Flanagan's study focuses on the shift from the egalitarian society to that of chiefdom with particular reference to the distinguishing marks of the latter as proposed by Colin Renfrew (1974:73). By way of simplifying Renfrew's categories, the following areas are suggested as significant markers: (1) centralization of polity/political structure, (2) territorial expansion/boundaries, (3) frontier defenses/fortification, (4) professional army, (5) building projects sponsored and undertaken by the state/crown, (6) surplus-producing economy due to regional specialization, (7) interregional and international trade under royal/state directive, (8) organized extraction of surplus (taxes and tributes), (9) growth of regional centers, (10) population growth, and (11) stratified society. These are not merely conceptual categories, but many of them, as John Holladay has shown in his valuable study, can be discerned through archaeological evidence (1995:368–98). These aspects are interrelated and mutually influential changes. They are critical to the task of understanding the process of evolution that modifies the society as a whole. Hence, any explanation of the emergence of monarchy in Israel has to be offered in a combination of both internal and external causes.

In most discussions, the precise nature of the threat posed by the Philistines is not addressed, although it is taken for granted. There are two important dimensions, one military and the other economic. From the military point of view, the Philistines were able to overcome the challenges of the Judean hilly terrain, which rendered the dreaded chariots of the Canaanite elite of the premonarchic period ineffective. This was accomplished by employing the chariot units as mobile infantry for short-range land battles (T. Dothan 1982:7). This gave the Philistines a military edge, especially if they were able to employ infantry units on a large scale. Here one would have to ask a simple question: Why would the Philistines take the trouble to bother with a community located in the Judean hill country? What was the incentive? The answer lies at the economic front. The Philistines realized that the Israelites of the premonarchic society had created an economic base in the hill country employing technological innovations such as use of iron tools, cisterns plastered with slaked lime, and terrace farming (Chaney 1986:62–63). The hitherto neglected and unenticing hill country had become an economic and population base worth controlling for the purposes of extracting surplus. The Philistines adopted the classic policy of the elite of allowing the primary producers just enough access to technology to keep production going. This is reflected in an account most likely to be glossed over in 1 Samuel 13:19–22. Chaney's comments on this section are perceptive and right on target (1986:67). The passage does distinguish between military weapons and agricultural tools. While the Philistines withheld the Israelites' access to weapons, they did allow them access to tools to continue production for the ultimate economic benefit of the Philistines. Had they wanted, the Philistines could have easily and summarily decimated the hill country population. They had the military wherewithal to accomplish that.

But instead they worked with a more complicated strategy which "sought to avoid 'killing the goose that laid the golden egg'" (Chaney 1986:67).

Monarchic Israel: Tenth Century B.C.E.

This section focuses on the United Kingdom under David and Solomon. From a systemic point of view, this marks a unique phase. David's rise to power changed the situation drastically. The emergence of a strong Israelite power under David's command subdued the Philistine threat. The Israelite control gradually extended to the Canaanite plains. The vast territorial expansion under David necessitated major changes in the governmental system. The administration and oversight of the vast territory was possible only through the creation of a bureaucracy. An extensive bureaucracy with a large retinue of civil and military officials became indispensable for the maintenance of a strong state. This had far-reaching consequences for the systems of land tenure.

The payment for the services of the different officials involved in the administration was primarily made through a system of land grants. This would constitute the prebendal domain where lands were granted to officials in return for services to the state. It is quite conceivable that these lands became heritable estates under patrimonial domain. The most valuable piece of information for the system of land grants in the early monarchic period comes from the story of Meribaal/Mephibosheth and David (2 Sam. 9; 16; 19). Zafrira Ben-Barak identifies three stages in this account (1981). In the first stage, Saul's paternal estate, which was earlier taken over by David (on the assumption that there was no heir to Saul's estate), is now restored to Meribaal, who is discovered to be the lone survivor to the house of Saul. In the second stage, the estate is confiscated from him by David on the grounds of treason and given to Ziba for his services and loyalty. In the third stage, subsequent to Meribaal's repentance, David rules that Meribaal and Ziba are to share the estate. In relation to the land tenure question, this account speaks volumes. Gone are those days when only Yahweh was seen to be the owner of all land. The story reflects a whole new reality in which the crown has complete authority to confiscate and dispose of land, as it sees fit.

There were several ways the crown acquired land. Military conquest was one. Through conquests, David brought much of the Canaanite plains under Israelite control. Along with the subjugation of the Canaanite landed elites came many large estates. Confiscating heirless land as seen in the story of Meribaal was another way of acquiring land. The practice of taking possession of vacant land is clearly reflected in the story of the Shunamite woman (2 Kings 8:1–6). Land was also bought by the crown as David's purchase of Araunah's threshing floor points out (2 Sam. 24:24). The acquisition of land in exchange for other commodities is also attested in the exchange between Solomon and Hiram of Tyre (1 Kings 9:11–14). Receiving land or cities as gifts was also a source of land acquisition. Solomon received Gezer from the Pharaoh (1 Kings 9:16). David received Ziklag from the Philistines (1 Sam. 27:5–6). Confiscation of land on charges of treason seems to be another way land could come under royal control, as the story of Meribaal illustrates. Interestingly, this account mirrors four different practices with regard to the system of land grants: (a) confiscation of land over which there is no apparent heir, (b) the restoration of paternal estate to the legal heir, (c) confiscation of land on charges of treason, and (d) land grant for services rendered to the crown. The story clearly highlights the complete authority the crown had in the acquisition and disposal of land. The system of land grants from the crown was a means of creating a landed elite who were dependent upon and loyal to the crown. Reciprocally, the system as far as the recipients were concerned was an incentive for loyalty and initiative (Ben-Barak 1981:74).

David's reign was a transitional point between the premonarchic and monarchic Israelite societies. The older institutions and structures were still probably in existence. But new changes and realities were set in motion. In relation to land tenure, under David there came to exist two different and conflicting systems (Chaney 1986:67–68). As shown earlier, because of expanding Israelite territory, a combination of the patrimonial and prebendal domains were operative probably in much of the area. But it is quite possible that the ancient practice of the communal redistributional tenure did continue to survive in some form in the Judean hill country, which was David's original constituency.

Solomon's reign marks a unique phase in the history of monarchic Israel in that it represents a full-fledged nation-state. Gone were the transitional aspects of the previous regime. The success of Solomon's rule lay not in his military accomplishments but also in his exploitation of the economic possibilities of the empire, particularly through internal taxation and foreign trade. Taxation was a major source of revenue for the crown. Solomon undertook a systematic reorganization of his districts. This involved tampering with the traditional tribal boundaries. Even though Gösta Ahlström has argued against any conscious attempt at such tampering, he does, however, see this district reorganization as "a political means of organizing the nation so that the king and the court could extract the most out of it" (1993:514). Solomon reorganized the districts of his kingdom to (a) ensure a steady flow of provisions to the court, (b) provide territorial basis for the imposition of compulsory state services, (c) weaken the tribal ties, and (d) strengthen the power of the crown through the process of centralization (Wright 1958:58–68).

The lucrative trade enterprises of Solomon brought wealth to the state. Since trade was carried out under the royal directive, the beneficiaries of trade were the members of the royal class as well. The biblical accounts in 1 Kings 10 give interesting information concerning Solomon's trade. The joint ventures of Solomon and Hiram of Tyre going as far as Ophir bought wealth and other fineries into the state coffers (1 Kings 10:11–12; 2 Chr. 9:10–11, 21). These voyages were carried out with the merchant fleet based in Ezion-Geber with the help and cooperation of the Phoenician sailors. The Tyrian connection was not restricted to sea trade expertise but also extended to securing specific items through trade and obtaining the services of the "Phoenician expert stonecutters, masons and architects" (J. Holladay 1995:380–81). The use of ashlar stones in building projects and the abundant presence of Phoenician pottery (possibly from Sarepta) at Hazor, for instance, reinforce the conclusion about the Phoenician influence (Holladay 1995:381). In addition to sea trade, Solomon was also involved in overland trade with Arabia (1 Kings 10:1–10). The trade with Southern Arabia brought in highly valued items such as spices and gems from East Asia, as well as incense, gold, ivory, blackwood, exotic animals, animal skins, and feathers from Africa (Holladay 1995:383). Taxes and transit tolls were collected from the trading caravans (1 Kings 10:15). The trading merchant groups chose particular destinations depending on familiarity, camping and reprovisioning facilities, access to water, grazing rights, and safe passage (Holladay 1995:383).

According to 1 Kings 10:28–29, Solomon is believed to have obtained horses and chariots in trade from "Egypt" and Que/Kue. Irrespective of how one reads *mitsrayim*, either referring to Egypt or emended to read *mutsri* (Gray 1970:264, 269; Peckham 1976:242 n. 59), the fact remains that Solomon was engaged in an export-import operation that was of major proportions, as Yutaka Ikeda has observed (1982:215–38). Solomon's trade in horses seems to have been carried out with the help and cooperation of the king of Hamath. Ikeda interprets the reference to "the store-cities of Hamath" (2 Chr. 8:3–4) to mean a strategic base which served not only as a relay station in the trade between Anatolia and Israel but also as place where horses were reared and kept until they were needed by Solomon (1982:237–38). It is also recorded that Solomon exported grain and oil in exchange for the cedar and the cypresses from Lebanon (1 Kings 5:8–11). Interestingly, absent from this list of exports is wine. Does it mean that the wine industry was not developed to the extent that it was in the eighth century B.C.E.? Solomon also traded cities to Hiram in exchange for cedar, cypress, and gold (1 Kings 9:10–14).

Since the ruling class initiated, maintained, and monopolized trade, they were also the beneficiaries of this enterprise. Trade was geared towards procuring luxury items to cater to the whims of the upper class and also military items, which would ensure their political power. The key aspect here is the military buildup that goes hand in hand with the process of ushering in a strong centralized state. The massive buildup of military forces consisting of chariots and horses begins with Solomon and further increases in the period of the Omrides. It does not peak during the Battle of Qarqar, as John Holladay suggests (1995:382), but rather in the early part of the eighth century. In addition to the actual military items themselves, the buildup of military forces also must have entailed other related expenditures involving the feeding of the animals, maintenance and repair of equipment, and skilled personnel such as stable attendants and charioteers (Holladay 1995:382). From a systemic viewpoint, the military component is critical because military power enables the elite to have political clout. As David Hopkins points out, "states exist at the confluence of economic, social and political power" (1996:122).

Under Solomon, the expenditure of the state far outweighed the income. One area of expenditure was the building projects. The temple was a major architectural achievement. Aside from the mammoth character of the temple in Jerusalem, Holladay finds the separate location of shrines and palaces at Megiddo and Lachish as an archaeological attestation characteristic of a state (1995:373). The temple in Jerusalem not only served the purpose of being a dynastic chapel but also functioned as a national shrine. This signals the transformation of Yahwism into a national religion under the aegis of the monarchy. The economic aspects of this undertaking are staggering. The only native/Israelite feature of the temple is the ark. Everything else–the materials, furnishings, motifs, artists, and craftspeople–were brought from abroad, particularly Tyre (1 Kings 5:10, 18; 7:13–14). The levy of compulsory/statutory labor provided the bulk of the labor force (1 Kings 5:13) (Soggin 1987: 259-67).

The palace complex (1 Kings 7:1) included several structures: the "House of the Forest of Lebanon," named after the cedar pillars that supported it (1 Kings 7:2); the "Hall of the Throne" (1 Kings 7:7); and the royal dwelling place (1 Kings 7:8). The House of the Forest of Lebanon seems to have served as a storage place for armory (1 Kings 10:16–17) and vessels (1 Kings 10:21).

Two specific areas among Solomon's building accomplishments deserve comment: the growth of urban centers, and the fortification of these centers with chambered gates and casemate wall system. In 1 Kings 9:15, Solomon is credited with building Hazor, Megiddo, and Gezer. However, the debate concerning the corroborating archaeological evidence relevant to these areas is far from settled. The partial remains of the casemate wall and a six-chambered gate with towers in Stratum XB at Hazor have been assigned by Yigael Yadin to the Solomonic era (1972:135–46). Similar six-chamber gate remains at Megiddo and Gezer were also assigned by Yadin to Solomon (1958). But Yohanan Aharoni (1972) and David Ussishkin (1980) have proposed that they could not be dated earlier than the ninth century B.C.E. For the purposes of this study, either proposal would work. The tenth and ninth centuries both experienced substantial building and fortification as part of governmental construction projects. An attempt adequately to represent the full debate is beyond the scope of this treatment.

Even if one were to disagree about whether or not a particular structure belongs in an earlier or later stratum, in looking at the question from a systemic point of view the observations by John Holladay and Volkmar Fritz are pertinent. In contrast to earlier Israelite settlements, Holladay finds evidences of a "radically transformed" complex of buildings with fortified governmental centers, each with its own casemate wall system, six-chambered gateway, and palace complex in Hazor, Megiddo, Gezer, and possibly in Lachish and Tel Masos (1995:371–73). Two features about these complexes are of tremendous significance for making some overall conclusions. First, the uniformity of the complexes and their strategic location "allows for but one interpretation: in these changes we are witnessing a major instance of secondary state formation in the southern Levant" (Holladay 1995:372). Second, the cluster of buildings, including components such as palaces, sanctuaries, storage facilities, stables, and others, with their different functions, suggest the probability that we might be dealing with some sort of a central place or administrative center (Holladay 1995:394 n.4). After a useful review of the key archaeological results pertaining to a few tenth-century cities, Fritz comes to the conclusion that the available archaeological information from this period points to a process of "reurbanization." He posits a causal relationship between this process and the establishment of monarchy (Fritz 1996:195). Fritz also makes a valid point when he says that the orchestration of the vast labor force needed for all the building projects could "only have been brought about through the new form of state—the monarchy" (1996:195). In connection with the fortified structures, mention must be made of the structures scattered throughout the Negev. Of the forty-five such structures surveyed, twenty-five have been excavated (Barkay 1992:323). Even though the date and purpose of these structures have not been conclusively established, one of the possibilities is that they were built as "a chain of fortresses defending the southern borders of the Solomonic kingdom in the mid-tenth century" (Barkay 1992:324). A case could be made for the existence of the structures under Solomon, because the inscriptions of Pharaoh Shishak (925 B.C.E.) mention the destruction of seventy sites in the Negev (Barkay 1992:324). Further, the whole question needs to be assessed in relation to the information gained from Tel Beersheba and Tel 'Arad (Barkay 1992:325). The Negev settlement may also have had an agricultural purpose. This is evidenced in the curious settlement in Ramat Matred. The excavations at Ramat Matred have uncovered several individual houses, corrals, cisterns, terraced fields with water channels, and storage pits (Aharoni et al. 1960:110).

One of the features that Hopkins associates with a defining character of a state is social stratification (1996:129). Archaeologically, this can be corroborated by looking at symbols and structures that maintain and project a certain status. Among other things, the quality, size, and location of residences and the distribution of elite goods give us valuable clues concerning class distinctions (Holladay 1995:377). Burial practices and paraphernalia could be another area with possible clues for discerning stratification levels within a society (Hopkins 1996:129–32). The specifics of the burial–including the location of the burial, the particular tomb type represented, tomb plan, and grave goods–are determined to a large extent by economic, social, and political considerations (Bloch-Smith 1992:17–19, 132–51).

The imposition of forced labor played no minor part in the administration of Solomon (1 Kings 5:13–15; 2 Chr. 2:17–18). In fact, it assumed such proportions that it became the main bone of contention in the division of the kingdom. The disproportionate burden of taxation and forced labor on the northern territories led them eventually to secede from the rule of the Davidides. That forced labor was the major cause of the division is seen from the fact that it was Adoram/Adoniram, the official in charge of the forced labor, who was sent to suppress the rebellion in the north (1 Kings 12:18). Further, it is also no accident that Jeroboam I rose to prominence in the north by building a power base through the institution of forced labor in the house of Joseph (1 Kings 11:26–28).

On the basis of this very brief survey, some general observations can be made. First, monarchy in Israel attains its full-fledged shape under Solomon. Second, we see here a strong centralized political structure with all the attendant social and economic trappings. Third, there is a degree of growth and development of the urban centers but by no means a high order of economic prosperity (Frank 1971:155). There is no indication of the kind of regional specialization as seen in the eighth-century Israelite and Judean societies. Fourth, Solomon did not exercise control over his neighbors. In fact, there seems to a sizeable shrinkage of the Israelite territory under Solomon. The Syrian revolt in the north resulting in the establishment of Rezon as the king in Damascus (1 Kings 11:23–25) appears to have affected Israel in two ways. The establishment of the Syrian kingdom meant the removal of that much territory from Israelite control. This reverses the indisputable control established by David over the Aramaeans (1 Chr. 18:3–6). Further, the revolt in Edom backed by Egypt (1 Kings 11:14–22) had a similar effect in that it took away the territory south-southeast of the Dead Sea from Solomon's control (Frank 1971:137). Also, the references in 1 Kings 9:16 (the burning of Gezer by the Egyptians) and 11:40 (escape of Jeroboam I into Egypt when he fell out of favor with Solomon) indicate that the Egyptians continued to pose a threat to Solomon's kingdom. Solomon was strong enough to protect a reduced and manageable Israelite territory.

Israel and Judah: Ninth Century B.C.E.

From a systemic point of view, the ninth century offers an interesting parallel to the tenth in more than one way. In the aftermath of the division of the kingdom, the accession of the Omrides to the throne of Israel signifies a systemic watershed in the history of the Northern Kingdom. Before proceeding any further it must be acknowledged that we are bypassing the curious set of developments associated with the accession of Jeroboam I in the north after the division. It is beyond the scope of this treatment to pursue in any depth the attempts on the part of Jeroboam I to reverse the trends set by Solomon. Even though he becomes a villain in the eyes of the deuteronomistic tradition, he is more sinned against than sinning. Establishing cult centers in Dan and Bethel and multiple capital centers could be seen as attempts at decentralization. The presence of uniform residential structures in Tell el-Far'ah (N) might be indicative of lack of sharp disparities between the dwellings of the elite and the rest (de Vaux 1956:134). Whether they were conscious attempts at reducing disparities remains an intriguing question. Unfortunately, the biblical traditions will not be of much help in giving Jeroboam I a fair evaluation. The leadership in the north at this time shows an earnest desire to move away from the Davidic/Solomonic models and structures. But this might not have translated into generating viable alternatives. Hence, following the death of Jeroboam I, a period of instability and chaotic rule marked the history of the Northern Kingdom. Out of this political vacuum emerged Omri, a military commander to take the kingdom in a new direction.

While it seems that Jeroboam I attempted to get away from the Davidic/Solomonic models and structures, the Omrides did precisely the opposite. Even a cursory look at the period of David and Solomon on one hand, and that of Omri and Ahab on the other, reveals interesting parallels. The many similarities in policies and practices suggest the possibility that they are more than mere coincidences. The Omrides deliberately set about adopting the policies of the David/Solomonic empires, particularly the latter. The parallels are reflected in many areas.

(1) The accession of Omri to the throne initiated a policy of centralization aimed at establishing a strong state. After several decades of instability and political chaos, the rule of Omrides brought stability to the Northern Kingdom. The founding of Samaria as the primary seat of government parallels the establishment of Jerusalem as the capital of the United Kingdom under David. The archaeological support for this comes in the form of royal structures and paraphernalia from the acropolis in Samaria (Holladay 1995:373–76). The scope and grandeur of the constructions in Samaria would rank the Omrides "among the greatest builders in the history of the Land of Israel" (Barkay 1992:320).

(2) The creation of a strong state was made possible by a strong military establishment. One could even say that it necessitated the services of a strong military force. The Assyrian annals chronicling the coalition against Shalmanesar III in the battle of Qarqar (ca. 853 B.C.E.) refer to the contingent of two thousand chariots and ten thousand foot soldiers fielded by Ahab (Pritchard 1969:279). Even if there is an element of exaggeration in this account, it seems possible that Ahab commanded a much stronger military force on a smaller land base in comparison to Solomon (1 Kings 10:26). Ahab knew the vital importance of the military for his rule. This is supported by his efforts to keep "the horses and mules alive" (1 Kings 18:5) when the whole land was reeling under the grip of severe famine. The economic implications of maintaining such an elite force of chariots and horses are staggering. The cost of maintaining the select horses, chariot-related equipment, and personnel such as stable-masters, charioteers, and the skilled workers who maintained and repaired the equipment must have been astronomical (Holladay 1995:382).

(3) Another parallel is the variety of building projects. One such undertaking is the development of urban centers such as Hazor, Megiddo, Gezer, and Lachish, which show evidence of rebuilding with improved wall systems and chambered gateways (Holladay 1995:373; Dever 1995:418–19; Barkay 1992:308). To this list can be added other newly fortified sites such as Tel Dan, Tell el-Far'ah (N), Shechem, Tell en-Nasbeh, and el-Jib (Holladay 1995:373). Another aspect of the building programs is the impressive array of water systems at Hazor, Megiddo, Gezer, Jerusalem, Beersheba, and el-Jib (Holladay 1995:373). The technically more complex water systems at Hazor, Megiddo, Lachish, and Jerusalem are a tribute to the

hydroengineering skills of the builders (Barkay 1992:332–34). The temple built by Ahab for Ba'al in Samaria (1 Kings 16:32) parallels Solomon's temple-building efforts.

(4) As in the days of Solomon, the "Phoenician connection" was revived. Ahab's marriage to the Tyrian princess, Jezebel, daughter of Ethbaal (1 Kings 16:31), paved the way for strong Phoenician-Israelite cooperation. Consequently, this had a deeper impact in the political, socioeconomic, and religious aspects of the Northern Kingdom. The Phoenician presence is more visibly attested in three areas: ashlar masonry, ivory inlays, and imported pottery. Judging by the sheer volume of the ashlar stone remains at Megiddo, Hazor, and Samaria, Holladay concludes that its use in the ninth century far outweighs that of the Solomonic period (1995:380). The remains of the walls in Samaria give evidence of the hewn-stone technique, which is of Phoenician origin (Frank 1972:74, 162–64). Also, the largest amount of carved ivory inlays recovered to date come from the ruins of the Samaria palace (Dever 1995:424; Barkay 1992:320–22). The imported Cypro-Phoenician pottery was of fine quality, with red slips and concentric circles painted in black (Barkay 1992:325). Based on the quantity of wares found in Hazor comparable to the type found in Sarepta along the Syro-Lebanese coast, John Holladay posits a dramatic increase in the appearance of this pottery in the tenth- and early ninth-century levels. Even though there is a drop in the levels coterminous with the Omrides, it is still high (Holladay 1995:381).

The parallels between the tenth and ninth centuries B.C.E. are too many and too close to be dismissed as mere coincidences. Even if one sees the changes under the Omrides as the natural consequences of an emerging centralized state in the north, it does not negate the possibility that they were in accordance with specific designs of the Omrides to model that state on southern experience.

Another parallel, though unintended, exists between the Solomonic and the Omride periods. This is in relation to establishing undisputed control over their neighbors. We see neither a subjugation of the surrounding kingdoms, nor territorial expansion, as we do in the time of Uzziah and Jeroboam II. In the ninth century, three factors restricted Israel's expansion.

First, the Aramean kingdom was a force with which the Omrides had to contend. The Arameans under Ben-hadad I (880–842 B.C.E.) managed to emerge as the dominant power in the region, eventually replacing Israel (Bright 1981:236).The reference to annexation of border towns by the Aramean king in 1 Kings 20:34 points to the powerful position of the Arameans. Ahab is said to have fought three battles with the Aramean king (1 Kings 20:1–34; 22:1–40; 2 Chr. 18:1–34). No convincing case has yet been made that the kings involved in these narratives were at first anonymous and were later identified with Ahab and Jehoshaphat. Ahab's advance against Ramoth-Gilead (1 Kings 22; 2 Chr. 18) was an attempt at extending his control over northern Transjordan.

Second, the rising Assyrian power was beginning to pose grave dangers. It began with the reign of Asshur-nasir-pal II (884–864 B.C.E.) followed by that of Shalmanesar II (859–825 B.C.E.) (Bright 1981:237–39). The gravity of the Assyrian threat can be surmised from the coalition formed by Damascus, Israel, and Hamath and several other kings from northern and central Syria. The battle at Qarqar must have weakened Israel considerably. With such Assyrian threat looming large on the horizon, it is small wonder that Israel could not forge ahead.

The third factor in the restriction of the Israelite control was the Moabite kingdom. Although Moab was supposed to have been under the rule of the Omrides, the actual reality might be far from that. The territorial expansion reflected in the Mesha inscription was a gradual process, the beginnings of which go back to the time of the Omrides despite the nominal vassal status of Moab. In Herbert Donner's words: "Mesha's activities constituted a territorial expansion which reveals that the Omrides were not able to play a totally successful role either politically or militarily in the area east of the Jordan" (1977:408). Thus the growing power of the Arameans, the Assyrians, and the Moabites prevented the Omrides from becoming the dominant power in the region. This would offer a significant contrast to the territorial expansion of the Israelite and Judahite kingdoms in the eighth century B.C.E.

Jehoshaphat of Judah, who was a contemporary and ally of the Omrides, also followed similar policies, which brought renewed strength and prosperity to Judah. He reorganized the royal administration along the lines of Solomon's reign (2 Chr. 17:2) by placing forces in all the fortified cities of Judah and setting garrisons. The Arabs and the Philistines are reported to have brought tribute to Jehoshaphat that enriched the coffers (2 Chr. 17:11). His building activity included fortifying cities and founding store-cities and garrisons (2 Chr. 17:12–13). The unsuccessful maritime ventures of

Jehoshaphat are referred to in 2 Chronicles 20:36. The uneasy vassalage of the Edomites under Jehoshaphat is reflected in the successful Edomite rebellion during Jehoram's reign (2 Kings 8:20–22; 2 Chr. 21:8–10). Jehoshaphat was, at best, only able to keep them at bay. There was no scope of undisputed domination. Both in the case of the Omrides in the north and Jehoshaphat in the south, there was severe restriction by their neighboring powers. This is not to deny the stability and strength that they provided at home.

3

Social Reality of Israel and Judah in the Eighth Century B.C.E.

This chapter delineates a working hypothesis regarding the systemic reality of the eighth-century Israel and Judah to be tested against the prophetic texts. The basic contours of the hypothesis entail the following aspects:

1. The eighth century B.C.E. was a period of tremendous political power and economic growth unlike any other period in their history.
2. The beneficiaries of this economic growth were the ruling elite who dominated the state bureaucracy. Through various means, they were able to extract great amounts of the economic surplus.
3. The vast amounts of economic surplus extracted went to (a) support the leisured and luxurious living of the ruling class and (b) provide for means of extending and maintaining their political control.
4. The cumulative effect of all the above-mentioned was the deterioration of the plight of peasantry who constituted the majority of the population. The gradual deprivation of the peasantry is hypothesized in terms of the process of latifundialization.

While scholars might generally agree on the state of economic affluence and political strength of the eighth-century Israel and Judah, very few systematic studies offer an integrated and comprehensive picture. The purpose of the following section is therefore to offer a cogent and comprehensive (as is possible) picture of the eighth century B.C.E. as a period of economic growth and political stability for Israel and Judah. This will be done on the basis of close attention to the following aspects: colonization, regional specialization, demography, and trade and commerce.

Colonization

The early part of the eighth century B.C.E. was a period in which Israel and Judah enjoyed political stability and strength as a result of the powerful reigns of Jeroboam II in the north and Uzziah in the south. Not only were they powerful in forging strong states domestically, they were also able to expand into neighboring territories and wield control over their neighbors. This process of colonization results from a policy of imperialism. Imperialism may take the form of political subjugation in a direct way. Economic exploitation is an indirect form of imperialism. These are, however, not mutually exclusive. Territorial expansion often results in economic gain. Conversely, a policy of economic imperialism may result in the establishment of political control. Often, the fundamental motivation for imperialistic designs is the extraction of surplus. In many instances, the mounting pressures of inadequate local resources and increasing expenditures necessitate it. The elaborate building projects, maintenance of a huge army, state bureaucracy, and the royal paraphernalia are of enormous economic consequences.

The economic benefits of imperialism are threefold: plunder, tribute, and trade. The predatory policy is a more primitive and short-term form of economic gain. To illustrate this from ancient history, Assyrian emperors before Tiglath-Pileser III followed a policy of conquest and plunder. In contrast, the extraction of tribute is a more steady and long lasting source of revenue. Tiglath Pileser III initiated a policy of subtle economic imperialism whereby he allowed just enough independence to his vanquished subjects so as to continue production in order to ensure a steady supply of economic surplus into the Assyrian coffers. The tribute paid to foreign powers is raised through internal taxation of the common people. Sometimes rulers had to pay tribute in advance to ward off foreign invasions. The colonization of new territories could and does result in the expansion of active trade. However, the establishment of trade relations may not always involve political subjugation as the history of the Phoenicians in the ancient Near East would illustrate. In the ancient world, political control over territories was crucial for gaining access to trade routes. The control of trade routes was a profitable way of regulating trade and thereby benefiting from it.

The early part of the eighth century saw a surge in the colonial activity of Israel and Judah. Historically, this period corresponds to the reigns of Jeroboam II in the north and Uzziah in the south. The colonization of new territories we see in this period was motivated by the desire to expand the horizons of economic influence. The establishment of undisputed political control over economically profitable areas opened the doors for the effective extraction of surplus. One can see such motivation in the military conquests of Uzziah of Judah in 2 Chronicles 26:6–8 as follows:

> He [Uzziah] went out and made war against the Philistines and broke down the wall of Gath and the wall of Jabneh and the wall of Ashdod; and he built cities in the territory of Ashdod and elsewhere among the Philistines. God helped him against the Philistines and against the Arabs that dwelt in Gurba'al and against the Meunites. The Ammonites paid tribute to Uzziah and his fame spread even to the border of Egypt for he became very strong.

This passage clearly reflects the expansion of the Judean boundaries in three directions: westward, eastward, and towards the south.

Expansion into the West: The general pattern of relationship between the Philistines and the Hebrew kingdom(s) was one of persistent strain and strife. The Philistine domination of the Judean hill country in the premonarchic period has already been discussed in Chapter Two. The attempt by the Philistines to control the Judean hill country was motivated by the desire to extract the surplus from the premonarchic cultivators. The circumstances leading to the emergence of monarchy under David, however, put an end to the imperialistic designs of the Philistines. David liberated many of the territories that were under the Philistine control. Several accounts (1 Sam. 17; 27; 2 Sam. 21; 23; 1 Chr. 11; 18, among others) record the movements and victories of David against the Philistines. Early in

Solomon's reign, the Philistine areas were under the Israelite control (1 Kings 2:39–40). But toward the end of his reign, the Egyptians began to assert themselves in the south. In the years following the division of the kingdom, Sheshonk I (Shishak) during his campaign around 917 B.C.E. captured cities that had been fortified by Rehoboam (2 Chr. 11:5–10; 12:2–4). Some of the cities were in the Philistine territory. With the decline of the Egyptian power in the next fifty years, the Philistines began to assert their independence. In the following centuries, we see a persistent rivalry between the Judean kingdom and the Philistines. The kings of Judah repeatedly made efforts to penetrate the Philistine plains with a view to gain control over the Philistine section of the Via Maris–the Way of the Sea (Oded 1979a:239).

The Via Maris was a major trade route that ran through the length of Palestine, connecting Egypt with Mesopotamia and Anatolia. From Egypt, the Via Maris ran north along the coast through the Philistine plain. Some of the important cities along this section were Ashdod, Ashkelon, and Joppa. The main route continued in the direction of the plain of Sharon and turned northeast toward the Jezreel valley. This section of the route, which went through the mountainous Ephraimite hill country, was very important. The passes on this road were strategically important, because they could be blocked easily (Aharoni 1979a:50). One such pass opens into Megiddo. It is small wonder that Megiddo played such a major role in the fortification system of ancient Israel. From there, the Via Maris branched off into several routes. One branch went northwest through the plain of Acco along the Phoenician coast to Ugarit and Anatolia. Another branch passed through Hazor. The strategic importance of Hazor lay in the fact that it controlled access to the Judean ford on the way to Damascus (Aharoni 1979a:53). Yet another branch turned east across the Jezreel valley in the direction of Beth-Shean. The Iron Age fortress system at Beth-Shean attests to its importance in the network of fortifications (James 1966). From Beth-Shean a second branch ran northeast as far as 'En-Gev and further on to the Golan Heights. The ancient settlement at 'En-Gev is assumed to have been a vital halting point for the caravans going up to the Golan Heights (Mazar et al. 1964:2). At 'En-Gev, the excavators uncovered a huge fortified settlement. Apart from its strategic location en route to the Golan Heights, 'En-Gev was known for its fertile lands, fishing, and other maritime activities because of its proximity to the Sea of Galilee (Mazar et al. 1964:1). The large storage jars and huge public buildings with stone walls suggest the possibility of a fortified storehouse on the caravan route. These structures have been dated to the eighth century B.C.E. (Mazar et al. 1964:14, 30).

The significance of the Via Maris can be deduced from the number of key cities and settlements that flourished along its course. The roads provided the essential geographical link between places. They served as the major lines of communication for the merchant caravans. This facilitated the movement of goods from one place to another. A well-organized system of trade routes promoted the expansion of the market by facilitating the movement of goods by land and sea. The contribution of the Phoenicians to the growth of trade and commerce in the ancient Near East is unparalleled in antiquity. The local settlements along the main arteries of communication and the merchant caravans had a symbiotic relationship. The local settlements depended on the caravans for various trade items and also derived income through the collection of tolls. The caravans, in turn, depended on these settlements for protection, safe passage, and trade.

It should be noted that such well-organized networks of trade routes were possible only under the aegis of a strong centralized power. We witness this phenomenon in the tenth, ninth, and eighth centuries B.C.E. in the history of the Hebrew kingdom(s). The colonizing activity of Uzziah included the territories of the Philistines and the Arabs. In 2 Chronicles 17:11 we read that the Philistines and the Arabs brought tributes and presents to Uzziah. Second Chronicles 26:6–8 describes a large-scale expansion of the Judean hegemony under Uzziah. This can be corroborated by some archaeological evidence. The destruction of the lower city witnessed in the eighth-century level in Ashdod is attributed to the campaigns of Uzziah (M. Dothan 1967:184). At Tel Mor, which lies about a kilometer from the Ashdod shore, the remains of a fortress were found. Moshe Dothan suggests that Uzziah may have built this (1959:272). The numerous imported pottery vessels found at Tel Mor point to the close trade relations with Phoenicia and Cyprus. At Tel Nagila, the remains of a fortress were found. The early excavators proposed that this be identified with the Gath of the Philistines (Bürlow and Mitchell 1961:110). Even though this identification is doubtful and is not accepted widely, for our purposes it is sufficient to note that Tel Nagila was a site located in the inner coastal Philistine plain and that it attests to Judean presence in the eighth century B.C.E.

In the passage concerning Jehoshaphat's extraction of tribute (2 Chr. 17:11) and the one relating to the military exploits of Uzziah (2 Chr. 26:6–8), it is striking that the Arabs are mentioned alongside with the Philistines. The importance of this reference could be understood in light of the economic relations. The trade enterprises of the Philistines with Egypt had to be undertaken through the desert routes. It was necessary to cross the Sinai desert in order to trade with the economic centers of the Nile delta (Elat 1978:28). The Arabs controlled the trade routes traversing the Sinai desert. This forced the trading parties to be dependent on the goodwill of the Arabs for safe passage. By establishing control over the Philistines and the Arabs, Uzziah ensured the movement of goods from Egypt to Judah. The need to import Egyptian goods such as fine linen, gold, garments, minerals, and papyrus was the main motivating factor behind the colonizing activity of Uzziah. It is interesting to note that the Neo-Assyrian empire followed a similar policy of gaining control over the Philistines and the Arabs in establishing economic ties with Egypt (Elat 1978:20–34).

Expansion into the East: One of the areas to come under the domination of Israel and Judah is the territory east of Palestine across the river the Jordan, often designated as Transjordan. This includes areas immediately east of the Jordan valley, the Dead Sea, and the 'Arabah. The Transjordanian areas included the more prominent biblical places of Bashan, Gilead, Ammon, Moab, and Edom. The control of this region was keenly sought by many powers for centuries for two reasons: its economic importance, and the trade route that plied the length of the Transjordanian plateau.

The Transjordan region is an elevated plateau of mountainous highlands. On the western flank, it has hills rising from the Jordan Valley. These high ridges help in cooling the atmosphere by trapping western winds, which in turn produce large amounts of rainfall in the region (Aharoni 1979a:36). On the eastern side, the highlands gradually merge into the desert. As a result, there is no natural barrier. This left the region vulnerable to the attacks of the desert inhabitants. Under such circumstances, the presence of a powerful central authority offered protection to the inhabitants of the land. Conversely, for the protector, it was an economic base from which to profit. The entire region is watered well by the rivers Yarmuk, Arab,

Jurm, Jabir, Jabbok, Arnon, and Zered. Bashan is the most fertile area of all with a substantial rainfall. Bashan was known for its wheat, oaks, and fine cattle (Cohen 1962:687; Aharoni 1979a:36–38). Gilead is a mountainous region. The economic importance of Gilead lay in its grapes, olives, and balm (Cohen 1962:687; Aharoni 1979a:39). The Ammonite territory consisted of an urban settlement surrounded by smaller settlements, which were agriculturally fertile. This was due to the relatively abundant rainfall (roughly 20 inches annually) in the region, which helped in the intensive cultivation of fruit trees and cereals and also pasturage for cattle, sheep, and goats (LaBianca and Younker 1995:403). Bustanay Oded points to another factor that not only contributed to the economic strength of this region but also helped to promote the unification of the Ammonite settlements. The process of active international trade "which was generally a royal monopoly facilitated the unification of the Ammonites as a national kingdom administered from a single center" (Oded 1979a:260). Moab contains mountains that rise to three to four thousand feet above sea level. The annual rainfall drops to 12–16 inches in comparison to Ammon (La Bianca and Younker 1995:403). The economy of Moab centered around the production of cereals, fruit trees, and herding (Cohen 1962:687; Aharoni 1979a:40; LaBianca and Younker 1995:403). Relevant to this discussion is the interesting reference in 2 Kings 3:4 to the king of Moab, Mesha, as a sheep-breeder. Edom lies at the southernmost part of the Transjordanian plateau. The annual rainfall drops to 4–8 inches (LaBianca and Younker 1995:403). In contrast to Ammon and Moab, the economy of Edom revolved solely around pasturing and herding activities (LaBianca and Younker 1995:403). Additionally, Edom's strategic location at the southernmost part of the major trade route served as a vital link to Arabia in the south and the African coast in the east. Its proximity to the copper mines of the 'Arabah also contributed to its economic importance (Aharoni 1979a:40).

During the United Monarchy, the Transjordanian territory was controlled by David and Solomon. After the death of Solomon, the Arameans began to make inroads into Transjordan. During the ninth century B.C.E., the control of this region was fiercely contested by the Arameans and the Israelite kings. According to 1 Kings 20:34, Ben-hadad I is said to have taken cities from Omri and established bazaars in Samaria. Later, Ahab was able to inflict defeat on the Arameans and win cities from Ben-hadad II and establish bazaars in Damascus.

This implies that the Aramean hold on the Transjordan region slackened during Ahab's time. In 2 Kings 3:4, we read that Mesha, the king of Moab, had to deliver to Ahab "a hundred thousand lambs and the wool of a hundred thousand rams." In the biblical accounts, we also read that the Ammonites and the Moabites sustained defeats at the hands of Jehoshaphat of Judah (2 Chr. 20).

In the early part of the eighth century, we see a resurgence in the power of Israel and Judah under Jeroboam II and Uzziah respectively, resulting in the complete domination of Transjordania. The resurgence of Israel and Judah corresponds with the weakening of the Aramaean kingdom under Ben-hadad III. Second Kings 14:25 records how Jeroboam II "restored the border of Israel from the Lebo-hamath as far as the sea of the 'Arabah." This implies that the entire length of the King's Highway, the major trade route plying the length of the plateau, was under Israelite control. Uzziah gains power as Jeroboam's weakens. With the decline of the Northern Kingdom, Uzziah establishes his control over the region. In 2 Chronicles 26:8, it is reported that the Ammonites paid tribute to Uzziah. Oded draws attention to an interesting phenomenon in the reign of Uzziah. Uzziah, according to Oded, set about a process of colonization whereby some of the Judean population were brought to Gilead and settled there. These families seem to have established large land holdings. The family of Tabeel-Tobiah was one such (Oded 1979b:262). That the settlement had been established under the royal directive becomes evident from the fact that Judah appointed Ben-tabeel as the governor of the region bordering on the Ammonite territory (Oded 1972:155–56). This very same Ben-tabeel later became subject to the manipulations of Rezin of Damascus in the context of the Syro-Epraimite war with the promise of the Judean crown in place of Ahaz (Isa. 7:6). In this situation, it is not hard to see the intentions of Rezin in undermining the Judean control of Transjordan. The Assyrian intervention put an end to Rezin's machinations. In the centuries following this period, the control of Transjordan passed to the Assyrians, to the Babylonians, and finally to the Persians.

The importance of the Transjordan region lay not only in its agricultural and herding resources but also in the international trade route, the King's Highway, that ran along the length of the region. The King's Highway, which connected Egypt and Arabia with Syria and Mesopotamia, promoted international trade and commerce and thereby bolstered the Transjordan's economic importance. The initial references to the King's Highway occur in Numbers 20:17 and 21:22 in connection with the wilderness wanderings of the early Israelites. The highway linked all the important settlements in Transjordan: Naveh, Karnaim, and Ashtaroth in Bashan; Ramoth-Gilead, Geresa, and Jogbehah in Gilead; Rabboth-Ammon in the Ammonite territory; Heshbon, Madeba, Dibon, and Kirhareseth in Moab; Sela and Bozrah in Edom; and then finally Ezion-Geber (Aharoni 1979a:56). From Bozrah, the highway split into two branches, both leading eventually to Egypt. One branch went in southwestern direction through the wilderness of Zin, through Kadesh-Barnea, to Egypt. The other one descended south through Teman, Rekam, along the southern part of the 'Arabah, to Elath (Aharoni 1979a:56). The nature of the terrain determined and, in fact, restricted the trade exchange to only these routes. The safe passage of the merchant caravans enabled the free flow of commerce. A strong power capable of providing protection to the caravans also benefited from the tolls collected from them. Further, the growth and survival of the settlements along these routes needed the defense of a strong power against the sporadic attacks from the desert on the eastern flank. In this connection, it is important to realize that it is precisely those times when the Hebrew kingdoms were strong that they were able to control this territory and benefit from it. To a certain measure, this was possible in the tenth century B.C.E. under David and Solomon, and in the ninth century under the Omrides in the north and Jehoshaphat in the south. But in the eighth century B.C.E., we see an undisputed control of this region jointly by Israelite and Judean kings. As pointed out earlier, Jeroboam II dominated the King's Highway from Hamath to the sea of 'Arabah (2 Kings 14:25). Under Amaziah of Judah, the southernmost part of the highway came under Judean control (2 Kings 14:7). His son and successor, Uzziah, is credited with the rebuilding of Elath (2 Chr. 26:2).

Expansion into the South: From the point of view of climatic conditions and agricultural resources, the expansion into the Negev may seem inexplicable. The Negev comprises the dry desert stretching from fringes of Beersheba southward for about 30 miles. It has an average rainfall of about 12–15 inches. The eastern part of the Negev has some mountain ranges, which are a continuation of the central hill country. The elevation of about 1500–1800 feet above sea level contributes to the minor differences in temperature and moisture that set conditions of agriculture and herding (Aharoni 1979a:31). The combination of intensive dry farming and herding may have supported a significant population in the Iron Age (Rosen and Finkelstein 1992:57). Despite the climatic and topographical limitations, the Negev continued to attract the Judean kings as an avenue for territorial expansion. The Negev had its own advantages. First, most of the roads leading to Egypt, Arabia, and Edom passed through the Negev. This network of roads was, in fact, a means of conducting international and interregional commerce. Second, the Negev served as a defense frontier on the boundary. It was an effective buffer zone against infiltrating desert groups and other enemies. Third, the Negev gave access to the 'Arabah with its economically important rich copper mines. Finally, the Negev provided another settlement space for the excess population of the Judean kingdom (Aharoni 1958:37; 1979b:290; Glueck 1959:146). The size of the desert population in the Negev depended on the availability of economic resources such as trade, stable political situation in the north, and climate (Rosen and Finkelstein 1992:57–58).

There were four main arteries in the Negev. The first one connected Kadesh-Barnea and Arad. It is referred to as "the way of Atharim" in Numbers 21:1 (NRSV). The second road went from Kadesh-Barnea through the Nissanah valley leading to the way of the Shur and then down south to Egypt. The third route went south from 'Avdat through Mount Ramon to the 'Arabah. The fourth one linked the 'Arabah with Edom and then continued south past Tamar to Elath (Aharoni 1967:11).

The network of roads outlined above facilitated the flow of international and interregional trade and commerce. Making these roads safe and passable necessitated the establishment of fortresses. One of the important archaeological findings in this region is the network of fortresses along the highways in this region (Aharoni 1967:2–11). The standard-sized fortresses were built on the tops of hills to have a wide range of view. There were also some fortresses located at crossroads and important points on the main roads. The general plan for these structures consisted of a row of rooms surrounding a large central courtyard. All these fortresses are dated within the time period of the tenth to seventh centuries.

Aharoni classifies these fortresses into several groups depending on their external features (1967:2–11). The first group consists of four major forts that were distinguished by towers. To this category belong the forts at Kadesh-Barnea, Arad, Horvat 'Uza (Khirbet Ghazzah), and Ezion-Geber. A casemate wall and eight projecting towers surrounded the fort at Kadesh-Barnea. Traditionally, this fort has been attributed to Jehoshaphat. But Moshe Dothan proposes that the fortresses could very well be attributed to Uzziah (1965:142). There are two clues for dating this to the eighth century B.C.E. First, the adaptation of the thick walls into casemate type construction with the rooms surrounding the inner courtyard is to be dated no earlier than eighth century. Second, the projecting towers from the casemate fortification belong to the eighth century. There is no proof that they were any earlier (Aharoni 1967:13–14). The fort at Kadesh-Barnea was of strategic importance because it guarded the defenses of the frontier areas.

The fort at Arad is similar to the one in Kadesh-Barnea in its general plan of a large courtyard surrounded by a casemate wall and towers (Aharoni and Amiran 1964:134–36). The contents of this fort provide some interesting evidence. There were traces of a large public building, which probably served as a storehouse. There were also dwelling units, which could have been used by the state officials and merchants in transit. The presence of a large number of weights attests to some kind of commercial transactions (Aharoni 1967:14). Further, the ostraca (inscribed fragments of pottery) found at Arad inform us of the strategic importance of the fort there. These ostraca contain instructions or requests for the issue of rations of wine, oil, and flour. It is conceivable that the fort at Arad served as a storehouse and that these rations were sent to other smaller fortresses as provisions for the merchant travelers, soldiers guarding the fortresses, or state officials stationed in these places (Aharoni 1967:14; 1979b:299). Since these forts were established and controlled under the royal directive, one can also assume a system of central provisioning for the project.

The fort at Horvat 'Uza (Khirbet Gazzah) was a border fortress located between the edge of the Negev and the steep descent into the Dead Sea. It guarded access to Edom. From here went the road to the 'Arabah and Edom. In construction, it is very similar to the other two with projecting towers, massive walls, large courtyards, and series of rooms. There were no traces of pre-Iron Age II material (Aharoni 1958:35; Glueck 1959:179).

The fort at Tell el-Kheleifeh was also one of the major fortresses, even though it differs in external features. The fort was oblong in shape with surrounding rooms and courtyards. It was the southernmost fort defending the borders and serving as a gateway to the kingdoms south of Judah. In addition to these four, there were more than twenty other forts, which Aharoni classified under the following categories: (1) square forts without towers, (2) oblong and round forts, and (3) forts surrounded by polygonal enceintes.[1] The existence of such a large number of fortresses at strategic points along the roads and settlements in the Negev testifies to a conscious policy and planned effort. The Judean kings systematically sought to extend the frontiers of the Negev for the purpose of defending the trade routes and promoting trade with neighboring kingdoms.

One other piece of evidence for the occupation of the Negev is the settlements found alongside the fortresses. The remains of what seem to be farming communities were uncovered in three places: Ramat Matred (el-Matrada), Mishor Haruah (Sahil al-Hawa) in the Nissanah valley (Wadi 'Ajram), and the Buqei'a valley. These settlements were agricultural in nature. In the Negev, which has a meager annual rainfall of about 8 inches, agriculture is not an easy venture. The main obstacles to desert farming are lack of suitable soils and adequate water. In the desert areas, cultivation is possible only where the runoff water collects. These depressions in due time become wadis. In the eighth century B.C.E., the Negev settlers countered these difficulties by directing the runoff water onto terraced fields (which not only supplemented the water supply but also enriched the top soil), and channeling the water into cisterns for drinking purposes and for animals (Borowski 1979:31). This agricultural method was called runoff farming.

The settlements at Mishor Haruah and Upper Nissanah valley at the edge of Maktesh Ramon offer important information regarding the eighth-century colonization of the Negev. The excavators found

---

[1]The square forts without towers were smaller in size located (1) in Nahal Raviv; (2) in Qasr el-Ruheibeh 3 miles north of Rehobot of the Negev; (3) on the northern edge of Kadesh-Barnea; (4) on the ridge of Beer-Hafir; (5) 10.5 km north of 'Avdat; (6) in the valley joining Nahal Haluqim, Nahal Besor, and Nahal Boqer; and (7) at Mishor-Haruah. The forts in the second category—oblong and round—were situated (1) at Giv'at Refed; (2) 2 km southwest of Giv'at Refed; (3) at Horvat Tov 5.5 km northeast of Arad; (4) at Yotbetah in the 'Arabah; (5) at Nahal Le'anah near Beer Hafir; (6) at Ezion-Geber; and (7) at 'Ain Qedeis in Kadesh-Barnea. The last category was not found in the Negev proper but in the Judean desert: one in Mispeh 'Ain Gedi and another one on Mt. Hesron west of Nahal Seelim. Furthermore, three of the *tells* in the northern Negev—Beersheba (Tell es-Seba), Tell Malhata (Tell el-Milh), and Tell Masos (Khirbet el-Meshash)—had forts in the monarchic period (Aharoni 1967:2–11).

two periods of settlement: Middle Bronze I (ca. 2000 B.C.E.) and Iron II (ca. 850–600 B.C.E.). In the Iron II levels, the remains of the settlement included terraced fields, a large farm house, water cisterns, and a stone wall covering the whole unit (Evenari et al. 1958:234–35). The pottery found was typical of the eighth century. This settlement was located along the main roads reaching Elath on the one hand and Kadesh-Barnea on the other. In the Buqei'a Valley, three such farm houses were found. These communities grew barley, wheat, and legumes (Stager 1976:145). Among the discoveries from the valley were forts, dams, and cisterns. The wheel-burnished water decanters of the eighth century appear in large quantities (Cross and Milik 1956:39–45). The crucial question raised with regard to these settlements is their relationship to the forts. There are two possibilities. One, the food supply for the soldiers stationed at these forts could have come from these farms. It is attested that in addition to terrace farming, substantial farming was done at wadi bottoms. Further, sheep and goats seem to have provided an additional source of living as the number of corrals attached to these farm houses show (Evenari et al. 1958:238). Another possibility is that the soldiers at these forts were also part-time farmers (Borowski 1979:32). These settlements in all probability depended on the commercial traffic for tolls and other merchandise.

When we put together the different pieces of the puzzle, it becomes clear that the settlement and development of the Negev were not part of a natural process. The network of trade routes, the system of strategically located fortresses, and the groups of settlements—all point to the conclusion that this was a conscious and well-planned drive on the part of the Judean monarchy to colonize this area. Uzziah certainly becomes the prime candidate for such an initiative. Scholars who have studied the Negev settlement process in depth corroborate this. Michael Evenari et al. write:

> This type of sedentary agriculture using the run-off water in the desert may have been the result of a concentrated statewide effort by the Judean kings to dominate this area. Uzziah is one of the kings to whom this enterprise could be attributed [2 Chr. 26: 10]. (1958:238)

In Oded Borowski's opinion, if the relationship between the forts and the farming settlements could be established, it becomes apparent that "these settlements were established by the central administration of the state" (1979:33). Commenting on the settlement at the Judean Buqei'a Valley, Cross and Milik conclude:

> The pattern of construction of the fortresses, their plans and masonry, their rock-cut cisterns together with the massive and similar irrigation system adjoining each and finally their identical pottery series suggests that the settlement of the Buqeiah was organized at one time by a central authority and not improbably built with the aid of corvée labor. (1958:15)

Besides pointing to the centrally organized aspect of these settlements, Cross and Milik have touched upon an important issue: the part played by corvée in the settlement process. This factor becomes important in examining the conditions that contribute to the worsening plight of the peasantry, because it was the peasants who supplied the labor force. Frequent and long corvée responsibilities affect the productiveness in agriculture. The energies of the peasants are overextended between agriculture and forced labor. It should be pointed out that the burden of forced labor was the main bone of contention in the division of the Hebrew kingdoms after Solomon's death.

Regional Specialization

This has to do with development of particular economic activities in regions that are conducive to such activities. Besides natural differences in terms of available resources, geographical differences suited to particular crops and conditions conducive to particular activities promote regional specialization. Fundamental to understanding regional specialization in ancient societies is the shift from a subsistence economy to a market economy. The shift toward a market economy brings about a change in the nature of productive units and the pattern of production. Under the subsistence economy, the productive units (most often basic family units) tend to be smaller, multipurpose, and all doing the same kinds of activity. There is very little division of labor among the productive units. But with the rise of a market economy, economic activities are no longer confined to the family units. There is increasing division of labor. This gives rise to specialized structures of productive units, which are engaged in production for the market. Under the subsistence economy, the units produced for their own consumption and consumed what they produced. But with the rise of a market economy, the production is for unknown consumers, which brings economic gain. The drive to produce commercial crops for the market with a view to gain maximum economic advantage reinforces the shift toward regional specialization. It can be argued with proper basis that such a phenomenon was at the heart of the economic life of the eighth-century Israelite and Judahite societies.

Second Chronicles 26:10 offers some clues concerning regional specialization in Judah under Uzziah. The traditional reading of this passage is exemplified in the translation of the *New Revised Standard Version:*

> He [Uzziah] built towers in wilderness and hewed out many cisterns, for he had large herds, both in the Shephelah and in the plain, and he had farmers and vinedressers in the hills and in the fertile lands.

This rendering does not adequately highlight the subtleties of the socioeconomic realities. In contrast, the proposals (independently arrived at) by Chaney and Rainey to rearrange the punctuation of the sentence do justice not only to the Hebrew syntax but also to the economic and geographic realities of Judah:

> He [Uzziah] built guard towers in the steppe and hewed out many cisterns, for he had large herds; and in the Shephelah and in the plains [he had] plowmen; and vineyard and orchard workers in the hill country and in the garden-land ... (Chaney 1986:73)

> And he [Uzziah] built towers in the *wilderness* and carved out many cisterns because he had so much cattle; and in the *Shephelah* and on the *plain,* farmers; and vinedressers in the *Hills* and in the *Carmel* ... (Rainey 1982:58)

What this passage reflects is regional specialization with the promotion of herding in the steppes by building guard towers and providing water by means of hewn cisterns; intensive cultivation of staples like wheat and barley in the fertile plains where there was adequate supply of water; and development of viticulture in the hill country that was best suited for it. Chaney's hunch that this might indicate a "command economy" under the royal directive has merit. Anson Rainey also talks of them as royal enterprises. Command economy originally referred to the authoritarian economic organization of the kingdom in ancient history (Heilbroner and Thurow 1975:90). The crown was the central economic authority, which controlled the flow of economic life in the society.

In terms of geographic potential, Israel and Judah offer a striking variety. The differences in the natural conditions and potential promoted regional specialization. The various specialized economic activities included viticulture, olive growing, mining and metallurgy, dyeing and weaving, and a perfume industry, in addition to farming and herding. It must be pointed out that the economic sphere attests to both private and royal enterprises. Under the subsistence economy, no such distinction exists, because in a tribal setting a strong centralized power is lacking. With the emergence of monarchy, there is a strong centralized power. Along with the private enterprises, the monarchical state began to play a key role in the economy.

Wine Industry

Archaeological excavations have brought to light a fairly extensive wine industry at Gibeon. It is a bit puzzling that the Bible is silent about this. The settlement at Gibeon flourished and prospered in the period extending from the tenth century B.C.E. to the beginning of the sixth century B.C.E. One main reason for the prosperity of Gibeon was the production and export of wine (Pritchard 1962:79). Pritchard calls it "an ancient 'bordeaux' of Palestine." The evidences for the wine industry were accumulated over a period of four seasons of excavation. Before the 1959 excavation, fifty-nine jar handles, a clay funnel, and more than forty clay stoppers were found (Pritchard 1964:24). In 1959, the excavators uncovered as many as sixty-three vats cut into the bedrock. On an average, the vats were seven feet deep and about six feet in diameter. These vats were used as storage cellars. Wine was stored in two-foot tall jars standing stacked up in these cellars. At a conservative estimate, the excavators place the capacity of these vats in the cellar to hold in excess of twenty-five thousand gallons of liquid (Pritchard 1962:90–92). It was also discovered through an experiment that these rock-cut cisterns could keep a steady temperature of 65°F required to preserve the wine (Pritchard 1962:83).

That Gibeon was an important center for the production of wine can be derived from two other clues. First, it is no mere coincidence that the very first report we get of the Gibeonites in the Bible depicts them as carrying "wineskins" to Joshua at Gilgal (Josh. 9:4). Second, even in modern times, vines grow in abundance at Gibeon (Pritchard 1962:99). Gibeon seems to have thrived as an important commercial center for four centuries between the tenth and sixth centuries B.C.E. It is puzzling that the Bible makes no mention of this. The peak period of wine production was probably the eighth century. James Pritchard places the peak period of wine production in the seventh century, but he does not rule out the possibility of an earlier date. He writes: "In the 7th century, and probably long before, wine was produced in great quantities" (1962:99).

The large number of stamped handles marked with the name of Gibeon and the name of the producer indicate that Gibeon was not only a large-scale wine-producing center but also an exporting center of some consequence. It is reasonable to assume on the basis of personal names and the lack of royal connections (that is, lack of *lmlk* connections, see below) that the wine production at Gibeon was a private enterprise.

The evidence for royal vineyards in Judah comes from the *lmlk* seal impressions, meaning "to/for the king," on storage jars. The origin and purpose of these jars have been the subject of many studies. A review of all the treatments on the subject is out of the direct purview of this book, although they will be referred to at appropriate junctures.[2] That the content of these jars was wine is not debated. Earlier, the *lmlk* seals were attributed to the time of Josiah. But in light of the evidence from Lachish stratum III, a late eighth-century B.C.E. date emerged as the consensus (Ussishkin 1977:54–57; Na'aman 1979:77–79; Rainey 1982:57).

Much of the debate centered around the origin and purpose of these jars with particular reference to the four place names found in these seal impressions: Hebron, Socoh, Ziph, and Mmšt. Aharoni had argued that these place names represent the four store-cities around which Hezekiah undertook a reorganization of Judean districts a few years before Sennacherib's invasion (1979a:398–99). Rainey has made a compelling case that the four place names represent four royal wineries in the Judean hill country (1982:59). It is significant that three of the four names occur in the list of the Judean hill country places in Josh. 15:48, 54, 55. Mmšt is the problematic one, since it is not attested. On a conjectural basis, Rainey locates it north of Hebron

[2]Key works on the *lmlk* seals include Cross 1964, Diringer 1949, Lance 1971, Lapp 1960, Na'aman 1979, Rainey 1965, Rainey 1982, Stern 1975, Ussishkin 1976, Ussishkin 1977.

(1982:59). The distribution of the places would be as follows: Ziph and Socoh in the southernmost hill country, Hebron in the center, and Mmšt in the north. Rainey seeks support for his interpretation in 2 Chronicles 26:10, which alludes to the crown properties and regional specialization. According to 2 Chronicles 26:10c, the vine dressers are to be located in "the hills and in the Carmel." In Rainey's view, "the hills and the Carmel do in fact represent two units of the Judean hill country" (1982:58). This is by no means conclusive but has much to commend it. Be that as it may, the relevant point for our discussion is the information that Uzziah had at his command vinedressers in the hill country and that these were royal vineyards. These could have been private holdings of the crown acquired through the descendants of David (Rainey 1982:59). The wine produced at these vineyards might have been sent for the use of the royal household. In the case of the *lmlk* impressions, as Rainey proposes, the wine could have been sent to certain strategic locations in an effort to accumulate supplies for the troops in the wake of the Assyrian invasion under Sennacherib (1982:58). Nadav Na'aman (1979:82–83) takes the occurrence of the seal impressions to indicate the borders of the Judean kingdom under Hezekiah. But the absence of the *lmlk* seals from some other places in Hezekiah's kingdom such as Tell Jemmeh, Tell esh-Shar'ia (Tel Sera'), and Tell el-Hesi does not substantiate this. Rainey's proposal, that the seals were found in great profusion in places that were chosen by Hezekiah to strengthen for military reason in anticipation of Sennacherib's invasion, seems likely (1982:61–62).

Another valuable source of information regarding the wine (and also oil) industry is the Samaria ostraca. In addition to testifying to the quantity of wine and oil production, they also attest to the existence of private and royal enterprises with regard to vineyards and olive orchards. Second, they also provide information concerning the taxation system. A third aspect is related to the previous one. It has to do with the administrative system. The debate concerning the Samaria ostraca revolves around two issues: the meaning of the *l* prefix to the personal names and the interpretation of the numerals as a guide to dating. Aharoni and Rainey interpret the prefix as the preposition *l* meaning "to." It follows from this that the personal names attached to the prefix would refer to the individuals who were recipients of the commodities listed. According to Aharoni and Rainey, the ostraca were records of shipments received by government officials or high-ranking court officials in charge of certain territories to whom income from these territories was allotted in accordance with their office or rank (Aharoni 1979a:363; Rainey 1962:62–63; 1967:32–41). Both reject the idea that these were tax receipts. In a later treatment, Rainey has suggested that "the life setting underlying the ostraca is the land-grant and patrimonial system" (Rainey 1967). The shipments were received from their family holdings by persons serving at the capital and also from other estates, which had been handed to them by the crown. The story of Meribaal (2 Sam. 9; 16) is cited as supporting evidence.

Yadin reads the *l* prefix as indicating possession (1959:184–87; 1962:64–66). This is in conjunction with the accepted principle in Hebrew grammar that *l* prefixed to a proper noun not preceded by a verb should be considered possessive (Gesenius 1910:419 #129). In addition to the *ledavid* superscriptions in the Psalms, Yadin also cites 1 Kings 2:39 and Ezekiel 37:16 as examples of the use of the *l* prefix (followed by a noun without a governing verb) denoting possession (1968:50–51). Consequently, the names of the persons attached to the prefix would, then, imply that they were owners of the estates from which consignments were sent. According to this proposal, the ostraca would have to be seen as tax receipts from private landowner to the royal courts. Yadin's interpretation is probable for various reasons. First of all, the interpretation of the *l* prefix in a possessive sense fits with the known conventions of Hebrew grammar. However, reading the *l* as a prefix of possession does not of necessity preclude the land-grant/patrimony theory that Rainey suggests. These private estates could very well have been grants from the crown as well as holdings through patrimony. Second, the shipments could have been sent either by the landed elite or more likely by the tenant farmers as taxes on behalf of their absentee landlords. It seems less probable that the royal court kept track of the provisions sent for the use of individual officials as suggested by Aharoni and Rainey. It is more likely that the royal administration would be more interested in keeping a record of its revenues (taxes) rather than provisions sent for the support of the officials.

Without going into details about the numerals found in these ostraca as a guide to dating them, for our purposes it is sufficient to say that, for the most part, the ostraca are placed either in the first or middle part of the eighth century B.C.E. Aharoni places one group as belonging to the reign of Joash, 800–785 B.C.E., and another to

Jeroboam II, 785–749 B.C.E. (1979a:366). Yadin attributes them to the reign of Menahem, 747–734 B.C.E. (1961:9–10).

The Samaria ostraca, thus, attest to the existence of private estates engaged in the production of wine and oil in the eighth century B.C.E. Another interesting piece of information brought to light by the ostraca is the clan names. Aharoni traced these clan names to the tribe of Manasseh (1979a:367). All the places mentioned in the ostraca are located in the northern part of Mount Ephraim. Ephraim has been known as a territory where "lived the richest and most advanced sector of the population" (Baron 1958:65).

The Samaria ostraca also give evidence for the existence of royal vineyards. It is possible that the two vineyards, Cherem-Hattel (referred to in the ostraca nos. 53, 54, 56, 58, and 61) and Cherem-Yehoeli (referred to in nos. 55 and 60) were, in fact, royal vineyards (Aharoni 1979a:367). The lack of reference to either personal names or clan names points in that direction. A survey conducted in the Jenin-Megiddo area, which is also in the Manasseh region along the edge of the Jezreel valley, uncovered as many as 117 wine presses over the entire area (Ahlström 1978:46). A more systematic excavation would produce additional information.

The various sources discussed above in connection with the wine industry point to its prominence in the economic sphere. More importantly, three aspects relating to the wine industry provide circumstantial evidence that there was an increase in the production of wine in the eighth century B.C.E. First, the repeated references to wine in the epigraphic sources, and also the increase in the number of epigraphic sources mentioning commodities such as wine and oil, are indications of the increase in wine production. Second, the proliferation of wine presses attested in the eighth-century levels of the many archaeological sites in Israel and Judah reflects a thriving wine industry. Finally, the appearance of wine and oil storage jars in the eighth-century layers of excavated sites is linked to the increase in the production of wine.

The production of commercial crops such as wine and olive was in response to the demands of the market economy. Commodities like wine and oil were more lucrative items to export because they were worth more than grain per unit of volume or weight. Besides figuring prominently in the conspicuous consumption of the upper class, wine and oil were exported in exchange for key military items and luxury goods. More will be said about this later in the chapter.

Oil Industry

Along with wine, olive oil was an important commodity in terms of both local consumption and export. The moderate climate in the Mediterranean region is best suited for its cultivation. While an olive tree needs a warmer climate than a grapevine, it does need cooler temperatures for limited periods in order to give fruit (Frankel 1999:36). It is precisely for such climatic reasons olives could never become a prominent crop in Egypt. Oil had to be exported to Egypt from Palestine. In return, horses and chariots and other luxury items such as fine linen, perfume, and jewelry were imported into Palestine from Egypt. The local use of olive oil included food preparation, lamps, anointing, libation, base for perfume, and treatment of wounds (Borowski 1979:180; Frankel 1999:43–46).

The importance of oil to the economy of Palestine is seen from the number of olive presses uncovered in the excavations in many sites and also reference to oil in the epigraphic sources such as the Samaria ostraca and the Arad ostraca. One of the largest oil presses to be excavated thus far comes from Beth-Shemesh. This comes from stratum IIc, which is dated to the early part of the eighth century B.C.E. (Grant 1939:76). A number of other smaller wine and olive presses were also discovered in the same stratum. These may reflect simpler rock-cut installations consisting of a sloping surface for treading or crushing and a collecting vat at the bottom connected by a channel (Frankel 1999:51). It is difficult to distinguish between presses used for wine and oil production. It is quite possible that the same presses were used for crushing grapes as well as olives. This is apparent from the presence of grape seeds and olive pits near the presses. The lack of a specific term for an oil press in biblical usage further illustrates this point (Frankel 1999:185–86). This also explains the hesitance on the part of some excavators to attribute these presses to one or the other industry.[3]

In a survey conducted in the Samarian hills, forty rock-cut installations identified as olive presses were discovered at Khirbet Banat-bar (17), Klia (15), Khirbet Khudesh (5) and one each at Dir-amar, Khirbet Kasfa, and Sanniriya (Eitam 1979:146). Some of these

---

[3]For a detailed treatment of wine and oil production in antiquity in Israel and other Mediterranean countries, with particular reference to basic processes and various types of installations and presses, see Frankel 1999.

presses were operated by means of a log fixed to a niche in the wall and pressure applied by adding weights. This type of press has been called the beam press. It is important to note that the introduction of the beam press was a technological improvement that facilitated the production of larger quantities of oil (Borowski 1979:177).

At Tell Beit Mirsim, in stratum A2 belonging to the eighth century B.C.E., a number of "free-standing central vats" (Frankel 1999:63) were found. Albright interpreted these installations as dyeing vats (1943:55–60). Even though many scholars accepted Albright's conclusions, Gustaf Dalman did not. He proposed that these installations were olive presses (1964:70–89). David Eitam (1979) further substantiated this. Albright based his conclusions on the following grounds: (1) the analogy of the Arab installations; (2) traces of slaked lime, which Albright took to be the fixative element for the dye mixture; (3) a light gray ash that was interpreted as potash, a necessary ingredient in dyeing; (4) scores of doughnut-shaped weights; and (5) square plastered basins, which were thought to be cisterns used in the dyeing process (Albright 1943:56–60).

Eitam countered Albright's conclusions as follows: (1) The Arab installations at Hebron are not like the installations at Tell Beit Mirsim. (2) The slaked lime residue in the basins could have been there for a number of reasons: for instance, for plastering or cleaning the basins. (3) The so-called potash was never analyzed in the laboratory. (4) The stone weights could have been the ones used for a beam press and not necessarily for a loom. (5) The rock-cut basins which Albright interpreted as cisterns were in fact used for crushing olives. The presence of such basins near the olive presses in Beth-Shemesh and Tell en-Nasbeh supports this (Eitam 1979:152). One other factor that works against Albright's conclusion is the geographic location of Tell Beit Mirsim. Tell Beit Mirsim is generally identified as the biblical Debir. If this is correct, the location of Debir according to Joshua 15:48 is in the sixth district of Judah along with Jattir, Anab, and Eshtemoh, southwest of Hebron in the hill country. Even if this identification is not correct, the location of Tell Beit Mirsim at a point where the hill country descends into the Shephelah is critical. The hill country, as is well known, is conducive to viticulture and olive groves. This further strengthens the case for taking these installations to be olive presses. However, it does not rule out possibility of dyeing and weaving as minor industry at Tell Beit Mirsim as in the case of Beth-Shemesh (Grant 1939:76). Other olive presses have been recovered from sites such as Tell en-Nasbeh (McCown 1947:62), Hazor (Yadin et al. 1989:24), and Dothan (Free 1959:22).

In addition to the discovery of oil presses, the information from epigraphic sources and the large number of jars bear testimony to the importance of oil in the economy of Israel and Judah. Two such sources have already been mentioned in the previous section. Among the Samaria ostraca, more than twelve ostraca refer to the shipment of oil. As has been pointed out earlier, most of the shipments seem to have come from private estates as taxes to the royal storage. It is also interesting to note that only the shipments from two vineyards, Cherem-Hattel and Cherem-Yeholi, identified by Aharoni as royal vineyards, refer to both wine and oil. A second source of information is the Arad ostraca. The provisions referred to here often include oil as a regular item. These ostraca bear instructions or requests for issue of rations of wine, oil, and flour from the Arad fortress. It seems possible that the provisions were sent from Arad to other smaller fortresses for the officials and/or soldiers stationed there. There were also royal vineyards and olive groves as suggested by 1 Chronicles 27:27.

The excavations at Dothan, particularly during the fifth and sixth seasons, have produced literally hundreds of storage jars (Free 1958:10–18; 1959:22–24). The contents of these jars have been identified as wheat and oil by the remnants of grains and olive pits in them. Several observations point to the fact that Dothan was an administrative center for collecting taxes in wheat and oil. Most of the jars were of a single type, which indicates that we may be dealing with some kind of standard operation or authority. Second, the concentration of a large quantity of these jars in a relatively small area suggests that they were stacked up in a storage facility (Free 1958:12). In light of this, one could make a case for Dothan serving as a local center for collecting taxes in wheat and oil.

Another valuable piece of evidence is an ostracon from Tell Qasile dating to the eighth century B.C.E. Mazar interpreted this ostracon to be a bill for a certain quantity of oil sent from the royal treasure house to one of the coastal towns in Phoenicia or Egypt. The sender is identified by an Israelite name, Hiyahu, who could have been an inspector of exports from the storehouses at Tell Qasile (Maisler 1950/51b:209). Tell Qasile was located close to the Yarkon River, which promoted not only a high standard of agriculture but also active trade. The number of grain pits; silos; storage facilities for wine, oil, and wheat; and other public buildings dating to the ninth and eighth centuries attest to its importance as an administrative center (Maisler 1950/51a:62).

What was said about the increased production of wine is also true of oil production. The increase in the references to wine and oil in the epigraphic sources, the increase in the number of epigraphic sources themselves, the proliferation of presses/installations, and the incidence of storage jars for wine and oil—all point to the increased production of oil.

Pottery

Pottery was probably the largest and most important industry of the time from a practical and utilitarian point of view. The thriving wine and oil industry, in a way, necessitated the large-scale production of receptacles to hold and transport the commodities. Certain innovations in the use of the potter's wheel resulted in producing not only large quantities but also standard shapes at a greater speed. The invention of the potter's wheel occurred many centuries before the eighth century B.C.E., but its use became much more common from about the eighth century as its increased occurrence in Megiddo, Gezer, Lachish, Hazor, and other towns shows (Heaton 1968:37). The technical improvements promoting mass production were twofold: speed techniques and the shift from hand to wheel burnishing (Silver 1983:15).

Speed Techniques: There were two kinds of speed techniques. One was used for the manufacture of large bowls. Producing large bowls required refined clay and a skillful potter who was an expert in throwing. But commercially, to cut corners, another technique was used. Instead of refined clay, cheaper clay was used. This was thrown to make a thicker bowl. When the bowl was of leather-hard consistency, the bowl was trimmed down to the desired thickness and shape (Kelso and Thorley 1943:97). Besides the use of cheaper clay, this method also had the advantage that it could be done by even less skilled or unskilled laborers.

Another speed technique was used in making the small "pinched off" juglets. Originally, the small juglets were made from separate pieces/lumps of clay individually. But in the "pinch-off" technique, a great mass of clay was placed on the wheel and was shaped into a tall cone. The juglets were formed at the tip of the cone in succession. The potter continued the process until the mass of clay was exhausted (Kelso and Thorley 1943:96). The advantage of this technique was that it not only saved time but, in fact, doubled the production of this type of ware. Thus, the introduction of speed techniques facilitated the mass production of pottery in standard shapes and sizes and also the employment of unskilled labor for such jobs.

Wheel Burnishing: Another simple technique that had far-reaching effects in the production of standardized pottery was the shift from hand burnishing to wheel burnishing. Olga Tufnell argues that this technique was introduced at the end of the ninth century B.C.E. and came into general use in the eighth century. For instance, about 34 percent of vessels excavated from Tomb 1002 at Lachish were wheel-burnished bowls. In comparison to other strata, the proliferation of wheel-burnished bowls in this strata shows how quickly the technique had spread (Tufnell 1953:47, 229–36). Even though the speed techniques facilitated the mass production of utilitarian pottery, artistry in pottery was not sacrificed. G. Ernest Wright comments that some of the most beautiful pottery of Iron Age Palestine comes from the early part of the eighth century B.C.E. (1965:155). A good example is the Samaria ware, which was made of extremely well-mixed clay, buff-colored and exceptionally light in weight (Wright 1965:157). In Israel, the potters adopted a technique of rubbing the vessel lightly over the area to be burnished with a cloth or leather before baking, so that when the ware was baked it acquired a shiny finish. Other of the finest vessels to be made in the eighth century were the ring-burnished bowls, water decanters, and big jars (Wright 1965:156).

From a systemic perspective, the mass production of pottery is related to the production of wine and oil. The need to store and transport these items required large quantities of storage jars. This need was effectively met by the introduction of speed techniques in producing pottery. The need to export wine and oil could have led to the standardization of measures, also made possible by speed techniques. The *lmlk* seals on the large storage jars seem to point in that direction. Even though there is disagreement as to what these impressions mean, one possible explanation is that it reflects the effort on the part of the Judean kings to standardize the volume held by the jars (Diringer 1949:81; Lapp 1960:12).

Metallurgy

One major source of copper and iron ore was the mines of wadi 'Arabah south of the Dead Sea. Beno Rothenberg assigns the Iron Age copper industries exclusively to Solomon. He contends that these industries did not function either before or after the days of Solomon (1962:40). The basis for his exclusive dating includes pottery from wadi Timna and wadi 'Amran/'Amrani and a questionable presupposition that runs as follows:

> The planning and maintaining of such large enterprises, problems of man-power [sic], supply, defenses and the safe-guarding of long lines of communication demanded the efforts of a strong monarch with ample supplies at his disposal. None but Israel's king Solomon seems to answer these requirements. (Rothenberg 1962:40)

Rothenberg assumes that anything mammoth and grand must belong to Solomon. The achievements of other rulers are overlooked. In this particular instance, he overlooks the achievements of Uzziah precisely in matters mentioned in the quotation. Uzziah's concerted effort to control the Negev has already been discussed above in the section on the colonization of the Negev.

Information concerning metallurgy is sparse. Tell el-Kheleifeh, located on the north coast of the Gulf of 'Aqaba, was considered to be a major source of evidence for a copper industry. Nelson Glueck interpreted the remains of a large building as a copper refinery (1938:3–18). Rothenberg successfully questioned Glueck's proposal and proposed an alternative, that the building was a large storeroom and a central stronghold of a fortress serving as a caravanserai since the time of Solomon (1962:49–56). Later, Glueck accepted Rothenberg's proposal that it probably served as a storehouse and/or granary (1965:75). But he continued to maintain that there was enough evidence to assume the possibility of some sort of metal smelting and refinery industry at Tell el-Kheleifeh. The identification of Tell el-Kheleifeh with either Ezion-Geber or Elath remains controversial. The basis of such identification is the fact that Tell el-Kheleifeh is the only site thus far excavated in this region whose pottery and other datable materials correspond with the history of Ezion-Geber and/or Elath. If Tell el-Kheleifeh is not to be identified with Ezion-Geber and/or Elath it must be considered to be an industrial and maritime satellite of the above two, serving as a fortified caravanserai and a granary city.

A significant piece of evidence emerged from Elath. The find was a signet ring with the inscription "belonging to Jotham." It could refer to Jotham, the successor of Uzziah, or an officer under Uzziah. More interesting is the representation on the ring: a horned ram and in front of it, a picture of a central body with four outstretched limbs. The latter has been identified by Nahman Avigad (1961:18–22) as a bellows used in metalworking. Similar bellows are attested in the wall painting from the tomb of Khnum-hotep III at Beni-Hasan (Albright 1960:207) and also in Robert Forbes's description of the typical bellows used by the gypsies (1964:111–13). The wall painting in the tomb of Khnum-hotep III represents the seminomadic Asiatics arriving in Egypt. The object in question, which Albright identified as portable bellows, was found on the backs of asses. Forbes explains that the bellows were made of animal skin attaching a pipe and tuyère (clay nozzle) to force a quick air blast to the fire. At the other end of the bellows, a wide slit with two wooden rims was used to pump fresh air into the bag. On the basis of the parallels, Avigad concludes that the image on the seal reflects the connection to metal working. The owner of the seal, Jotham, therefore could have been an officer in charge of royal mining and smelting in the 'Arabah and of the refining plant in Elath (Avigad 1961:21). This seal reflects the continuation of metallurgical activities in this region since the time of Solomon.

Wool Industry

Second Chronicles 26:10 locates transhumance pastoral activity in the Negev. Uzziah is said to have had large herds. One of the by-products of herding is wool. Albright proposed that Tell Beit Mirsim functioned as a major textile center, mainly on the basis of the structures that he identified as dye vats and loom weights. In reading Albright's report, one cannot but wonder with Wright that "it is curious that the whole town of Debir was given over to this one industry" (1962:191). Albright's intereptation has been questioned by Dalman (1964) and Eitam (1979). Dalman and Eitam (see section above on Oil Industry) have argued that what Albright identified as dye vats were, in fact, olive presses. This calls into question the proposal that weaving and dyeing were a major industry in Tell Beit Mirsim. However, this does not rule out the possibility of woolen textiles as a minor industry. The proximity of Tell Beit Mirsim to the southern Shephelah between the Judean hill country and the Philistine plains supports this.

Tell en-Nasbeh, located south of Bethel on the border of Judah, seems to have been another woolen weaving center. The excavators point out that wine and oil were two prominent sources of wealth. The large number of spindle whorls and loom weights reflects the functioning of a textile industry, perhaps centered in the home

(McCown 1947:62). It is quite conceivable that producing woolen textiles was a minor industry at Tell en-Nasbeh as well.

One other possible center of wool production was Lachish, also located in the Shephelah. In the living quarters excavated (Rooms H. 15:1003; G. 14:1001, 1005, 1006, 1007, and 1008), vast numbers of loom weights (an average of 25–50 per room), spindle whorls, and hammer stones were discovered. The charred remains of a wooden beam set upright at the end of one room were identified as part of a vertical loom (Tufnell 1953:109). At Tell Beit Mirsim, Tell en-Nasbeh, and Lachish, the strata where the objects in question were found have been dated to the eighth century B.C.E.

Perfume Industry

Perfume seems to have been a standard component in the production of cosmetics, anointing oil, medicine, and libation oil. The aromatic plants such as aloes, gelbanum, laudanum, myrrh, balsam, cassia, cinnamon, and calamus were some of the sources of perfume (Stern 1979:261). Even though perfume was one of the items imported into Palestine from places like Arabia and Egypt, some plants were native to Palestine. There is evidence to conclude that henna and balsam were cultivated as perfumes at En-Gedi (Stern 1979:263). According to the excavators, the tropical climate and abundance of spring water at En-Gedi facilitated the cultivation of plants with aromatic and medicinal qualities (Mazar, Dothan, and Dunayevsky 1966:7). The unique finds at En-Gedi included concentrations of clay barrels, small juglets, clumps of henna, and small bowls in the courtyards of the Israelite houses (Mazar, Dothan, and Dunayevsky 1966:26). These findings, along with scales, weights, silver ingots, and grinding stones, reflect the operation of perfume and/or medicinal production (Stern 1979:264). En-Gedi was one of the settlements that was consciously developed by the Judean kings. The welfare of the settlement depended upon a strong central administration capable of providing adequate irrigation facilities, economic organization, and protection (Mazar, Dothan, and Dunayevsky 1966: 8). Consequently, the site showed decline during periods of weak governments.

Demography

The third indicator of growth and development in the eighth century is the change in the demographic situation. The growth of economy does bring about change in the demographic pattern. The increase or decrease in economic activities unique to particular areas is bound to affect the population numbers. This correlation can be easily documented in contemporary societies. But it is not so easy when it comes to societies of antiquity such as ancient Israel and Judah. For one thing, paleodemographic studies are few and far between. At best, estimates can be made on the basis of circumstantial and indirect information. One such clue is the growth of cities. On the basis of the increased building activity seen in the eighth-century levels of sites such as Hazor, Samaria, Tell Beit Mirsim, Tell el-Kheleifeh, Tell es-Sa'idiyeh, Tell en-Nasbeh, Beersheba, Megiddo, Tell el-Hesi, and Jerusalem, it is possible to assume changes in the nature and number of the population. Albright estimated the population of Tell Beit Mirsim at 2000–3000 people based on the 150–200 houses occupying an area of 7.5 acres (1943:39). Based on this analogy, other tentative estimates have been made: eighteen acres of Lachish would have supported 6000–7000 people, and thirteen acres of Megiddo 3500–5000 people (Wright 1962:189). Even though Magan Broshi and Israel Finkelstein estimate a lower number for Tell Beit Mirsim in particular, they do point out that the Shephelah region as a whole was one of the most densely inhabited areas in Israel and Judah (1992:52).

Wright comments on the increase in population and standard of living in the eighth century (1962:91). Broshi and Finkelstein corroborate this observation more systematically in their study of several regions in Palestine. The population of Israel and Judah reached an all-time high of 460,000 in the eighth century B.C.E. This is nearly three times the size of the population at the end of the eleventh century (Broshi and Finkelstein 1992:55). This number is considerably lower than some of the earlier estimates—as high as eight hundred thousand by Albright (1963:56) and up to three hundred thousand more by Salo Baron (1972:61–62). Broshi and Finkelstein point out that large-scale agricultural development, general economic well-being, peace, and security contributed to this population increase (1992:55). This corresponds with the profile of Israel and Judah in the eighth century. Besides overall growth of the population, Broshi and Finkelstein also find demographic balance between different regions in Palestine. Once again, this picture is congruent with the growth of regional centers and specialized activities witnessed in the eighth century. But this situation changed drastically as a result of the series of Assyrian military campaigns beginning with Tiglath-Pilesar III in 734 B.C.E. Two waves of refugees following the destruction of Samaria in 722 and the campaign of Sennacherib in 701 resulted in the tremendous growth of the city of Jerusalem (Broshi and Finkelstein 1992:47). The thriving regional centers of the eighth century were destroyed, leading to the increased geopolitical and economic importance of Jerusalem in the seventh century.

Trade and Commerce

Another area that reflects the growth and development of an economy is trade and commerce. This can be seen in the expansion of the market both internally and abroad. At the systemic level, it reflects a shift from subsistence to a market economy. With the growth of a market economy, goods and services are increasingly drawn into the market sphere. The presence of a strong centralized power facilitates this process. Involvement in trade expands the horizons of the market network. Establishing trade relations at the interregional and international levels further augments the profits from local trade. This development is linked with the emergence of a class of people specializing in trade, probably under the auspices of the crown.

Not much direct information is available about trade and commerce in eighth-century Israel and Judah, but a hypothetical reconstruction is possible through a systemic approach. Data pertaining to various other aspects of the Israelite and Judahite societies allow us to reconstruct the international trade relations. For instance, the control of trade routes is a case in point. As pointed out earlier with regard to the colonizing activities of Jeroboam II and Uzziah, Israel and Judah had control over the area from Hamath to the Sea of 'Arabah (2 Kings 14:25). This meant that the King's Highway running through the Transjordanian states was controlled by Israel and Judah.

Second Chronicles 26:6–8 also attests to the control of the Transjordanian kingdoms, Philistine territories, and the Negev by Uzziah. The geopolitical sovereignty enjoyed by Israel and Judah in the first part of the eighth century had enormous implications for their trade relations. In specific terms, this translates into control of major trade routes plying through Palestine: in particular the King's Highway, and the Via Maris and smaller routes in the Negev. The elaborate network of trade routes protected by a system of fortresses was an important feature of the Judean royal administration in an effort to promote international trade. The repeated attempts by Judah to penetrate the Philistine plain were intended to gain access to the Philistine section of the Via Maris. Important cities and fortifications were found along the main arteries of communication.

In the eighth century B.C.E., Israel and Judah extended their hegemony over many of their neighboring states. But interestingly, one group with whom they did not seem to have had military encounters was the Phoenicians. There is a good reason for that. The Phoenicians, being a mercantile community, played a key role in the arena of trade and commerce. Their expertise in the field of sea navigation made them invaluable allies. The Hebrews of antiquity were not particularly known for their seafaring abilities. But a Hebrew seal made available to Avigad by an American collector raises interesting questions (Avigad 1982). The seal has the picture of a sailing ship with the following inscription: "belonging to 'Oniyahu, son of Merab." The seal is dated to the period of the eighth–seventh centuries B.C.E. based on the semicursive formal type of Hebrew (Avigad 1982:61). The name appears to be an Israelite name, and hence the picture could be a representation of an Israelite ship modeled after a Phoenician prototype (Avigad 1982:61). Israel could have slowly acquired some measure of expertise in shipbuilding through its long contact with the Phoenicians. It is important to note in this connection that Jehoshaphat was offered help and advice by Ahaziah for their joint maritime venture (1 Kings 22:49–50; 2 Chr. 20:35–37).

The Phoenicians dominated the mercantile world because of their exceptional navigational abilities. Like any other maritime society, trade interests primarily motivated the Phoenicians. They had no political aspirations. Their main industry was the production of the purple dye extracted from snail shells. In fact, the name "Phoenicians" may be derived from the Greek word *phoinos* meaning ruddy. The Greeks used *phoinike* to refer to the place where purple dye was produced, the place being the coast of Canaan. Thus, it also came to mean the merchants who traded in this product (Oded 1979a:224). Similarly, the Hebrew term *kena'ani*, "Canaanite," has a double entendre. The colorfast dye produced by the Phoenicians was in demand in places like Tell en-Nasbeh, Lachish, and Tell Beit Mirsim, where excavations have brought to light evidence of a textile industry. The Phoenicians also traded in cedar, cypress, and oak

(Oded 1979a:228; Silver 1983:57). The proximity to seaborne transportation aided the trade of lumber that would have been required in great demand for the many building activities of the state. That the Phoenicians had experts trained to work in gold, silver, bronze, iron, stone, and wood is attested to in 2 Chronicles 2:14. The Phoenician exports to Israel included items such as costly vessels, ivory carvings, and jewelry made out of bronze, gold, and silver for the benefit of upper-class women.

Some of the raw materials came from other countries. For instance, silver was imported from Spain by the Phoenicians (Tsirkin 1979:553). Jeremiah 10:9 refers to the export of beaten silver from Tarshish, identified with Tartessos in Spain. The rise of Tartessos into prominence came about in the eighth century B.C.E. (Tsirkin 1979:553). Gold was imported from Ophir. The identification of Ophir is debated. Some locate it in India and others in Arabia. Irrespective of where it is located, Ophir was known for its gold. An ostracon found at Tell Qasile offers some useful information. The ostracon seems to be an official note certifying the dispatch of thirty shekels of gold from Ophir to Beth-Horon (Maisler 1950/51a: 210). There are two possibilities of interpreting Beth-Horon. It is possible that Beth-Horon was a treasure city in the Ephraimite territory, one of the store-cities fortified in the days of Solomon (2 Chr. 8: 5). The second possibility is that it could refer to the temple of Horon, a Canaanite deity worshipped by the Phoenicians. If so, it would seem that Tell Qasile was a center facilitating gold trade from Ophir to Phoenicia (Maisler 1950/51b: 210). From another ostracon (referred to in the section on Oil Industry), possibly a bill for a certain amount of oil sent from the royal storehouse, it is inferred that Tell Qasile was an important center for export and import. Its proximity to the Yarkon River supports its function as an important seaport. Mazar suggests that the river was used for bringing logs to Tell Qasile and from there they were transported by land to Jerusalem (Maisler 1950/51a: 63).

The hewn-stone technique in architecture is attributed to the Phoenicians (Katzenstein 1973:199). Close trade relations with Phoenicia explain the spread of this technique in Israel. The Phoenician trade connection of the Northern Kingdom is also hinted in the Samaria ostraca. A large number of personal names with the Baal component occur, which might suggest that the enterprising Phoenician merchants could have acquired large estates in Israel. Or it could simply indicate the cultural intermingling between the Israelites and the Phoenicians.

The existence of trade activities between Israel and Phoenicia is also indicated by the large quantities of pottery salvaged from underwater excavations along the coast of Israel (Barag 1963). Three observations are of particular interest for our purposes. First, of the five hundred or more vessels recovered, with exception of a negligible amount, a majority were native to Israel. Second, the majority of the vessels came from the period between the eighth and fourth centuries B.C.E. Third, more than half the objects recovered were large storage jars dating from the eighth century B.C.E. (Barag 1963:17–18). This would indicate that the jars were used for transporting items of trade. Dan Barag comments that "the large percentage of storage jars is definitely connected in some way with trade in wine and oil" (1963:18). This corroborates the picture of the eighth-century economy. The nature and extent of Phoenicia's commercial activity was very diverse and stretched to distant lands, as Ezekiel 27 illustrates. It also points to the regional specialization and the resultant pattern of commercial activity. Generally, a sixth-century dating is ascribed to this chapter. While it may be true that the immediate referent of the lament could be experiences of the sixth century B.C.E., the economic reality depicted in the passage reflects a long period of history. From this point of view, the passage is a gold mine of information regarding trade and commerce in the ancient Near East in the periods preceding the more immediate context that the passage seems to presuppose.

The source of spice trade for Israel and Judah was Arabia. The Arabian export activity largely depended on the trade in frankincense and myrrh. Myrrh was used as a component in cosmetics, while frankincense was used as a medicine to stop bleeding (Silver 1983:61). The export items from Egypt included fine linen, garments, flax, papyrus, gold, and perfumes (Elat 1978:21–22). In addition to luxury items, key military items were also imported. The import of horses and chariots is attested to in the Bible (1 Kings 10:28–29). But the source of supply of these items is disputed. Customarily, the reference to *mitsrayim* is taken to mean Egypt. Elat challenges this interpretation. He reads *mitsrayim* as *mutsri,* a place northeast of the Anatolian peninsula, and *Kue* as reference to the kingdom of Que, on the Cilician coastal plain in the southeastern Anatolian peninsula (1979a:183).

Before concluding this section, it is relevant to take note of one factor that had enormous implications for the facilitation of trade and commerce: the increase in storage facilities associated with the shift from subsistence to market type of economy. Under a subsistence economy, producers consume what they produce and produce for their own consumption. There is very little exchange of the produce outside the productive unit. But with the growth of a market economy, the productive unit, consumptive unit, and the nature of production undergo a vast change. The production is no longer confined to the familial units. The producers produce for unknown customers. Therefore, there is a need to produce items that are in demand in the market. The increase in storage facilities serves in two ways. First, storage facilities increase the chances of preserving the goods for a longer period of time. Second, preservation for a longer period of time, in turn, helps in controlling the forces of demand and supply. Apart from the economic advantage this may bring, storage facilities are essential for the accumulation of the agricultural surplus.

There was a significant increase in the number of storage facilities in eighth-century Israel and Judah. Aharoni points out that one of the major elements in the city was the storehouse unit. A typical structure consisted of a long hall divided by two rows of pillars (usually referred to as the pillared structure). Examples of this type of building were found in Hazor, Tell Qasile, Tell Abu Hawam, Beth-Shemesh, Beersheba, and Arad (Aharoni 1982:222–23). The storehouses along with the granaries were aboveground facilities for storage. The underground storage facilities included grainpits, silos, and cellars. A classic example of the grainpit comes from stratum III in Megiddo attributed to Jeroboam II. The pit was twenty-three feet deep and thirty-six feet in diameter at the top and twenty-three feet across at the bottom (Lamon and Shipton 1939:66). The seventh season at Dothan uncovered four huge storage pits of the nature found at Megiddo. The first one was attributed to the ninth century and the last three to the eighth century B.C.E. (Free 1960:7–9). The underground wine cellars at Gibeon with the capacity to hold more than 25,000 gallons of wine in jars are another instance of increased storage facilities.

The widespread storage system in important cities such as Samaria, Arad, Megiddo, Dothan, and Tell Qasile suggests the strong possibility of a central provisioning system. This is evident even in earlier periods. The storage system in the time of David is referred to in 1 Chronicles 27:25–28. We also read that Rehoboam "made the fortresses strong and put commanders in them, and stores of food, oil, and wine" (2 Chr. 11:11). In the later part of the eighth century, Hezekiah is said to have had storehouses "for the yield of grain, wine, and oil" (2 Chr. 32:28). On the basis of the information derived from the Arad ostraca and the system of fortresses and roads in the Negev, it has already been suggested (see section above on Colonization) that the settlement of the Negev was a conscious economic venture on the part of the Judean kings. The part played by storage facilities in this system goes without saying.

Another aspect of the storage facilities was their function in the taxation system. They not only functioned as provisioning centers but also as places of collecting and storing produce that was received through taxation. The information from the Samaria ostraca and the Tell Qasile ostracon supports this. In this connection, one cannot but take note of the function of increased storage facilities in providing for local consumption all year around. At a systemic level, there is connection between the increased storage facilities and the consumptive pattern of the upper class. Increased storage facilities ensured a steady and year-round supply of food items. As we can infer from the data available, these facilities either belonged to rich private estate owners or the crown. This clearly shows who controlled the distribution of goods.

In sum, the overall picture we derive is that of thriving trade and commerce in the eighth century B.C.E. The available information indicates that interregional and international trade was initiated, maintained, and monopolized by the crown. It is precisely at the times when there was a strong centralized power that there was also thriving trade under the royal directive. The geopolitical advantage enjoyed by Israel and Judah in the eighth century B.C.E. enabled them to control trade and commerce through the control of trade routes. Hence, the beneficiaries of the lucrative trade enterprises were also the members of the ruling class. The profitable nature of interregional and international trade prompted the production of commodities or articles that had good exchange value. Accordingly, some items were more in demand than others. Commodities such as wine and oil were worth more in terms of their exchange value per unit of volume and weight in comparison to grain. The production of cash crops, such as grapes and olives, had drastic consequences for the production of staples. The plots that were formerly used for the production of cereals and vegetables were now used for the production of the cash/commercial crops for the market. These items were used as exchange items for the procurement of luxury and military items for the benefit of the upper class. In this way, trade and commerce provided the ruling class with its luxurious and leisured lifestyle.

The Extraction of Surplus

The preceding section aimed at establishing the eighth century B.C.E., particularly the early part, as a period of economic prosperity and growth for Israel and Judah. Colonization, regional specialization, demography, and trade and commerce were used as indicators of the growth and expansion. This section will focus on the question: Who were the beneficiaries of this growth and prosperity? This dimension is often overlooked in discussions of the eighth-century economic situation. Scholars agree that this period was a period of economic prosperity but often neglect to ask who were the beneficiaries of this growth and prosperity, or at whose expense such prosperity and growth were achieved. This results from not attending to the comparative data from the field of social sciences regarding agrarian societies.

A cursory familiarity with the nature of agrarian societies would quickly convey that we are dealing here with a stratified society. In a stratified society, the power and status of individuals dictate the distribution of goods and services, whereas in a less stratified society, the distribution of goods is dependent on need (Lenski 1966:27). A stratified society implies a condition where a dominant class of people control and dictate the distribution of goods. The basic concern of the dominant class is how to extract the maximum surplus from the primary producers. It requires achieving a delicate balance between extracting maximum surplus but allowing just enough for the producing class to survive in order to continue production. This has implications for the structure of the society. When such exploitation embodies and expresses itself in social structures, class struggles are said to exist (Ste. Croix 1981:43). Focusing on the class conflict helps to delineate the divisions within a society. Failure to note this dimension does not do justice to the nature of agrarian societies. A classic example of such failure is the work of Morris Silver (1983). His book *Prophets and Markets* is important for a variety of reasons. First of all, it is probably one of the more extensive treatments on the political economy of eighth-century Israel and Judah. Second, his training as an economist is clearly evident in his handling of the enormous amount of data with regard to the political economy of Israel and Judah. But, unfortunately, the conclusions he derives from those data reveal a lack of insight into the systemic realities of agrarian societies. This is also indicated by the notable gap in his bibliography in the area of comparative and historical sociology of agrarian societies. In light of this, some of his conclusions remain unconvincing. A statement characteristic of this is:

> Whether or not the income distribution became more unequal, there is no reason to believe that the poor became poorer and abundant reason to conclude with Heaton [1968:35] that "an appreciable number of Israelite citizens became men of means" during the 8th and 7th centuries. (Silver 1983:118)

To support his position, Silver invokes the aid of archaeological evidence, or, more accurately, its absence: "The archaeological evidence does not, at this point, convincingly demonstrate the existence of trends in income distribution" (1983:116). The statement is problematic for a variety of reasons. First, it is a rather sweeping generalization. Second, it may point to the nature of the resources upon which Silver is drawing. The problem is not so much the lack of data; rather, as William Dever points out, "the extensive archaeological data for the Iron II period in Palestine have rarely been utilized to comment on the social structure of ancient Israel" (1995:429). Clearly, herein lies the problem. If one does not use the archaeological information to draw conclusions about the systemic reality of a society, even if they are only suggestive, of what value is the information? Also, much of old-world archaeology concentrated on uncovering the acropolis, citadels, structures, palaces, and the like, which do not reflect the material culture of the whole society. Much depends on how one uses the information and what sort of interpretive scheme one brings to one's study. The handling of the archaeological data pertaining to the Iron II period by John Holladay and Dever illustrates this very well. Holladay offers insightful comments on the nature of the monarchical state in Israel and Judah illustrated through archaeological information (1995). One such comment is pertinent to our discussion here. Holladay points out that wealth and class distinctions are observable in the form of the distinctive nature and preferred location of residences, and the presence or absence of elite goods (1995:377). Dever uses information pertaining to the process of urbanization, evidence from tombs and burial customs, architecture, art, and literacy to draw implications for the social structure of ancient Israel (1995). In discussing the social implications of the rapid process of urbanization in the Iron II period, Dever rightly points to its consequences: concentration of "population, resources, and power in a relatively few cities" (1995:418). These cities dominate the rural periphery. What this fosters, in terms of societal organization, is stratification that is closely linked to "differential access to goods and services" (Dever 1995:418). It is possible to discern trends in "income distribution" as the treatments by Holladay and Dever demonstrate.

In an agrarian state, the members of the elite have the dominant access to goods and services. This is made possible through organized means of extraction of surplus. There are two ways of surplus extraction: (1) direct and individual, and (2) indirect and collective.

Direct and individual: This refers to the extraction of surplus by individuals such as employers, landlords, and moneylenders in their own immediate context. This could take the form of (a) exploitation of wage labor, (b) exploitation of "unfree" labor like slaves, serfs, and debt bondspeople, or (c) through lease of land and house property to tenants in return for rent in money, kind, or services (Ste. Croix 1981:53). The scope of this extraction is limited in comparison with the indirect and collective way. The latter is more effective in laying hold of larger portions of surplus.

Indirect and collective: The agent of this mode of extraction is the state. The state apparatus controlled by a dominant class may extract large portions of surplus in indirect ways. The extraction of surplus may take the form of (a) internal taxation, (b) imposition of compulsory state services (i.e., corvée or forced labor), (c) military conscription, and/or (d) a policy of imperialism (Ste. Croix 1981:53).

Internal taxation was probably the major and most continuous source of revenue for the state. However, there is no extensive data in the biblical records about this. On the basis of this, it is argued sometimes that the Israelite and Judean population did not pay taxes apart from occasional contributions. But this flies in the face of what we know about agrarian monarchies from comparative data. Besides, there are enough clues to infer that regular taxation was a source of income for the state. Taxes were collected both in cash and/or kind. The systemic changes associated with the emergence of monarchy are portrayed well in 1 Samuel 8:10–18. This passage, apparently, comes from a later time. The actual experiences of the effects of monarchy on the common people must have given rise to this antimonarchical passage, which is put in the mouth of Samuel as a prediction. One of the evils mentioned here is with reference to taxation: "He [the king] will take the tenth of your grain and of your vineyards and give it to his officers and to his servants" (1 Sam. 8:15). "He [the king] will take the tenth of your flocks and you shall be his slaves" (1 Sam. 8:17). This certainly reflects the practice of appropriating the surplus through taxation. It is also significant that these verses cover the three areas of the economy: farming, viticulture, and herding. Solomon's reorganization of the territorial boundaries was with a view to derive maximum economic benefit (1 Kings 4). The twelve officers set in charge of the twelve regions were to provide the king and the royal household with food. Each region was required to provide for a whole month. Solomon's administration levied toll on imported goods and goods in transit (1 Kings 10:14–15). 2 Chronicles 17:5 reports that all of Judah brought tribute to Jehoshaphat. This, in all probability, was an annual tax like the tribute of the vassal states (de Vaux 1965:140). The word *minhah* used in this context (usually translated *offering*) represents a tax payment (Paul and Dever 1974:187; Rainey 1982:61).

The Samaria ostraca give valuable information concerning the system of taxation. The ostraca are to be read as records of tax receipts for the wine and oil sent mostly from the private estates. There were also some sent from the royal estates. (See sections above on Wine and Oil Industries.) There is also some indirect information from the *lmlk* seal impressions. It has been proposed elsewhere in this study (see section on Wine Industry) that the place names on the seals represented royal centers of wine production in the Judean hill country. The absence of *lmlk* seal impressions around Beersheba and Arad is notable. Rainey has proposed that the absence of the *lmlk* impressions in Beersheba and Arad does not mean that they were not important fortified settlements but that the support of the military establishments came from private landowners. This is based on the supposition that the *lmlk* impressions were found in places where there were military establishments supported by provisions from the royal estates (Rainey 1982:61). The supply of commodities from private estates to Beersheba and Arad is supported by two ostraca (Aharoni 1973:71–72; 1975:52–55). The Arad letters were addressed to one Eliashib, son of Ashyahu, who was in charge of the stores of the royal fortress, containing instructions or requests for the dispatch of provisions. It seems likely that the provisions came from both private and royal estates. Another interesting but ambiguous piece of evidence is the letter from Metsad Hashavyahu near Yavneh Yam (Avigad 1979). A large jar fragment contains fourteen lines of inscription. It records the petition of a poor worker to a military official in charge of a fortress, probably located in the place where the document was found. The worker complains that his immediate supervisor named Hoshaiah has seized his garment for allegedly not fulfilling his obligation. The petitioner asks for a redress of the situation. In the letter, the nature of the obligation is not clear. Two possibilities have been proposed. One possibility is that the worker may have been part of a work force (forced labor) engaged in harvesting. The overseer, Hoshaiah, confiscated the garment of the worker for not fulfilling his share of work. Thereupon, the worker complains to a higher official (Avigad 1979:32–34). Cross raises some pertinent objections to this interpretation. First of all, if the worker were part of a conscripted work force, there is no place for an agreement concerning fulfillment of an obligation. Further, in the event of the nonfulfillment of forced labor, punishments such as nonpayment of wages, corporeal punishment, confinement, or increased workload would be more appropriate (Cross 1962:46). A second possibility, a much more likely one, is that the worker was a tenant farmer working in an agricultural estate under the royal control, and the confiscation of the garment was retaliation for not paying the overseer's claim on the crop (Cross 1962:46). That the issue here was the claim of a creditor is supported by Exodus 22:25–26 and Deuteronomy 24:10–13. The dating of this letter is placed between the eighth and seventh centuries B.C.E. If the second interpretation is correct, we have here some information on the taxation process. The context of the letter and officials mentioned therein suggest that we are dealing with the claims of the state.

Taxes were collected in kind and in "money," or metals, especially silver (discussed in chapter 4). The rural population probably paid in kind. The local tax collectors received the agricultural products and delivered them to the royal storehouse (1 Chr. 26:24; 27:25–31; 2 Chr. 11:11; 32:27–29). Taxes were also paid in money. It is conceivable that the urban population paid in silver (2 Kings 15:20; 23:35; 2 Chr. 24:5). Menahem's levy of a thousand talents of silver on all the wealthy landowners, at the rate of fifty shekels per head to ward off the threat of Assyrian invasion, is a good example of taxes collected in money. However, it should be pointed out that, in this particular instance, it seems to have been an exceptional tax. A similar occurrence is mentioned during the reign of Jehoiakim, when he raised a hundred talents of silver and ten talents of gold demanded by the Pharaoh by taxing the people of Judah according to their wealth (2 Kings 23:33–35).

Corvée refers to the imposition of compulsory state service on the population for the purpose of accomplishing building projects, roads and canals that were state-operated. The state could accomplish its projects by using free labor or very cheap labor. Corvée was a means through which the dominant class in the society provided for and ensured its own affluent lifestyle. This is in keeping with the disdain of physical labor by the upper class. The peasants were the ones who bore the brunt of the forced labor. The energies of the peasant were overtaxed by agricultural production and performing forced labor. 1 Samuel 8:16 associates the institution of corvée with the emergence of monarchy: "He [the king] will take your menservants and maidservants and the best of your young men and your asses, and put them to his work." That the institution of forced labor was a major operation is known from the fact that a separate officer was needed to oversee it. In the list of officials from the later years of David's reign, Adoram is mentioned as the official in charge of corvée (2 Sam. 20:23–26). In an earlier list (2 Sam. 8:15–18; 1 Chr. 18:14–17), there is no mention of Adoram. Adoram continued to be in charge of corvée even during Solomon's reign (1 Kings 4:6; 5:14 [Heb. 5:28]). The connection between the mammoth building projects and the need for corvée is not hard to see. The building of the temple, the palace, the fortification of Jerusalem, and other garrison towns must have required a considerable amount of labor force. According to 1 Kings 5:13 (Heb. 5:27), Solomon raised a levy of forced labor out of all Israel, and the levy numbered thirty thousand people. Solomon is also said to have had seventy thousand porters and eighty thousand stonecutters who were employed with Hiram's masons and carpenters (1 Kings 5:15–18 [Heb. 5:27–32]). Corvée was the main cause of the division of the Hebrew kingdom after the death of Solomon. This is seen from the fact that Adoram, who was in charge of corvée, was sent to quell the rebellion in the north (1 Kings 12:18). It is also relevant to note that Jeroboam built his power base and rose to prominence within the context of corvée among the tribe of Joseph (Chaney 1986:70). Specific references to forced labor after the breakup of the kingdom are not many. Asa of Judah employed corvée to carry stone and timber to build Geba and Mizpah (1 Kings 15:22). The kings of Israel and Judah must have used forced labor for their huge building projects. The building achievements of the Omrides, particularly under Ahab, must have used vast forced labor. Since the Omride Israel reflected so much of the David-Solomonic empire, there is no reason to think that it did not reflect the same conditions with regard to corvée. The same thing would be true of eighth-century Israel and Judah. The building of palatial mansions, storage silos, and administrative centers under Jeroboam II implies the use of a large labor force. In the south, the building of the network of fortresses and system of highways in the Negev and the establishment of administrative centers again reflects the employment of a tremendous amount of forced labor force. It is not possible to conceive how else such projects could have been carried out except by the imposition of corvée.

The role of military conscription in the extraction of surplus is closely related to the policy of imperialism. (See below.) Like the institution of corvée, military service takes the peasant away from agricultural work to accomplish things that are imposed by and of interest to the ruling elite. The military duty was to be performed in addition to the agricultural production. The energies of the peasant are expended between the two. Among conditions that contribute to the burden of the peasantry, war is one. The production and supply of war materials is a drain on the economy. This includes provision of supplies like weapons, food items, building of defense systems, and water works to provide water during times of siege. It is the peasants who are pressed into service for such projects. The burden on the peasantry affects agricultural productivity. The conscript army should be distinguished from the professional army. In Israel, the professional army did not come to play a major role until the later part of David's reign. These professional troops, consisting of mercenaries, formed a special contingent and were distinct from the troops that the citizens furnished in times of emergency. In war operations, the professional army would launch the offensive, and the contingents of the conscript army were held back until the final assault (2 Sam. 12:26–29). It is in the reign of Solomon that the chariot force came into prominence, overshadowing the foot soldiers. The conscript army consisted of "men of war" who were called for military service in times of war and would return home after it.

Officers were responsible for recruiting in several districts (Deut. 20:5–9). Some categories of people were exempted from military service: people who owned a new but unoccupied house, people whose vineyards had not yielded harvest yet, and men who were engaged to be married (Deut. 20:5–9). Newlywed men were also exempt from military service for a year (Deut. 24:5). The conscription was done according to *bet 'ab* (2 Chr. 17:14; 25:5), which Gottwald interprets as an extended family group organized as economically self-sufficient households (1979:237). Every male who was twenty or over was drafted (2 Chr. 25:5). This conscript army was provided with arms by the state. The practice of central provisioning is reflected in 2 Chr. 26:14, where Uzziah is reported to have supplied the army with shields, spears, helmets, coats of mail, bows, and stones for slinging. The practice of conscription was evidenced in the reigns of David (2 Sam. 24:1–9), Asa (2 Chr. 14:8), Jehoshaphat (2 Chr. 17:14–18), Amaziah (2 Chr. 25:5), and Uzziah (2 Chr. 26:11–13). Military conscription by the state was only part of a larger imperial policy. Since the policy of imperialism is a multifaceted issue, it will be dealt with separately in the next section.

Imperialism is another aspect of surplus extraction. It could take either an overt or covert form. The overt form of imperialism entails establishing military superiority or territorial conquest. Economic imperialism is a more covert form. This distinction is not pure and simple. It is quite possible that territorial expansion often resulted in or was undertaken for economic gains on a short- or long-term basis. The converse would be true, that the policy of economic imperialism might result in political control. The fundamental motivation for a policy of imperialism was the extraction of surplus. Most often, this was necessitated by the mounting pressures of inadequate local resources and ever-increasing expenditures. The elaborate building projects, the maintenance of a huge army, big bureaucracy, and the royal retinue were of no small economic consequence. They were a tremendous drain on the local economy. The personnel involved in the royal paraphernalia in no way contributed to the productive aspect of the economy. Further, most of the population was concentrated in urban centers due to the lure of urban life. The population of these cities was dependent on supplies from outside, mainly from the agricultural periphery. The economic surplus from agriculture flowed into the urban centers to support the agriculturally nonproductive population. What we witness here is a phenomenon of top-heaviness of the urban centers accentuated by the relative poverty of the surrounding areas. The decreasing local means and the ever-increasing demands of the nonproductive layer of the empire necessitated a policy of imperialism.

The economic benefits of imperialism are threefold: plunder, tribute, and trade. The predatory policy is a more primitive form of surplus extraction. The policy and practice of the Assyrian rulers before Tiglath-Pileser III are examples of this. Levying of tribute on the vanquished is a more steady and long-lasting source of revenue. The tribute will continue to flow as long as the military threat from the conqueror is felt to be real. Establishing trade relations with vanquished territories is a subtler and more effective way of ensuring uninterrupted flow of revenue. It involves a clever policy of allowing the territories enough freedom to continue their economic activities with a view to benefit from them. The economic policy of Tiglath-Pileser III toward the Phoenicians and the Philistines is a good illustration of this.

A strong policy of imperialism is possible only under a strong centralized power. In the eighth century B.C.E., Israel and Judah enjoyed unprecedented power. It was a period of vast territorial expansion. Jeroboam II is said to have controlled the territories from Hamath to the sea of 'Arabah, while his contemporary Uzziah extended control over the Philistines, Arabs, and the Ammonites. The extraction of surplus in this context seems very likely. These two kings also successfully exploited the avenues of trade for economic gain. The most important mechanism in this regard was the control of the trade routes. Israel and Judah together commanded the two major highways: the King's Highway and the Via Maris plying through the land of Palestine. Through this control, they benefited from direct and/or transit trade with countries such as Phoenicia, Philistia, Egypt, Arabia, and kingdoms of Transjordan. In addition to facilitating the movement of goods, these trade routes were also lucrative sources of tolls. Uzziah's control of the Negev facilitated active trade and thereby ensured the inflow of surplus. The entire operation was possible because of a strong state power.

In the process of surplus extraction, the beneficiaries are the extractors. This has dire consequences for the economy of the extracted. The tribute paid by the vassals had to be collected from the common people. Very often, the tribute paid to foreign powers is raised through internal taxation. The basic question is, who can establish the most effective political control? In the history of the ancient Near East, the destiny of one country was very much linked to that of another. The rise of Israel and Judah coincided with the political vacuum in the area. After the death of Adad-Nirari III in 784 B.C.E., the Assyrian power plunged steadily into decline. The Aramean state was also in a decline. Israel and Judah promptly made use of the opportunity. But the situation began to change with the appearance of Tiglath-Pileser III on the scene in 745 B.C.E. Under Tiglath-Pileser III, the Assyrian power reached its zenith. The Assyrian empire adopted a policy of extensive political campaigns and subtle economic imperialism. Tiglath-Pileser III gave up the predatory policy of his predecessors and established a system of collecting tribute on a regular basis through elaborate bureaucratic machinery.

The foreign policy of the Assyrian empire was shaped by its commercial and trading interests. In this connection, the Phoenician cities came to play a key role in the Assyrian empire. By controlling the Phoenician city-states and their maritime expertise, Assyria was able to dominate the international economic scene. By the end of the third quarter of the eighth century, the Assyrian power had extended well into Syria and Palestine. By 738 B.C.E., Assyria had subdued most of Syria and Palestine including Hamath, Tyre, Byblos, Damascus, and Israel. Tiglath-Pileser's inscription (Pritchard 1969:283) and the biblical account (2 Kings 15:19–20) report that Menahem paid tribute to the Assyrian king. This tribute money was raised by Menahem from wealthy landowners by the levy of special taxes. From a systemic perspective, these two factors—foreign threat and payment of tribute—had far reaching consequences on the local economy. The threat of foreign invasion accelerated the preparations for war. The urgent need to increase war supplies, build defense systems, and secure adequate water supply in case of siege involved huge spending. The military buildup drained the coffers of the crown. Agricultural production was the most vulnerable area. The resources to equip for war had to come by way of taxation of the local population. Further, the payment of tribute was an additional liability for the state. As Menahem's episode points out, the proceeds for the tribute came through internal taxation. Sometimes tributes had to be paid in advance to avert possible invasion. Conditions of war, thus, contribute to the misery of the peasants, because it is they who bear the brunt of taxation. In addition, the increased emphasis on military technology during a war period affects the productive sphere.

In relation to the part played by Assyrian imperialism, a discussion of the Syro-Ephraimite war becomes appropriate, since it played such a major role in the politics of the later part of the eighth century B.C.E. Traditionally, the threat of the Assyrian invasion has been taken to be the occasion for the formation of the Syro-Ephraimite coalition. But this has been questioned in recent times. That the Syro-Ephraimite coalition was formed to wage war against Judah could not have been occasioned by the impending Assyrian threat is argued on three counts. First, in anticipation of a serious foreign threat, Syria and Israel would not have wasted their energy and resources in coercing Judah to join the union. Second, from time to time hostilities between Judah and Israel were triggered for other reasons but never at the approach of an enemy. Finally, 2 Kings 15:37 indicates that Rezin and Pekah went against Judah even in the days of Jotham, which would put the Syro-Ephraimite coalition before 734 B.C.E. (Oded 1972:153–54). The reason for the coalition was not the impending Assyrian invasion but the desire to dislodge Judean control from Transjordan. The key to this understanding is 2 Chronicles 27:5. According to this verse, Jotham is supposed to have controlled the Ammonite territory. The granary, oaks, and cattle of Bashan, the grapes and olives of Gilead, and the pastoralism of Edom were always a lure to the vying powers. In the eighth century, Uzziah established a firm control over Transjordan. Rezin wanted to break this monopoly. The very fact that the coalition threatened to replace Ahaz with Ben-tabeel from Transjordan suggests their ulterior motive. This move would make Ben-tabeel a puppet in their hands. History shows that the control of Transjordan was fiercely contested from time to time by vying powers precisely for such economic reasons. Hence, the cause of the Syro-Ephraimite coalition was the dislodging of Judah from Transjordan and not the impending Assyrian invasion. Assyria did intervene in the process of the war at the request of Judah, and defeated the coalition. Thus, the Assyrian invasion was the end of the war and not the cause. Here again, the effects of this war on the local economies need not be belabored. Excessive and continuous surplus extraction had devastating effects on the majority poor. The extracted surplus went mainly to support the needs of the upper class. Items of luxury were necessary to make their living comfortable. The strategic military items were necessary to strengthen their political control, which in turn was essential to ensure a steady flow of surplus. The process of ensuring military superiority, political control, and economic gain went in a vicious cycle. The net result was the impoverishment of the peasantry. The economic relationship between the urban centers and the agricultural periphery could be illustrated through the imagery of a leech feeding on and draining off the blood of a human body. If, as Silver claims, there is no reason to believe that the poor become poorer (1983:118), how is it that such a prosperous economy collapsed in the following decades? How can one explain the calamities resulting from economic distress? The answer for that should be sought in the lopsided concentration of wealth in the hands of, and for the benefit of, a small group of ruling elite. The ever-increasing chasm between the ruling minority and the peasant majority took the economy to a breaking point, as it is frequently attested in agrarian societies.

The Use of the Surplus

The earlier sections have been devoted to examining (1) how the eighth century B.C.E. was a period of economic prosperity and political supremacy for Israel and Judah, and (2) who were the beneficiaries of such economic growth, and how they acquired the economic surplus. In this section, the use of the economic surplus will be the issue. How was the economic surplus spent? The answer to that is twofold. First, the economic surplus went to support an elaborate and luxurious lifestyle of the ruling elite. Second, the economic gains were invested in providing for means to extend and maintain political control, which is essential for gaining further economic advantage. In other words, this aspect refers to the securing of strategic military items.

The two key words that describe the lifestyle of the upper class are *leisure* and *luxury*. Leisure is the nonproductive consumption of time. This derives from a disdain of productive physical work and a sense of superiority in being able to afford an idle life (Veblen 1912:43). Luxury is written all over their lifestyle. It applies to where they live, what they consume, what they wear, and what they do in their leisure time. One common feature of their leisure and luxury is conspicuous waste. But from the point of view of the ruling elite, they constituted symbols of prestige and status.

Living Quarters: Archaeological excavations have yielded evidence of the high quality of the residential buildings of the city dwellers. The burgeoning building activities are attested in Hazor stratum VI, attributed to Jeroboam II. Commenting on these buildings, particularly in Areas G and A, Yadin writes: "The buildings themselves are amongst the nicest found so far in the Israelite periods and testify to the prosperity of the citizens of Hazor. This fact is further corroborated by the objects found in the houses which include fine ivory vessels" (1972:179). Some of the houses in Hazor even had an upper story. The houses belonging to the eighth century B.C.E. at Tell el-Far'ah (N)/Tirzah show remarkable improvement in quality. Roland de Vaux observed a difference between the tenth-century and eighth-century dwellings. Whereas the buildings of the tenth century were uniform and modest, thus indicating perhaps an absence of disparities of social classes, the buildings of the eighth century point to the contrary. The occupation was much denser. Sections of occupation were rich in quality distinct from sections that were apparently poor. The quarters where the rich lived had "a group of lovely private houses" that were separated by a long wall from the poor quarter where "smaller houses were huddled together" (de Vaux 1956:133–37). The eighth-century level had splendid private houses and other public buildings. The eighth-century buildings at Samaria also manifest high quality. During the reign of Jeroboam II, the palace was extended to the western and northern wings, and a defensive tower was also erected at the southwest corner (Reisner, Fisher, and Lyon 1924:117).

The excavations at Tell Beit Mirsim have also brought to light evidences of well-preserved houses. The structures of the houses varied from simple to elaborate. Most of the houses had staircases, which have also been preserved well. This indicates that the houses had an upper story as well (Albright 1943:49–55). This is further supported by the use of pillars in construction, which became popular in the eighth century B.C.E. At Lachish stratum III, there are indications that the growth of the city reached its peak in the eighth century. The buildings were numerous and well constructed and the finds from these buildings "indicate the wealth of their inhabitants" (Aharoni 1975:41). Stratum VIII at Shechem (810–748 B.C.E.) also reflects extensive building activity (Wright 1965:155). The common houses were made out of mudbrick. The more well-to-do could afford houses of hewn stone. The art of ashlar stone masonry came to Israel through the Phoenicians. Remnants of hewn stone slabs were found off the coast of Cyprus and the harbor of Tyre (Katzenstein 1973:199).

The houses of the rich were decorated with ivory inlays. The great store of ivory, in fact as many as five hundred pieces, recovered from excavations at Samaria supports this (Barkay 1992:320). By far the greatest number of them were found in the ruins of the Samarian palace (Dever 1995:424). First Kings 22:39 corroborates this by its reference to the "ivory house" built by Ahab in the ninth century B.C.E. Dever's comments on the ivories as an eloquent witness to social stratification are very pertinent (1995:424). First, they were rare luxury items. Second, they were acquired from foreign countries through trade. Phoenicia was the main supplier of these luxuries. Third, the concentration of these ivories in the royal palace suggests for whose benefit they were obtained. Such penchant for the "exotic," quality housing, and other architectural achievements was one of the ways the upper class used the economic surplus.

Consumption: Conspicuous consumption is a mark of the lifestyle of the upper class. It becomes a way of life. It is no longer "eat to live, but live to eat." Voluptuous consumption becomes a way of showing off economic strength. This is associated with status and maintaining reputation. Wine and oil figured prominently in the consumption of the elite in antiquity. The thriving wine and oil industry in eighth-century Israel and Judah supports this. The *marzeah* feast epitomizes the consumptive pattern of the elite. The *marzeah* was a celebration held in honor of both the dead and the group who celebrated. The membership included upper-class individuals. As an association, it owned houses and vineyards. The Ras Shamra fragment 18.01 (230) refers to a vineyard that was divided between the men of *marzeah* of Ari and the men of *marzeah* of Siyannu (Schaeffer and Nougayrol 1956: Plate LXXVII). This points to the place of vineyards and wine in the *marzeah* celebrations. There are some key texts from Ugarit that contribute to our understanding of the *marzeah.* One of the early references comes from a fragment (Ras Shamra 14.16) published by Virolleaud (1947:173–79). The text is fragmentary with two important references: "men of *marzeah/ marzih*" and a large sum of "10,000 shekels." Two other fragments refer to the "house of the *marzih/ marzeah* men" (Ras Shamra 15.70; 15.88).[4] A more informative text is the mythological text describing the banquet offered by El (Ras

---

[4] The text of Ras Shamra 15.70 and 15.88 can be found in Schaeffer and Nougayrol 1955: Plates XVII and XX.

Shamra 24.258).[5] The picture of *marzeah* is one of drinking and eating. Very often, drinking went to the point of making them delirious and unconscious:

El sat in his *mrzh,*
El drank wine to satiety,
   strong wine until drunk.
[Then] El went to his abode;
   he descended to his court.
TKWN and SNM supported him.
Then approached him a creeper
   with two horns and tail.
He wallowed in his excrement and urine;
El collapsed, El like those who go down the earth.
(Ras Shamra 24.258 lines 15–22)

El's *marzeah* is nothing but a projection of the ruling elite's delirious drinking and conspicuous consumption to the realm of the gods. In this connection, an interesting piece of evidence has come to light in the excavations at Kuntillet 'Ajrud located approximately twenty-three miles south of Kadesh-Barnea. The architectural remains included Structure A (locus 15), a spacious room surrounded by benches. The structure identified as the "bench room" (locus 6) is divided into two wings with stone benches along its walls (Meshel 1992:104).[6] The main function of the room was associated with the benches (Meshel 1992:104). The bench room contained stone bowls of various sizes, flasks, lamps, and juglets (Meshel 1992:105). Two other structures identified as "kitchens" (locus 51, 101) had three ovens each (Meshel 1992:106). There has been considerable discussion regarding the nature and function of the building. The epigraphic references to "Yahweh of Samaria" and "Yahweh of Teman" in particular have prompted the view that Kuntillet 'Ajrud was a religious center (Meshel 1992:108). Judith Hadley has argued strongly against this suggestion and presents a case for its function as a desert way station (1993:115–24). Inscriptions similar to the one found here were also found at Khirbet el-Qom in a burial context (Hadley 1993:122; Hadley 1987:50–62). The burial context raises an

---

    [5]Ras Shamra 24.258 was originally published in Virolleaud 1968. Some key treatments of this text include Pope 1972, Pope 1977, and Margalit 1979/80.
    [6]Kuntillet 'Ajrud was excavated by Z. Meshel. The results are published in Meshel 1978.

intriguing third possibility of the structures at Kuntillet 'Ajrud serving as a *marzeah* structure. Further study is needed in this connection, however. The paraphernalia found here certainly fit the information available about *marzeah*. The very name *marzeah* sums up the nature of the association. It is the association "of those who keel over" (Coote 1981:38). Ras Shamra 1957.702 offers glimpses into the administration of economic matters in relation to the *marzeah* association.[7]

Increased affluence induced changes in the habit of consumption. Items of tastier quality were consumed. Wheat and rye replaced secondary cereals like barley. Finer bread was preferred to coarser bread. The increased consumption of meat instead of cereal protein satisfied both taste and nutritional quality. There was not only increased consumption of beef and mutton but also the substitution of fattened animals for unfattened ones (Silver 1983:91–93). The consumption of bread is inferred by the presence of ovens excavated in places such as Hazor, Gibeon, Tell Halif, Tell es-Sa'idiyeh, Dothan, and Tell en-Nasbeh (Silver 1983:96).

Dress: Another indicator of affluence was dress. For the ruling class, dress becomes an expression of sophistication, higher culture, and standard of luxury. Different layers of clothing adorned by many ornaments distinguished the rich. The use of fine linen and colored cloth was preferred to coarse and plain clothes. Egypt was the main supplier of fine linen to Israel and Judah. Women adorned themselves with scores of ornaments, either imported or made locally with the expertise of Phoenician craftspeople. Hundreds of items such as necklaces, earrings, bangles, rings, and bracelets have been uncovered in excavations throughout Israel and Judah.

Pastime: The favorite pastimes of the upper class consisted of war-sports, music, and merrymaking. Such a leisurely and luxurious living was made possible by the large economic surpluses. The unproductive and voluptuous living took its toll on the economy. The unbalanced spending on items catering to the needs of the wealthy minority had far-reaching adverse effects on the majority of the peasant population.

---

[7]The exact nature of the text is unknown. It seems to be a contract or agreement having to do with the establishment of the *marzeah*. For detailed treatments see Miller 1971, Dahood 1971, Halpern 1979/80, and Friedman 1979/80.

The Process of Land Accumulation in the Eighth Century B.C.E.

The adverse effects on the peasant majority of lopsided economic growth coupled with the extraction of an economic surplus, the bulk of which went to support the leisured and luxurious living of the ruling elite, can be described in terms of the process of latifundialization. At the heart of this process is the steady worsening of the plight of the peasantry, which is directly related to the loss of easy and secure access to arable land.

This process did not happen overnight. The beginnings go back to the time of David with the emergence of the monarchy. In the introductory section of this chapter, the emergence of monarchy in Israel was described as a systemic watershed. With the expansion of the Hebrew kingdom through the incorporation of the alluvial plains of Canaan came conflicting systems of land tenure. The need to oversee and administer the expanding kingdom resulted in the establishment and maintenance of a huge bureaucracy. The members of the bureaucracy were awarded lands for their services. Thus emerged the systems of acquiring land through patrimony and land grants. Under the subsistence economy, there was maximum security and minimum risk in the peasants' access to arable land. But this privilege was lost with the growth of the large estates. The peasantry faced maximum risk and minimum security in terms of access to cultivable land.

The change in the systems of land tenure, the growth of large estates, coupled with an orientation to market economy, brought about a change in the productive pattern. Under the subsistence economy, there was mixed farming with intercropping of cereals and vegetables. But with the growth of market orientation, there was a shift toward producing commercial crops for earning maximum economic gain. The production of cash crops such as grape and olive became prominent. The thriving wine and oil industries in Israel and Judah attest to this situation. Wine and oil became important commodities, not only for the local conspicuous consumption of the ruling elite but also for export. They were easier items to export in exchange for luxury items and military items because they were worth more than the grain per unit of volume and weight. Commercial crops require extensive plantations, and thus they came to occupy large expanses of land in response to market pressures. The priority of producing the cash crops affected the production of staples. The subsistence needs of the majority were at stake. The peasants had to buy the staples that once they themselves produced. This forced them into an unfamiliar market system where the merchants took advantage of their unfamiliarity by using false measures, weights, and rigged scales. The peasants could not even have access to staples without being deprived.

A variety of factors forced the peasants into debt. One was the schedule of the cyclical cultivation required by cash crops like grapes and olives. In the off-season, the laborers were jobless and hence were forced to borrow to buy food. Foreign invasions and natural disasters like earthquake, drought, and agricultural plagues destroyed the accumulated fruits of labor. Again, the peasants were forced into borrowing. A third factor was rent capitalism. This refers to the process of splitting up the means of production into several units to which monetary value was attached. The peasants had not only to pay rent for the use of the land but also for the various means of production such as water, seed, and work animals. Such a process of segmentation of the means of production with high monetary value forced the peasants into debt. Unable to pay for these means, the peasants had to take recourse in loans.

The demands of cyclical cultivation, the vagaries of rain agriculture, pestilence, and the effects of rent capitalism forced the peasants into borrowing. It was borrowing out of desperation and not, as Silver points out, for the purposes of investment. Here again the logic of Silver misses the target. "An increase in the number of debt-slaves may reflect not economic depression but an expanding economy in which an increased number of people are borrowing in order to invest" (1983:70). The first part of the sentence may be true in that the increase in the number of slaves reflects an expanding economy. What Silver ignores is the adverse effect of the expanding economy on the common majority of peasants. The expansion was at their expense. Most often loans were obtained on the value and security of the next harvest. If the crops failed due to a bad season, the peasant went deeper in debt. This meant that the peasant's capacity to repay further diminished. The diminishing capacity to repay did not restrict the need for loans. The demand for loans and the desire on the part of the creditor to capitalize on the misfortunes of the peasants contributed to skyrocketing interest rates. (See the discussion of debt in chapter 4.)

In addition to the usuriousness of the terms of loans, there were other ways the landlords and moneylenders tried to squeeze the peasants out of their due. The peasants were forced to sell their crops at the time of harvest when the price was always the lowest. Further, during crop division, the peasants were often shortchanged through false weights and measures. The peasants were subjected to undue exactions. The outcome of all this was the heavy indebtedness of the peasants leading to foreclosures. Foreclosures through debt instruments became an effective way of land accumulation in the process of latifundialization. There were provisions for redressing the situation through legal courts. But the legal courts, instead of safeguarding the interests of the peasants, in fact served as means of sealing their fate, because the court officials were controlled and manipulated by the ruling elite. The legal courts became instruments in their hands to lend a touch of legality to their corrupt practices.

It is precisely these various aspects of the process of latifundialization to which the prophets refer and/or allude. The prophets were not only shrewd observers but also analysts in their own right. They understood the economic dynamics well. Silver denies any credit to the prophets in this regard: "Unfortunately, most modern writers on this period, in this as in other cases, have uncritically taken over the prophets' huge biases but even their primitive inchoate economic analysis as well: This is unacceptable" (1983:74). The observations of the prophets are not "huge biases." What the prophetic oracles reflect is an accurate picture of the process of latifundialization attested well in the comparative data derived from agrarian societies. A cursory acquaintance with these data would have given Silver a more realistic picture of what goes on in the agrarian societies, instead of prompting him to ask:

> Why in a period of "prosperity" did the agricultural population sell their land? Where did they go once they had sold out? Why were "large-city dealers" and "bureaucrats" more interested in acquiring land than the farmers were, in keeping it? In what respect did the buyers enjoy a "privileged" economic position? Did the "absentee landlords" take the land by force? If not, why was land consolidation a "detriment to the population as a whole?" (Silver 1983:75)

In this passage, Silver is responding to Samuel Yeivin's characterization of eighth-century Israel and Judah (1979:163–64). The basic problem in Silver's approach is that it is not systemic. The various aspects of the economic picture are not looked at in relationship to one another. For instance, his approach fails to take note of the relationship between the mode of production and social formation. Consequently, the basic issue in production–the extraction of surplus–is completely ignored. He writes, "To say the least, it is not at all obvious why the process of land consolidation must be accompanied by the impoverishment of the former free landowners" (1983:76). This statement is the result of not addressing the basic problem in production: the extraction of surplus. It is not enough just to describe the nature of economic growth. One needs to focus on the agents. Who controlled the conditions and factors of production? Who extracted the surplus, and how, and at whose expense? Even where he does grant that there was a call for social justice, Silver does not stop to analyze the conditions prompting the call. He comments, "Since an appreciable number of Israelites became men of means, it is not surprising that the eighth and seventh centuries reverberated with the call for social justice" (1983:248).

The correlation between the economic growth and the call for social justice remains incomprehensible without any reference to the ill effects. Economic affluence in and of itself does not give rise to the call for social justice. The demand for social justice arises out of the ill effects of economic influence on the majority of people who, in this case, happen to be peasants. To use Yeivin's words:

> Prosperity brought in its wake a much more acute differentiation between the agricultural population which became more and more landless and the nouveaux-riches absentee land lords, living in cities as large dealers and high grade bureaucrats exploiting their privileged economic position to the detriment of the population as a whole. (1979:163–64)

In sum, the regional specialization, demographic changes, active trade and commerce, and colonization activities witnessed in the eighth century B.C.E. demonstrate that this was a period of economic prosperity and political power. The beneficiaries of this economic growth were the ruling elite who successfully managed to extract the economic surplus through the state apparatus. The economic surplus thus obtained was spent for supporting the luxurious lifestyle of the upper class and for building military strength to secure political control. The cumulative effect of all this on the common peasantry is what we hypothesize as the process of latifundialization. These various particulars of the process of latifundialization are either explicitly mentioned and/or alluded to in the eighth-century oracles of Amos, Hosea, Isaiah, and Micah.

4

Land Accumulation in Amos, Hosea, Isaiah, and Micah

This chapter will be devoted to examining the prophetic oracles in the books of Amos, Hosea, Isaiah, and Micah. The purpose is to test extensively the hypothetical reconstruction of the systemic reality of eighth-century Israel and Judah proposed in the previous chapter against the data in the prophetic oracles. Through this analysis, the author hopes to demonstrate how significant aspects of the oracles not covered by previous exegesis can be explained and/or illumined by the process of latifundialization hypothesized.

The various aspects relating to the process of land accumulation as proposed in chapter 1 will provide the main framework for organizing the prophetic texts. Under each aspect, the listing of passages will be according to the following criteria. First, passages with explicit references to the process of latifundialization and its various aspects and whose dating is generally agreed upon by scholarly consensus to be eighth century B.C.E. will be discussed. Second, passages with allusions to the process of latifundialization and its various aspects and whose dating is generally agreed upon by scholarly consensus to be eighth century B.C.E. will be analyzed. Third, passages containing explicit references to the process of latifundialization but whose eighth-century dating is debated will follow. Finally, passages containing allusions to the process of latifundialization with controverted dating will be taken up. In this chapter, all translations are the author's.

Land Accumulation

Central to the process of latifundialization is the growth of large estates. The small plots of land to which the common peasants have access for residence and cultivation of staples are taken over by the landed elite. The accumulation of land grows in inverse proportion to the number of people owning land. The landowning class decreases but the land held by this group increases. This deprives the common peasants of their right of access to land.

Isaiah 5:8–10

> 8 Woe to those who accumulate house to house,
>   and field to field
>   until there is no small landholding;
>   and you have been made possessors of land
>   all by yourselves in the midst of the land.
> 9 In my hearing…Yahweh of Hosts:
>   "Indeed the large estates shall become desolate,
>   large and beautiful, no one to sit in possession.
> 10 For ten acres of vineyard shall but make one bath,
>   and a homer of seed shall yield but one ephah."

These verses reflect the growth of large estates. This passage, along with Micah 2:1–5, is a classic statement on the central reality that characterizes the Israelite and Judean societies in the eighth century B.C.E. The preceding section (vv. 1–7) contains the song of the vineyard. The very use of the form of the song of the vineyard seems to be intentional in that it relates to the content of what follows. Verses 8–10 is one of a series of six woe oracles authentic to Isaiah from the later part of the eighth century prior to the Syro-Epraimite war (Brueggemann 1998:63; Clements 1980:61; Kaiser 1972:65; Seitz 1993:51; Sweeney 1996:129; Watts 1985:63; Wildberger 1991:197).

One of the key words in this passage is *bayit*. The meaning cannot be restricted to simply "house." William Moran has studied extensively the use of the Akkadian *bitu* in Ugaritic documents from the second millennium dealing with the transfer of immovable property. On the basis of his analysis, he concludes that property in these texts was referred to as house (*bétu/bitu*) or as field (*eqlu*) or as house and field (1967:549–52). Building on Moran's treatment, Chaney in his discussion of the Tenth Commandment has argued that the *bayit* "of one's neighbor originally referred to a plot of arable land held in redistributional domain by an Israelite extended family which, as a unit of both production and consumption as well as of residence, farmed the plot in mixed, subsistence agriculture" (1973:6). It is significant that the Ugaritic formula linking houses and fields occurs in this condemnation of land accumulation as well as in Micah 2:2. Consequently, it seems likely that Isaiah is using large houses to mean large landholdings. The same phrase also occurs in Amos 3:15. Ronald Clements writes: "The joining together of houses and fields evidently refers to the formation of large cultivated estates by neighboring property" (1980:62). As a consequence, a group of rich landowners emerged that "not only contrasted with abject poverty of other citizens but had actually been the cause of dispossessing the latter of their properties and legal rights" (Clements 1980:62–63).

In verse 8, the Hebrew word *maqom* (usually translated as "place") has been rendered here as "small landholding." This translation is based on William Johnstone's study of some technical expressions in the Old Testament with regard to property holdings in light of the Ugaritic texts. According to Johnstone, *maqom* in a technical sense refers to estate or property in addition to its general meaning of locality, place, or spot (1969:314). He follows G. R. Driver's translation of *mqmh* (1956:30) as a "share of his estate" (1969:315). Johnstone further cites the following biblical passages in support of his argument: Genesis 23:20; Judges 9:55, 19:28; 1 Samuel 2:20, 27:5, 29:3; and 2 Samuel 19:39 (1969:314). However, Johnstone does not cite Isaiah 5:8, where *maqom* is used in a technical sense to refer to the small landholding of the peasant.

Crucial to the rendering of the last part of verse 8 is the word rendered as "possessors." The semantic field of the Hebrew verb *yashav* includes the ownership of land. Albrecht Alt recognized the upper class political nuance of this term in his discussion of Judges 5:23 where it designates the proprietors or lords of the aristocratic Canaanite political structure ("die Besitzer und Herren des aristokratisch verfassten Kanaanischen Gemeinwesens") (1953:276). In more recent times, Gottwald has concluded that the possessors

> are leaders in the imperial feudal statist system of social
> organization, with primary reference to every king, but

embracing other functionaries in the statist system. As Israel developed statist sociopolitical organization of its own, the term was increasingly applied to Israelite functionaries in the state apparatus and, on occasion, referred to persons of power in the upper socioeconomic strata irrespective of their holding political office. (1979:532)

It is these members of the ruling elite class who owned large estates. In Isaiah 5:8–9, the verbal and nominal forms of *yashav* should be seen in the context of the process of land accumulation. The phrase "in the midst *(bqrv)* of the land," far from being a casual reference, may have a deeper significance. Isaiah may be hinting at the absentee landlords living in the "middle" or "center" of the land, namely, in the urban centers, which were pivotal to the elite (Wildberger 1991:198; see further discussion in the next section).

The accusation in verse 8 is followed by judgment in verses 9–10 calling for a total desolation of these large estates of the upper class. In this context, the use of these terms about possession and houses underlines the magnitude of their possessions. It is significant that the judgment in verse 9 ends with the reference to possessors. The prophet predicts that there will be no one to possess land–there will be no landlords. The rich landlords will be bereft of their large landholdings. There is a sense of retributive justice in Isaiah's judgment. Their crime of accumulating large estates by joining the small plots of land, which were the peasants' inheritance, was a violation of the sacred ordinance, the principle of distribution of land under Yahweh's ultimate ownership.

Consequently, to the avaricious motivations of the landed elite to gain maximum economic advantage through the cultivation of cash crops, Yahweh will respond with a total failure of the harvest. It is noteworthy that verse 10 lists two of the major items of export from Palestine: wine and grain. These items were exported in exchange for luxury and strategic military items. Thus, the local economic resources went to support the elite and their lifestyle. The primary producers benefited in no way from the fruits of their labor. The firm control of the distributive process by the ruling elite was responsible for this. The judgment speaks of depriving the rich of the very things of which they had deprived the peasants.

The present treatment differs from previous treatments of the passage in question on three counts. First, it is different in its systematic use of the comparative evidence. The process of land accumulation reflected in Isaiah 5:8–10 is analyzed with the help of categories drawn from the studies of agrarian economies past and present. Comparative perspective can lead to asking useful and new questions. Second, the present treatment has sought to propose a context for the passage as a whole, while at the same time making sure that the various details in the passage fit together cogently in relation to the overall context. Thus, the interpretation of *bayit, maqom,* and *yashav* all belong in the context of the growth of large estates and the deprivation of the peasantry. Third, the present treatment has tried to understand the context of the passage in its *systemic* interrelatedness. The growth of large estates is a multifaceted phenomenon. Hence, the force of verse 10 cannot be understood if one does not see the place of cash crops in the consumption of the elite and their export/import operations. That is why the judgment is rendered precisely in terms of failure of these crops.

Among earlier scholars, Bernhard Duhm had some perceptive comments on the Isaianic passage, pointing out that access to land was important for the ancient Israelites and to be without land was to be without kinship affinity. He also recognized the landowning nuance of the term *yashav* (1922:56–57). Otto Kaiser's comment on the change in the ownership pattern reflected in this passage as a violation of the sacred ordinance concerning land is pertinent (1972:65–67). He does identify the main reason for this crisis as the rise of monetary economy but does not develop the thesis, giving little attention to the details of the text. The means by which the large estates were formed, according to Clements, "can only be guessed at, but analogies would suggest that it was achieved by the taking over of common land and by the buying up of neighboring properties" (1980:62). I am not certain whether Clements is thinking of comparative evidence from the field of social sciences or from passages such as Micah 2:2 and 1 Kings 21:3. I suspect it is the latter. In relation to the accumulation of land, Clements also recognizes the role of the legal process in legitimating corrupt practices. He does not, however, elaborate on this aspect, and, again, very little is said about the individual details of the text. Hans Bardtke's exposition of this passage misses the mark both in trying to provide a general background for this passage and also in some details (1971:135–54). His argument that Isaiah 5:8–10 reflects the condition of the second half of the eighth century B.C.E., particularly during the time of

Hezekiah, is not convincing. Also, his explanation that the indebtedness and impoverishment of the common populace are to be seen in the context of protracted payment of tribute paid to the Assyrians has limited relevance. It is true that the common people bore the brunt of taxation for raising the tribute money. But this does not explain why the condition of the peasantry deteriorated even at a time of unprecedented political supremacy and economic growth as seen in the Israelite and Judean kingdoms in the first part of the eighth century. The reference to "joining house to house" is interpreted by Bardtke as the acquisition of actual buildings in cities (1971:238). William Holladay also sees this as "buying up" of real estate (1987:54). Bardtke argues further that "the poor and the unpropertied" were not affected by this buying of houses in the cities. This argument is baffling, as it shows a lack of familiarity with the agrarian reality. Comments such as these only go to show the need to take comparative evidence on agrarian societies more seriously. Insights from the field of social sciences concerning agrarian societies are crucial in bringing to light aspects of the text that have been overlooked, misunderstood, or not covered by previous exegesis.

Micah 2:1–5

1 Woe to those who scheme wickedness
    and who devise evil upon their couches,
    and at the break of dawn they execute it,
    for it is in their power.
2 They covet fields and seize them,
    and houses they take away from them.
    They oppress individuals and houses,
    people and their inheritance.
3 Therefore, thus says Yahweh:
    I am devising evil against this family
    from which you cannot remove your necks,
    and you shall not walk proud, for it is an evil time;
4 on that day, a taunt song will be raised concerning you,
    a lament shall be sung, saying,
    "We are utterly ruined;
    the property of my people is measured;
    how he removes mine.
    For [the purpose of] reparation our fields are divided.

5 Therefore, no one will be there for you to cast
   the measuring line by lot in the assembly of Yahweh.

The eighth-century oracles of Micah are among the most direct
and descriptive of the references to the process of latifundialization.
The present passage is a classic portrayal of the growth of latifundia.
The eighth-century dating of this oracle is not generally disputed.
Verses 1–5 form a unit. There is a definite structure and pattern to the
progression of thought. The first two verses describe the wicked
planning and activities of the ruling elite. Verse 3 warns about the
threat of punishment. The details of the retribution are given in verse
4. Verse 5 concludes the unit with retributive justice having been
established.

This oracle is a strong invective against the accumulation of
landed property by the ruling elite to the deprivation of the peasantry.
Along with Isaiah 5:8, this passage depicts the growth of large estates
through a process of land accumulation. The wealthy landowners
carefully plotted their strategy for depriving the small peasants. Micah
castigates: "Woe to those who scheme wickedness and who devise evil
upon their couches."

The verse also alludes to the mode of execution of their plans.
The reference to dawn is important, because it was in the morning
that the courts met at the city gate to decide legal disputes (Köhler
1956:151; Chaney 1973:11). The powerful landowners controlled the
court officials. Micah is aware of the fact that they could carry out
their wicked plans because they had the power in their hands.

The formulaic reference to "houses and fields" also occurs in
Genesis 39:5; 2 Kings 8:3; Isaiah 5:8; and Jeremiah 32:15. (For a
discussion of the formula, see the treatment of Isa. 5:8.) The passage
makes it clear that the reference here is, in fact, to the small plot of
land under ancestral allotment. This is implied in the use of *nahalah*
("inheritance"). The full import of the landowners' crimes has to be
understood in the context of this ancestral allotment. It was an assault
on the fundamental principle on which the family structure was built
(Hillers 1984:33). The growth of the latifundia was a violation of the
old sacred ordinance of Yahweh based on the principle of "a man [*sic*],
a house and an inheritance" (Alt 1959:373–74).

The Mican passage refers to the process of land accumulation
through foreclosures (v. 2a) and expropriation (v. 2b). This refers to
oppression by extortion as Chaney recognizes (1973:12). Verse 3

warns against the coming judgment. The wicked intention of the landlords to grab the lands of the poor will be avenged by the scheme of Yahweh. The parallel is established by the use of "scheme" in verse 1. The threat underlines the inevitability of punishment.

Verse 4 spells out the actual details of the judgment. The oracle reaches its climax in this verse. The judgment in every detail matches the crimes. It predicts the complete bankruptcy of the ruling elite. The punishment would consist of stripping the elite of their prominent and powerful socioeconomic and political position in the society. The fate of the rich landowners is conveyed in the form of a lament from their own mouths. They give expression to their plight. This is done in four short lines. In the first line—"we are utterly ruined"—the fallen condition of the elite is set forth. Following Alt's suggestion, the second line is emended to read, "The property of my people is measured" (Alt 1959:377). The third line reads, "How he removes mine." meaning that the lands that they had appropriated to be their possession are now taken away from them. The fourth line should read, "For reparation our fields are apportioned" (Brown, Driver and Briggs 1978:998). Wolff links this reparation with the previous sentence: "O how he takes from me [the land] as retribution" (1990:68), with the meaning of "to mean to bring back or pay back." The redistributive justice is achieved through a repartition of the large estates into small landholdings. The punishment thus corresponds to the crime. In the end, the rich landowners who appropriated the small landholdings to build large estates will be deprived in order that the large estates can be redistributed into small plots.

The clincher comes in verse 5: "Therefore, no one will be there for you to cast the measuring line by lot in the assembly of Yahweh." "The assembly of Yahweh" occurs as a designation for the sacred assembly of Israel (Deut. 23:2; Num. 16:3, 20:4; and 1 Chr. 28:8). The traditional practice of convening the community for the purpose of measuring and apportioning land took place here (Alt 1959:380). Consequently, the original order of the peasants would come into force with the measurement and redistribution of the latifundia, now rendered ownerless by the judgment of Yahweh. Those who are guilty of the crime will have no rights in the sacred assembly. The extreme form of humiliation is envisioned for those who have violated the sacred practice of Yahweh's inheritance. They will lose their inheritance rights. To be without inheritance rights in the sacred assembly was to be without any kinship affinity–the worst that could happen to an ancient Israelite.

Hosea 5:10

> The court officials in Judah have become like removers of
>   boundary landmarks;
> upon them I will pour out my fury like water.

These verses are taken to originate from the period following the death of Jeroboam II and before the outbreak of the Syro-Ephraimite war (Andersen and Freedman 1980:402; Mays 1969b:16; Mackintosh 1997:202; Wolff 1974:xxi). Generally, this passage has been interpreted to reflect Judah's invasion of the Northern Kingdom. The context is the impending advancement of Tiglath-Pileser III of Assyria against Syria and Palestine. It is argued that, encouraged by the success of the Assyrian power in the north, Ahaz began to move the northern boundary for the protection of Jerusalem (Wolff 1974:113). Similar interpretation is offered by Francis Andersen and David Noel Freedman: "The crime here is not a case of social injustice with regard to personal property; the vocabulary has been extended to the relationships between the nations who were formerly members of the tribal league. Thus the annexation of territory may be described as moving intertribal boundary marker" (1980:408).

It does not seem probable that Judah was the aggressor in the Syro-Ephraimite war. The historical information we have points to the contrary. Syria and Israel were the aggressors. In the previous chapter, it was proposed that the cause of the Syro-Ephraimite war has to be sought in the economic realm. Syria and Israel wanted to end Judah's hegemony over Transjordan. Hence, it was Syria and Israel who came down repeatedly against Judah and not the other way around. Since the text does say that the Judean officials have been involved in some kind of boundary shifting, we will have to seek an explanation in another direction.

The context of Hosea 5:10 reflects the process of land accumulation. It refers to the process of land accumulation by the court officials. The deliberate tampering with the boundary marks has violated the old tribal inheritance practice of holding small plots. To remove landmark implies the changing of the boundaries of one's landed property (Birch 1997:64). Relevant to this understanding are two passages from Deuteronomy: "You will not shift the boundary marks of your neighbor which the ancestors have established in the inheritance which you will possess in the land which Yahweh your God gives you to possess" (Deut. 19:14). "Cursed be the one who shifts the boundary marks of his neighbor" (Deut. 27:17a). It is striking that the combination of neighbors and boundary marks not only occurs in Deuteronomy 19:14, 27:17a; Proverbs 22:28, 23:10, but also in Hosea 5:10. In all the references, the concern is preserving the boundary limits established by the ancestral practice of allotting the land by casting lots in the assembly of Yahweh. The growth of latifundia was a violation of that practice. The peasants were stripped of their freely held plots as a result of the growth of large estates. It is precisely this phenomenon to which Hosea 5:10 refers. Two other scholars have seen a similar emphasis in this passage. Julius Wellhausen first identified such a concern in this passage. He places it with Isaiah 5:8 and Micah 2:2 for its condemnation of the tampering with the ancient ancestral allotment practices (1963:114). Alt also sees the similarity of concern in Isaiah 5:8; Micah 2:2; and Hosea 5:10 but is skeptical whether Hosea, being from the north, would have been so concerned with what was happening in Judah. Hence, Alt is in favor of emending Judah to Israel (1959:171–72), but there is no textual basis for it.

Growth of Urban Centers

The growth of urban centers is very much related to the growth of a market-oriented economy. A market-oriented economy gives rise to the emergence of privileged social groups such as ruling class, officials of the royal administration, wealthy landowners, merchants, and moneylenders. Conversely, the whole market economy is geared toward catering to the whims and fancies of these privileged groups. The best of the goods and services flowed into a handful of urban centers. The importance of the urban center/city stems from its political (administrative and military), economic, and religious functions. The social groups associated with these various functions had to be supported. Being the productive base, the vast agricultural periphery was the main provider of goods and services to the urban centers. In the initial stages of the development of agrarian societies, this might have been an arrangement of mutual benefit. The primary producers provided goods and services in return for military protection. But with the balance of power tilted in favor of the ruling class, the mutual dependence soon degenerated into outright exploitation. The cities as administrative centers of the state functioned effectively in extracting the surplus from the rural areas. The urban centers virtually lived off the rural areas. One may compare this to a leech living off a human body by draining its blood.

Amos 3:9–11

9 Make known upon the fortified palaces in Ashdod,
   and upon the fortified palaces in the land of Egypt,
   and say: "Gather upon the mountain of Samaria,
   and witness the great commotion in it;
   and those who are oppressed by extortion in its midst.
10 They do not know right action," says Yahweh,
   "those who store up violence and plunder in their
   fortified palaces."
11 Thus says the Lord Yahweh:
   "The enemy! The land is surrounded!
   He will bring down your strength from you,
   and your fortified palaces will be plundered."

Many scholars consider this oracle to be authentic to Amos (Andersen and Freedman 1989:37, 402; Auld 1986:60–61; Coote 1981:12; Mays 1969a:5; Paul 1991:115; Wolff 1977:107). Even though the addressees of this oracle are not specified, from the context and the content it becomes clear that they are the leading citizens of Samaria. The opening lines draw attention to the violent and oppressive crimes of the upper class. The city of Samaria stands as a symbol for the excesses of the urban culture. In the eighth-century oracles of the prophets, the references to the city serve an important function. The cities represent the prosperity and development achieved at the expense of the rural areas. In the perception of the prophets, cities become symptomatic of the malaise they saw in the society at large. The antiurban sentiment stems from an awareness of the effects of the urban culture on the lower economic strata of the society.

Amos calls Ashdod and Egypt to witness the violence and oppression in Samaria. The reason for the invitation is the nature of the genre. Being cast in the form of a covenant lawsuit, it reflects the practice of witnesses providing evidence in legal procedures (Hayes 1988:127; Stuart 1987:329). This refers to the oppressive acts of the powerful ruling elite, which have been detrimental to the life of the peasantry. As is characteristic of Amos's accusations, we have here a mention of the victims of oppressive extortion, with a connection between the terrorizing activity of the elite and their accumulation of wealth.

The occurrence of "fortified palaces" four times is significant. It refers to the fortified section of the royal palace (King 1988:67). Such strongholds apparently would be the residential quarters of the upper class or the military officials. In this sense they are visible symbols of urban growth and thus the power of the ruling elite and their wealth. It was a constant reminder of the stark difference between the rich and the poor. The rich are described as those who "store" violence. Since the elites have amassed wealth through violence and oppression, Amos equates their treasures with violence, using terms that refer to the assault on the body of an individual and to crimes against goods and property. Thus, this word pair sums up the violence committed against persons and property (Paul 1991:117; Wolff 1977:194). The punishment predicts a total destruction of the strongholds of the rich (v. 11). The scene of the crime becomes the scene of punishment. The punishment corresponds to the crime. The robbers will be robbed. The symbols of the elite's power and their devious activities will be brought down.

Amos 6:1–3

1 Woe to those who are at ease in Zion,
   who trust in the mountain of Samaria,
   the select elite of the prominent of nations,
   to whom the house of Israel come.
2 Pass over to Kullani and see;
   then go from there to Hamath the great;
   and go down to Gath of the Philistines.
   Are you better than these kingdoms?
   Is your territory greater than their territory,
3 you who put away the evil day to a distant future,
   who bring near the reign of violence?

This passage, part of a larger unit in verses 1–7, is generally assigned to Amos (Andersen and Freedman 1989:61, 550–51; Coote 1981:12; Hayes 1988:183–84; Mays 1969a:12–13; McKeating 1971:49; Paul 1991:200; Wolff 1977:107). The oracle is a condemnation of the carefree and complacent attitude of the ruling class. Thematically, this passage picks up on Amos 3:9–11 (Jeremias

1998:110 n. 14). The common theme is the role of the cities/urban centers. The city was the center of urban life where the members of the upper class, officials of the royal administration, and members of the royal household thronged. Being the capital city of the Northern Kingdom, Samaria must have been even more important. Omri purchased the hill of Samaria and built his capital city there. Hence, it was a crown possession. The lure of the city life attracted the members of the upper class. The importance of the city/urban center stems from its political (administrative and military), economic, and religious functions. The aristocracy was able to underwrite its affluent lifestyle through the extraction of surplus from the agricultural producers. The urban centers, in fact, lived off of the agricultural periphery. The best of everything flowed into the city. The persistence of this pattern of exploitation was pushing the economy to its brink. The civil and military officials had to be supported by the revenue, but they contributed nothing towards production. Agriculturally, they were a nonproductive group, but they were strong competitors for the agricultural produce of the rural areas. As long as the surplus flowed into the city, the ruling class was happy and secure, and they made sure that the flow continued.

Amos 6:1 refers to the upper crust of the society. The comparison with other nations was to indicate how Israel was doing. Kullani and Hamath were important commercial centers in Syria, which were taken over by Tiglath-Pileser III in his campaign of 738 B.C.E. (Paul 1991:201–202; Wolff 1977:275). These two places are mentioned not only to show that Israel compared with them in socioeconomic importance and the crimes of which it was guilty, but also to drive home the point that a similar disaster will overtake Israel. Verse 3 reinforces that idea. The ruling class was totally oblivious to the consequences of their actions. They refused to see the impending danger. But by their actions, they were only hastening the prospects of a violent judgment upon themselves.

Isaiah 1:21–26

21 How the faithful city has become unfaithful,
    she who was full of justice;
    righteousness used to lodge in her;
    but now murderers.
22 Your silver has become like oxide of lead;
    your beer diluted with water,

23 Your court officials are rebellious,
  and partners of thieves;
  everyone loves a bribe,
  and pursues after gifts.
  The orphans, they defend not;
  and the lawsuit of the widow does not come to them.
24 Therefore the oracle of the Lord Yahweh of hosts, the Bull
      of Israel:
  "I will satisfy myself, O my enemies! I will take
  vengeance, my foes!
25 I will bring back my power upon you;
  I will refine your oxide of lead like potash;
  I will remove all your impurities;
26 I will restore your judges as formerly,
  and counselors as in the beginning;
  after this you shall be called a faithful city."

Many scholars take this passage to be original to Isaiah (Clements 1980:35; Hayes and Irvine 1987:80–81; Sweeney 1996:85; Wildberger 1991:63). But some express uncertainty in dating this section (Gray 1912:32; Kaiser 1972:19). However, there are no serious arguments offered. Kaiser and Hans Wildberger see the connection between this section and Isaiah 3:12–15; 5:22–24; and 10:1–4 on the basis of similarity of thought (Kaiser 1972:19; Wildberger 1991:63). This, in fact, strengthens the case for the authenticity of this passage. And, as Brueggemann points out, we may have here "in a nutshell the primary claims of the early Isaiah tradition" (1998:22). Isaiah's characterization of the city captures, in essence, the total failure to be faithful to the covenant principles.

Verses 21–26 form a self-contained unit, with the phrase "faithful city" functioning as an inclusio (Duhm 1922:32; Sweeney 1996:84). This passage is highly critical of the leadership in Jerusalem and calls for a complete change of the present order to make way for a more just and responsible group of leaders. Isaiah uses the symbol of the city, which brings out several implications. The city serves as a symbol of the urban life. It signifies the political, civil, and military hierarchy. It also refers to the highly stratified society with the concentration of wealth and power in the hands of a small group of ruling elite. The city epitomizes commercialism, and in a more fundamental way, the disappearance of the old tribal system and its values. All these systemic changes came into force in Israel with the inauguration of monarchy. These disastrous effects operated to a maximum degree in the eighth century. The prophet bemoans this development by using the form of an elegy/dirge (Kaiser 1972:19; Skinner 1915:10; Sweeney 1996:85).

The first two verses (21 and 22) bemoan the unhealthy moral, social, and political aspects of the city. This is expressed through the images of a harlot, silver that has become impure, and beer that is diluted. In verse 21, the political leaders are referred to as "murderers." This description is fitting because of their inhuman and oppressive activities. The officials are also called "rebellious." Isaiah does not have in mind any specific act of political rebellion but the rebellion against Yahweh, only that they have violated the commandment for a just order of society (Clements 1980:36).

The term usually translated as "princes" does not necessarily mean those of royal descent but officials of authority who held key positions in the civil and administrative structures. The officials are also described as business associates (Elat 1979b:539). The verbs used to describe the unsuccessful joint sea expedition of Jehoshaphat and Ahaziah to Ophir (2 Chr. 20:35, 37) are derived from similar roots (cp. Job 40:30). The existence of joint business enterprises is further supported by the Hubur system, a company of wealthy merchants engaged in maritime trade (Pritchard 1969:27). The ruling class is described as a business association of thieves, because they deprived the common people. They appropriated by illegal means what rightfully belonged to the peasantry. The later part of verse 23 draws attention to the crimes of the judiciary officials. The judges could be swayed from their responsibility and integrity through bribes and gifts. They not only accepted bribes and gifts but also eagerly sought after them. This made them completely subservient to the power of the ruling class. Thus, they failed in their obligation to deal fairly with cases relating to the orphans and widows. These two groups of people along with the foreigners constituted vulnerable groups who were in danger of being marginalized in the society. (For a discussion of their status and the problems they faced, see the section on Judicial Courts below.)

Yahweh promises to avenge the officials' unfaithfulness. Because of their misconduct, they have become Yahweh's enemies. Their impurities will be removed. Yahweh also promises the restoration of judges and counselors as in the former days. The precise meaning of this is not clear. It could not possibly mean that they would go back to the system of the period of the judges. But in a more general sense, it could mean leaders who would be chosen by the people rather than appointed by the crown. A change in the situation for the better would come about only with a change in the order of the society.

Isaiah 2:12–17

> 12 For Yahweh of hosts has a day
>   against all that is haughty and lofty,
>   against all that is conspicuous and high;
> 13 against all the cedars of Lebanon, lofty and high;
>   against all the oaks of Bashan;
> 14 against all the high mountains;
>   and against all the conspicuous hills;
> 15 against every lofty tower,
>   and against every fortified wall;
> 16 against all the ships of Tarshish,
>   and against all the luxury liners.
> 17 The haughtiness of humans shall be humbled,
>   and the pride of the people shall be brought down;
>   Yahweh alone will be exalted on that day.

This oracle is part of an extended collection of threats against Judah and Jerusalem found in 2:6–4:1. Though the collection may have undergone expansion, the Isaianic origin of the collection as a whole, and of the passage in question in particular, is undisputed (Clements 1980:43; Fohrer 1960–61:9; Kaiser 1972:33; Skinner 1915:lxxvi; Sweeney 1996:103–104; Wildberger 1991:119; Willis 1980:104). Isaiah's portrayal of the day of Yahweh as a time of punishment has affinity with Amos 5:18–20.

The judgment is aimed at the urban paraphernalia. The dimension of height and loftiness plays a key role in this oracle and, in fact, throughout Isaiah 1–39. The dimension of loftiness and height symbolically represents human pride. In Isaiah's scheme, human pride undercuts the sovereignty of Yahweh, for Yahweh alone is exalted and lifted up. Hence, the pride and loftiness of humans, or whatever seeks to undercut the loftiness of Yahweh, shall be brought low. In keeping with the emphasis on a lofty dimension, Isaiah lists things of lofty dimension in this oracle: the cedars of Lebanon, oaks of Bashan, high mountains and hills, towers and fortified walls, and ships. Most of the things listed here have allusive implications. The "cedars of Lebanon" is a stock phrase in the Hebrew Scriptures. The cedars were items of export from Lebanon. Cedars were used to make masts for ships (Ezek. 7:5). Ezekiel 27 offers a comprehensive picture of the trading partners of Tyre in the ancient Near East with the relative export specialties of each country. Even though the immediate context of Ezekiel 27 is to be related to the developments in the sixth century B.C.E., it reflects the picture of trade and commerce developed over many centuries.

There are also many references to the oaks of Bashan in the Hebrew Bible. Bashan was one of the productive areas in Transjordan because of its adequate rainfall. It was known for its wheat, oaks, and fine cattle (Aharoni 1979a:36–38; Cohen 1962:687). It is of interest that oars were made out of oaks (Ezek. 27:6). The allusion to masts made out of the cedars of Lebanon, and oars of the oaks of Bashan fits well with the ship imagery in Isaiah 2:16. However, at a more general level, they allude to the trade and commercial activity in which cedars and oaks figured prominently, being the export items from Lebanon and Bashan.

The "lofty tower" and "fortified wall" stand here as symbols for the urban centers. In Palestine, the ancient acropolis was marked by the bastion system with fortified walls and guard towers. One may take them to be symbols of human achievement. But these achievements have become objects of contempt and devastation because they were built on the suffering and misery of many. The growth of the urban centers was at the cost of, and with the resources from, the rural areas. In agrarian societies, a minority of the population managed to extract agricultural surplus from the majority of the peasants to underwrite its own lifestyle. Only a strong and secure state could exploit the economic advantage. This, in turn, depended on the military establishment and fortification systems. The establishment of fortification systems was aimed at providing security against both internal and external threats. These elaborate undertakings materialized through the surplus extracted from the peasants. It should also be mentioned that the peasants were pressed into corvée by the state for these building projects. In this sense, these structures were built on the sweat and blood of the peasantry. Hence, they became objects of contempt in the eyes of the prophet.

Verse 16 evokes the theme of trade and commerce. "The ships of Tarshish" can be interpreted in several ways. It could refer to a refinery fleet (Köhler and Baumgartner 1951:1042). Tarshish is also identified as a place name for Tartessos in Spain. The Phoenicians imported silver from Spain. Jeremiah 10:9 refers to the export of beaten silver from Tarshish. Tartessos became active in international commerce in the eighth century B.C.E. (Tsirkin 1979:553). In light of both these interpretations, the reference in verse 16 is to cargo ships. The next line of verse 16 may well refer to luxury liners used by either the royal household or members of the ruling class; the Hebrew term has an Egyptian parallel (Köhler and Baumgartner 1951:921; Wildberger 1991:101). The predominance of ship imagery in this oracle suggests that the prophet is also alluding to the impact of the growth of trade and commerce on the lives of the poorer sections of the society. In antiquity, interregional and international trade was monopolized by the state. The beneficiaries of such trade were the royal household and those who were close to the royal circle. The majority of the population did not benefit from this. If anything, such extensive trade and commerce helped only to widen the gulf between the rich and the poor. Hence, the divine judgment rails against the ruling class who have set themselves against Yahweh by depriving the poor.

Micah 1:5b–6

5b What is the transgression of Jacob?
   Is it not Samaria?
   What is the prominent place of Judah?
   Is it not Jerusalem?
6 And I will make Samaria into an open field with stones,
   a planting ground for viticulture;
   I will throw down her stones into a valley,
   and I will uproot her foundations.

In these lines, Micah prophesies the destruction of Samaria. Why should Micah specify a particular place? Even the way Micah frames the charges is revealing. Samaria is described as the transgression of Jacob. In the same way, Jerusalem is also singled out for special mention. From a rhetorical point of view, this way of symbolic representation or personification is very effective in terms of its emotional impact (Shaw 1993:54). There is also another aspect to this. Samaria and Jerusalem are picked out not only because they are the capital cities of the respective kingdoms, but also because they are symbolic of a certain social reality. It pertains to the development of the urban centers. The growth of the urban centers is not an isolated phenomenon. It has its repercussions for the rest of the society. In the eighth-century Israelite and Judahite societies, the mode of production was the result of an interaction between two distinct socioeconomic and political units. There was a large agricultural periphery, which was the locus of production. Then there was the powerful centralized state. The state, whose power was located in the urban centers, depended on the rural areas for agricultural products. The rural areas, in turn, depended on the state for protection. The relationship between the two units, which began as one of mutual dependence, soon deteriorated into a relationship of exploitation. The state began to wield its power in the political and economic spheres of the society. The cities, as the administrative centers of the state, functioned effectively in the process of penetrating and extracting the economic surplus from the rural areas. The ruling class used the economic surpluses to build palaces, fortifications, and temples; to build, equip, and maintain armies; and to underwrite their luxurious lifestyle.

The city was the haven of the privileged classes. The best of everything flowed into it. If such is the case with urban centers, one can imagine the importance of the capital city. As the administrative center of the whole kingdom, it assumed enormous importance. It stood for the political and economic power of the state. On the one hand, cities were an embodiment of human achievement and pride. But it was an achievement wrought from the misery and suffering of many. The city stood as a symbol of the social stratification, which was based on a relationship of exploitation. The prophet predicts the demolition of the city and its paraphernalia, which are the symbols of power and affluence. All the proud structures will come down. The stones and foundations will be razed to, and uprooted from, the ground. In their place, there will now be an open field, an ideal place for planting vineyards (v. 6a). Through this imagery, the prophet is envisioning a radical shift in the social reality.

Micah 6:9–16

9 The voice of Yahweh calls to the city,
    and he will deliver the one who fears his name;
    fear O tribe, what he has appointed.

12 "Its [the city's] rich are full of violence,
and its aristocracy speaks falsehood;
and there are deceitful tongues in their mouths.
10 Shall I forgive storehouses that are evil,
and reduced measure that is cursed?
11 Shall I approve as clean, the crooked scales,
and a bagful of false weights?
13 Indeed I have begun to smite you;
desolation because of your sins.
14b What you put aside you will not save;
what you will save, I will give to the sword.
14a You will eat but will not be sated;
15 you will sow but will not reap;
you will tread olive but will not anoint with oil;
and [you will tread] grapes but will not drink wine.
16 You have kept the statutes of Omri,
and all the deeds of the house of Ahab;
and you followed their plans.
Hence I am giving it [the city] for desolation,
and its rulers for derision;
you shall lift up the disgrace of my people."

Many scholars question the authenticity of this passage. James Mays assigns it to the period of the Babylonian crisis (1976:30–33, 146–48). On the basis of stylistic and substantive differences, Wolff considers this to originate after Micah's time (1990:23, 189). George Gray denies the authenticity of 6:1–7:6 as a whole (1913:219). Theodor Lescow places 6:9–12 in early exilic times and 6:13–16 in the period immediately following 609 B.C.E. (1972:204–205). In Georg Fohrer's opinion, there is no concrete evidence for Micah's authorship (1968:446). However, the Mican authorship of these verses has its advocates (Hillers 1984:82; Shaw 1993:171; Wolfe 1956:899–900). In Kaiser's view, unless 6:9–16 is related to Samaria, this passage could hardly be claimed for Micah (1975:229). One of the problems in dealing with this section is the difficult nature of the Hebrew text. In some places, the Hebrew text needs emendations. And in some places, the order of the sentences also needs to be rearranged for a better flow of thought. (Note the inversion of several verses.)

The contents of the oracle concentrate on some specific aspects of the process of latifundialization witnessed in the eighth century B.C.E.

On the basis of these references, it is possible to claim that there is some genuine eighth-century material preserved in this oracle. However, the oracle has gone through a lot of editorial history. The oracle opens with the call of Yahweh to the city (v. 9a) and ends with the threat of desolation of the city (v. 16c). Verse 12 in the Masoretic text (MT) should be transposed immediately after verse 9 since it dwells on the theme of the city and its rulers. The feminine pronominal suffix at the end of the two nouns in verse 12 refers back to the city. Those who *yashav* in the city, in this context, are not to be translated as inhabitants. It does have the specific connotation of landed aristocracy.

Verse 12 echoes the familiar theme of Micah's tirade against the ruling elite. Here again, as in Micah 1:5b, the city becomes symbolic of the effects of urban life on the poor. The rich are full of violence that they contrive against the innocent. The aristocracy speaks falsehood by fabricating their cases. Verses 10 and 11 in the MT should follow verse 12. The storehouses mentioned in verse 10 not only symbolize elitist power but also economic strength. The storehouses were used for accumulating the agricultural surpluses extracted from the peasants. The prophet brands them as evil because they housed ill-gotten surpluses. The peasants were milked of the produce of their land by way of extractions at harvest. In verse 10a, "shall I forgive" is parallel to "shall I approve" in the following verse. The speaker is Yahweh enumerating the charges. In verses 10b and 11, the charges relate to the illegal practices rampant in the market system. "The reduced measure," "the crooked scales," and "the false weights" were the means used by the merchants to cheat the peasants. This aspect of the process of latifundialization finds repeated mention in the eighth-century prophetic oracles. (See discussions of Am. 8:4–6 and Hos. 12:7.) Verses 13–16 give expression to the judgment. It is no surprise that the judgment lists aspects pertaining to the lifestyle of the elite. They will eat and not be satisfied; they will sow but not reap. In other words, there will be no agricultural surpluses. The surpluses that supported their extravagant lifestyle will no more be forthcoming. The judgment also predicts the failure of wine and oil. This cuts at the root of the rich class's lifestyle. Failure of wine and oil meant that there would be no more wine for voluptuous consumption, no more wine to exchange for the luxury items for their perusal, and, most importantly, there would be no more wine and oil to export in exchange for the strategic military items. That strikes at the very heart of the power structure that sustains the political machinery of the elite. In light of the overall thrust of this section, it is very appropriate that verse 16 refers to Omri and Ahab. Earlier scholarship has failed to see the systemic significance of the reference to the Omrides. The earlier part of the eighth-century systemic reality has a lot in common with the reign of the Omrides in the ninth century. As pointed out in chapter 3, there is a commonality between the ninth and eighth centuries. Israel and Judah were strong powers in the region. Trade and commerce flourished. But only the royal class benefited from this wealth. The lot of the common peasantry deteriorated. The Omrides' attempt to imitate the Solomonic model of society had its detrimental effect. The building of a strong state, maintenance of a huge army, and the vast building projects brought heavy expenditure to the state. Needless to say, the burden of taxation was heavy on the peasantry. In the eyes of the prophet, history was repeating itself, only more severely this time. A systemic perspective enables us to see the full import of verse 16 and also the overall context of Micah 6:9–16. The oracle, which opened with a call to the city, comes to a close with the threat of punishment on the city and its aristocracy.

Micah 5:10–11 [Heb. 9–10]

> 10 An oracle of Yahweh: On that day
> > I will cut off your horses from your midst,
> > and I will destroy your chariots;
> 11 I will cut off cities of your land, bring down your
> > fortifications.

Generally, verses 10–15 [Heb. 9–14] are seen as a unit. The authenticity of this unit has been debated. In Mays's view, the basic oracle could hardly have come from Micah. He regards verses 10–13 in particular as early exilic redaction of the Mican tradition (1976:124). John Marsh and Lescow also subscribe to this view (Marsh 1959:106; Lescow 1972:77). Several scholars rule out a preexilic origin (Fohrer 1968:446; Kaiser 1975:228; Stade 1881:169–70; Wolff 1990:154). There are some who defend the authenticity of this oracle (Willis 1969:353–68; Hillers 1984:74; and Shaw 1993:139). According to G. B. Gray, fragments of preexilic prophecy, if present in chapters 4 and 5, are to be located in 5:10–14 (1913:219). G. A. Smith finds much in this passage that is suitable to an eighth-century dating (1929:394).

Most critics who reject the authenticity of this oracle do so on the assumption that the genuine Mican material is to be found only in the first three chapters (following Stade 1881) and that all of the authentic oracles should be arranged under one major heading in an analysis of the book. This is further based on another assumption that the hope passages in Micah are attempts by later generations to offset the vitriolic nature of the doom oracles of the preexilic prophet. Once these assumptions are brought under scrutiny, other possibilities open. Even granting that the genuine Mican material is to be found in chapters 1–3, it would not preclude the possibility of a later editor taking earlier material and arranging it for his/her purposes. There is a distinction between saying that a particular passage originated from Micah and that a particular passage reflects the social reality of the eighth century. The book of Micah lends itself to symmetrical arrangement. The most widely held view concerning the division of the book is as follows: chapters 1–3; 4–5; and 6–7. John Willis proposes another division based on an alternating pattern of threat and hope: 1–3 (threat); 4–5 (hope); 6:1–7:6 (threat); and 7:7–20 (hope) (1969:195). Willis shows, quite convincingly, that the individual sections also contain the doom-hope pattern. In chapters 4–5, he isolates seven oracles exhibiting this pattern. The oracle in 5:10–15 [Heb. 5:9–14] shows a similar pattern with doom in verses 10–14 [Heb. 9–13] and hope in verse 15 [Heb. 14] (Willis 1969:212). Willis's analysis calls into question the often taken-for-granted assumption that the genuine oracles are to be found in Micah 1–3 because they proclaim a message of doom. Even if one works with the assumption that the genuine Mican materials are doom oracles, one has to account for the doom oracles elsewhere in the book. Following this criterion, the oracle in 5:10–11 [Heb. 9–10] should be attributed to Micah. Significantly, the content of this oracle is closer to the social reality of the eighth century B.C.E. Further, this oracle has a parallel in Isaiah 2:6–8, which is dated to the eighth century B.C.E.

The judgment in Micah 5:10–11 [Heb. 9–10] is aimed at the destruction of the symbols of elitist power: horses and chariots, cities and strongholds. These are the instruments of the elite's political and military power. The ruling class established and maintained their political control by means of a powerful military establishment. A strong military was needed to dominate the local population and to protect against outside attack. A powerful state also served an economic function. The extraction of surplus could be carried out effectively only with the help of a supportive power structure. As it has been discussed earlier on many occasions, the symbols of elitist power come under heavy fire from the prophets precisely because of their effect on the poorer section of the society.

Since the cities became the hub of civilization, they attracted the best of everything in terms of goods and services. The rural areas had to bear the burden of supporting the parasitical urban centers. The economic implications of the prophets' cry can be understood better when the urban-rural dynamics are analyzed from a systemic perspective. Earlier interpretations tended to obscure this dimension by concentrating on the religious dimension. The contrast between trust in Yahweh and other objects of false trust has been overextended. While this may be true, the analysis of the prophets is much more comprehensive than that. It does take into account the socioeconomic, political, and religious aspects of the problem.

Hosea 8:14

> Israel has forgotten its maker and has built palaces;
> and Judah has proliferated the walled cities;
> hence, I will send fire on their cities,
> and I will burn down their strongholds.

Many consider this verse to be a secondary addition. The objections to Hoseanic authorship are raised on the basis of several factors. First, the reference to Judah is problematic (Harper 1905:324; Ward 1969:145). Second, many draw attention to the parallel refrain in Amos 1:3–2:5 (Harper 1905:324; Knight 1960:93; Landy 1995:110; Mays 1969b:123–24; G. A. Smith 1929:301; Wellhausen 1963:122). The suggestion is that the style is more characteristic of Amos than Hosea. Third, the conception of Yahweh as Israel's creator is considered to be of much later origin than Hosea's time (Mackintosh 1997:332). Fourth, the content is seen to be out of place in this section, which is devoted to religious syncretism (Harper 1905:324). Finally, the natural conclusion of this section is taken to be verse 13 (Harper 1905:324). These objections are not irrefutable. The reference to Judah is not unusual in Hosea. In 5:8–6:6, Hosea does address Israel and Judah. The similarity to Amos's style may point in the direction of stereotypical formula. It is also possible that Hosea could have been familiar with the sayings of Amos. The reference to

Yahweh as creator being uncharacteristic has no strong basis. Creation theology may have an earlier origin than the exilic period. What is being affirmed is the sovereignty of Yahweh. Concerning content, verse 14 fits quite well with the context of the chapter as a whole (Wolff 1974:136). It is not totally out of place.

There is no question that this verse mirrors the social reality of the eighth century B.C.E. under the reigns of Jeroboam II in the north and Uzziah in the south (Andersen and Freedman 1980:196–97; Mackintosh 1997:333). It must be granted that the building activity suggested in this verse would not have occurred in the time in which the rest of the chapter is set. As Mays points out, "probably the oracle was a floating piece which the redactor thought would bring 8:1–13 to a good conclusion" (Mays 1969b:124). The key to understanding this verse is to be sought in the words "palaces" and "walled cities." Why are these isolated for special mention? At a systemic level, palaces, walled cities, and fortifications stand for wealth and power of the ruling elite. The urban centers became important in terms of their political (administrative and military), economic, and religious functions (Sjoberg 1960:87). The urban growth mentioned in Hos. 8:14 (proliferation of walled cities) should be understood as a reflection of the distribution of power in the social structure. Only through the mechanism of a well-developed power structure could the urban centers carry out their economic function: extraction of the largest shares of surplus from the rural areas. The peasants were not only forced to turn over their agricultural surplus but also had to perform compulsory state services for the state's building projects. The palaces and fortifications are classic examples of the elite's indulgence to provide for their political security. Very often these structures were also the residential quarters of the elite. The prophet recognizes the adverse effects of such undertakings on the overextended peasants. They were overextended in the sense that they supported these urban centers economically. Further, they also provided the work force for the building projects. As a result, the plight of the peasantry worsened. The prophetic oracles deplore such deprivation of the peasantry. In this oracle (Hos. 8:14), the judgment portends the destruction of the very symbols of elitist power. In other words, Yahweh's judgment is a judgment on the oppressive political and socioeconomic structures of the ruling class.

Militarization

The dominance of the ruling class over the peasant group is possible because of the military power of the former. There is a concerted effort to ensure that the state has a strong military force at its disposal. The ruling class understood the basic equation that the stronger one's military power, the more powerful one can be politically. The more political power one has, the more social and economic benefits one can derive. The more social and economic benefits one has, the more one can pump into the military. And so goes the vicious cycle.

Hosea 12:1 [Heb. 12:2]

Ephraim seeks companionship with the wind,
chases the east wind all day long;
lies and destruction they multiply;
they make an agreement with Assyria,
and carry oil to Egypt.

In most translations the Hebrew verse 12:1 is taken as part of the previous chapter. The authenticity of 12:1 [Heb. 12:2] is not questioned (Andersen and Freedman 1980:605; Mackintosh 1997:479; Mays 1969a:16; Wolff 1974:xxxi, 221). The foreign policies of Israel come under scrutiny in this verse. It is described in metaphorical terms. The phrase, "seeks companionship with the wind" (Köhler and Baumgartner 1951:899), expresses in metaphorical language that the efforts of Ephraim are futile and useless. The text is talking about the futile foreign policy of Israel and its effects on the internal economy. The historical context behind this is the later part of the eighth century B.C.E., the aftermath of Jeroboam's death. The prophet probably had in mind the vassal treaty that Hoshea signed with Shalmaneser V (2 Kings 17:3). The biblical account mentions that Hoshea paid tribute to Assyria. But Hoshea broke the treaty by turning to Egypt for help (2 Kings 17:4). This is referred to in Hosea 12:1c–"They make an agreement with Assyria, and carry oil to Egypt"–once it is recognized that both verbs should be third person plural in order to be parallel.

The demands made by the state in times of war were burdensome on the local economy. From the Assyrian point of view, Hoshea's tribute was an extraction of surplus. Tribute was one of the ways a strong power could lay hold of the agricultural surplus of another country. From the point of view of Israel, paying periodic tribute was a heavy burden on the economy. The tribute, in all likelihood, came from internal taxation, the sources of which were the common population. Such conditions of war or the efforts to avert such a calamity cost a fortune for the tribute payer. The delivery of oil refers to the tribute paid in kind.

There is another possibility of interpreting the delivery of oil to Egypt. Here we may be dealing with the export of oil in exchange for strategic military items. The militarization process was aimed at securing the state. The security of the state was important for two reasons. First of all, there was a need to protect the state from foreign invasions. Second, the economic advantage that the ruling elite could derive from the local economy depended on their effective political control. This, in turn, could only result from a strong military basis. The consignments of oil exported to Egypt were a drain on the local economy. The peasants bore the brunt of such expensive undertakings. The economic pressures on the peasantry increased constantly, resulting in the process of latifundialization.

Isaiah 30:6–7 and 31:1–3

30:6 An oracle concerning the beasts of the Negev:
    a land of trouble and distress,
    lion and lioness, viper and flying serpent;
    through which they carry their wealth on the sides of the
        donkeys
    and upon the humps of camels, their treasures,
    to a people who cannot be of help;
7 Egypt whose help is worthless and empty.
    Therefore, I called that one
    "Rahab who sits still."

31:1 Woe to those who go down to Egypt for help
    and depend upon horses,
    who trust in their chariots, for they are many,
    and in their cavalry, for they are mighty.
    They do not look upon the Holy One of Israel
    nor do they seek Yahweh.
2 He is wise and will bring disaster;
    he will not revoke his words;
    he will rise up against the house of evildoers,
    and against the helpers who work evil.

3 The Egyptians are human and not God;
   their horses are flesh and not spirit.
   When Yahweh stretches forth his hand,
   the helpers will stumble; the one who is helped will fall,
   and all of them together will perish.

These two oracles are very similar in content. The authenticity of both the passages is undisputed (Clements 1980:244, 254; Fohrer 1960-61:21; Kaiser 1974:289, 311; Skinner 1915:238; Wildberger 1978:1150, 1228; Willis 1980:301–302, 310). The historical situation reflected in these oracles belongs to the later part of the eighth century B.C.E. The context is that of seeking military help from Egypt in the wake of an Assyrian invasion.

Most commentators see these passages as a condemnation of the political diplomacy of Judah. The full implications of this situation can be seen only from a systemic perspective. The need for military buildup had risen out of the impending Assyrian invasion. The project of militarization was undertaken at an enormous cost. Strategic military items were obtained in exchange for the local export items. Since the local specialties of Judah consisted of agricultural products such as wine, oil, and grain, they figured prominently in export. In fact, they were sources of wealth for Judah. Isaiah 30:6–7 alludes to the phenomenon of international trade. The mention of donkeys and camels is a reference to the active trade. The description suggests the movement of caravan traders to and from Egypt. It is of particular interest that the passage mentions the Negev. As pointed out in the section on Colonization (in chapter 3), Uzziah is credited with making the Negev traversable with a well-planned system of defensive fortresses and networks of roads connecting important trading centers. It seems conceivable that these continued to be in use even during Hezekiah's reign as well.

Isaiah 31:1 describes what was imported from Egypt in exchange for the items from Palestine: horses and chariots. In his discussion of Solomon's horse trade (1 Kings 10:28–29), Elat points out that the *Mitsrayim* mentioned in this passage refers not to Egypt but to the land of *Mutsri*, which lay northeast of the kingdom of Que/Kue along the Cilician coast. Horses were exported to various kingdoms from the breeding centers in the mountains of Cappodocia (Elat 1979a:183). However, in both the Isaianic passages, *Mitsrayim* seems to refer to Egypt. There are two clues for this reading. First, the reference to the hazardous travel through the Negev (Isa. 30:6) indicates travel in the southern direction leading to Egypt. Second, the expression "go down" (Isa. 31:1) also implies the destination to be Egypt. Since the kingdom of *Mutsri* was located in the northeastern part of the Cilician coast, that possibility is ruled out. The basic point is that horses were imported into Palestine from outside.

The prophet criticizes the wisdom of seeking military help, which would be of no avail. From an economic point of view, such extensive military expenditures were a great liability for the state. They were acquired at a great cost. Second, the huge military expenditure was aimed at providing state security, which meant the security of the ruling elite who controlled the state. But it was the peasants who bore the brunt of these military extravagances. Conditions of war, in addition to causing economic strain on the lives of the peasantry, took them away from their agricultural work to engage in performing draft services and other compulsory state services related to situations of war, such as establishing defensive and water works. Thus, the full import of the political diplomacy of the Judean monarchy could be realized only in the light of the socioeconomic implications of such endeavors for the lives of the common peasantry.

Hosea 10:13–15

13 You have plowed wickedness,
>   you have reaped injustice,
>   you have eaten fruits of lies.
>   Since you trusted in your chariots
>   and in the abundance of your warriors,
14 an uproar shall rise amidst your cities,
>   and all the fortifications shall be destroyed,
>   like the destruction of Beth-arbel by Shalman on the day
>   of battle;
>   mothers were dashed into pieces with children.
15 Thus it shall be done to you, O house of Israel,
>   because of your numerous evil.
>   At dawn the king of Israel shall utterly be silenced.

The oracle is addressed to the members of the ruling elite. Wolff suggests that Hosea may have spoken these words in the presence of the political leaders in Samaria (1974:183). The ruling class's dependence on military strength comes under judgment. The process of military buildup is condemned for several reasons. It promotes a false sense of security. Further, from an economic point of view, militarization comes with a heavy price tag. This cut at the very heart of the subsistence of the peasants. The opening lines of the oracle summarize the wicked activities of the ruling class in a general tone.

Is it accidental or intentional that Hosea uses imageries from agriculture in this context? "You have plowed wickedness, you have reaped injustice, you have eaten fruits of lies." The choice of images seems to be deliberate. Hosea is alluding to the devious ways in which the governing class controlled and dominated the economic sphere for their own benefit. It is fitting that Hosea's condemnation of the ruling elite's wicked activities is followed by his condemnation of their sense of complacency and pride resulting from military strength (v. 13d). Hosea's intent becomes clear when we look at this from a systemic perspective. The growth of military force was achieved at the expense of the welfare of the peasantry. Military power paved the way for establishing firm political control, and the above two were essential to gain maximum economic advantage through the extraction of surplus.

In verse 13d, the Hebrew text should be changed from "way" to "chariot" to fit the context better. The Septuagint supports this reading. The current MT reading could be explained as a misreading of the Hebrew consonants *rkb* as *drk*. The chariots were dreaded military items of antiquity. The Northern Kingdom enjoyed a measure of expertise in commanding chariotry from the time of Ahab. This may be a reference to the royal military force. Mays sees the historical context of this passage to be the reign of Hoshea ben Elah when he was beginning to revolt against his Assyrian masters (1969b:148). A. A. Mackintosh suggests that verses 13–15 belong to the period of prosperity under Jeroboam II (1997: 426–27). Verses 14 and 15 spell out the details of punishment for the crimes of the ruling elite. The judgment foretells the shattering of the very sources of their strength and protection. Their fortifications will be brought down. In verse 14a, "in/among your people" should be emended to "uproar shall rise amidst your cities." There will be a commotion in the ranks of the ruling elite on the day of disaster.

According to Hosea's prediction, the urban centers will become the targets of devastation. The identity of Shalman and Beth-arbel is not known. It is conjectured that Beth-arbel could have been a city in Moab and Shalman, a Moabite king. It could be the same Shalmanu mentioned by Tiglath-Pileser III (Pritchard 1969:282). It becomes clear that Israel will experience a gruesome devastation just as did Beth-arbel. It is revealing that the king is singled out for special mention. As the head of the state, the king symbolized the monarchical system and its policies. Since the system and its policies were a violation of Yahweh's principles, the king will be the first one to go.

Isaiah 2:4 = Micah 4:3–4

4 He [Yahweh] shall judge between the nations,
    and he shall arbitrate for many peoples.
And they shall beat their swords into plows,
    and their spears into pruning hooks.
A nation shall not lift a sword against another,
    Nor shall they learn war any more. (Isa. 2:4)

3 He [Yahweh] shall judge between the many peoples,
    and he shall arbitrate for numerous nations from afar.
They shall beat their swords into plows,
    and their spears into pruning hooks.
A nation shall not lift a sword against another,
    nor shall they learn war any more.
4 Each one will sit in possession under one's own vineyard
        and fig tree,
    and there shall be none to terrify;
    for the mouth of Yahweh has spoken. (Mic. 4:3–4)

These verses are part of larger units in Isaiah 2:2–4 and Micah 4:1–4 dealing with the theme of the pilgrimage of the nations to Zion. The poem in its present form may come from the exilic or postexilic period (Clements 1980:40; Fohrer 1960–61:9; Kaiser 1972:25; Marsh 1959:106; Mays 1976:93–94; Stade 1881:170; Sweeney 1996:98–99; Wolfe 1956:899–900; Wolff 1990:118). The oracle seems to preserve a tradition of promise oriented to Zion (Brueggemann 1981:189; 1998:24; Kapelrud 1961:395; Wildberger 1991:88).The stimulus for such a vision comes from the perception and experience of the kind of sociopolitical reality witnessed in the eighth century B.C.E. In this sense, the vision need not be "an invention of convenience by the postexilic community" but may very well come from Isaiah of Jerusalem (Watts 1985:28). The case for a late dating of the passage cannot be built only on basis of the presence of Zion tradition. The key motifs associated with the Zion tradition can be traced back to times well before the eighth century (Roberts 1973).

The close correspondence between the Isaian and Mican forms of the poem (except Micah has a fuller version) has raised questions of its authorship and dependence of one on the other. The position in Isaiah indicates that it is a quotation. Isaiah could not have borrowed it from Micah because Micah's prophetic ministry did not begin till later. It is possible that both the prophets are drawing upon a common tradition. This common tradition embodies elements that are germane to the prophetic critique of Isaiah and Micah, because they pertain to the social reality of that time. The poem as a whole is designed to lead Israel to an alternative reality. The promise presents the change to be effected in the present inadequate system of reality. There will be a new arrangement on earth. Brueggemann sees the new arrangement in the process of transformation of public policy (1981:192). What is envisioned is a demilitarization strategy. The prophet calls for a radical shift from military technology to productive technology.

The process of militarization involved securing strategic military weapons, conscription, and taxation. In agrarian societies, one of the conditions that contributes to the impoverishment of the peasantry is war. In a condition of war, the state not only took the peasants away from agriculture but also levied additional burden on them by way of taxation. Hence, the passage calls for a radical replacement of the present order. It is interesting that the passage uses the expression, "nor shall they learn war any more." Gottwald's comments on this line are illuminating:

> Nations learn war. War is not blind fate. It is learned. It is an instrument of social change in which many of our unconscious and unadmitted instincts find expression. Those instincts can find other outlets; war can be unlearned. (1983:72–73)

The Mican version of the poem is longer. The additional verse in Micah reinforces the idea of a shift from military technology to productive technology using an agrarian dream. The dream of demilitarization is juxtaposed with "a personal agrarian dream of well-being" (Brueggemann 1981:193). Each person owning his/her own vine and fig tree envisions a self-sufficient, secure, and autonomous life. This vision cannot become a reality as long as there is war or even threat of war. Brueggemann makes several perceptive observations that highlight the systemic nature of the issue (1981:193). First, he sees a close connection between the militarization process and the achievement of the peasant dreams. It is not only the military operations that are detrimental but also a tax system that provides for and sustains such enterprises. Second, Brueggemann also points out the dual emphasis on "not simply a cessation of war, but the dismantling of the war apparatus" (Brueggemann 1981:193). This is a radical call driven by a sense of realism. Third, he also sees, rightly so, a hidden agenda in the process of militarization. Hidden underneath the rhetoric of protecting the country is the greedy desire to preserve the special interests of a small group. "For the arms serve primarily either to usurp what belongs to others, or to guarantee an arrangement already inequitable" (Brueggemann 1981:193). Hence, realizing the vision of *shalom* would require giving up the arms and "abandoning swollen appetites as well" (Brueggemann 1981:193). The military buildup is for the purpose of maintaining the power structure of the elite to protect and further their interests. In this sense, it perpetuates an unjust and inequitable order of reality. The prophet calls for the dismantling of this oppressive and hence fearsome order of reality. The oracle ends with an assurance: "And there shall be none to terrify." The reference echoes the sentiments of Lev. 26:6: "And I will give you peace in the land, and you shall lie down, and there shall be no one to terrify you." The same phrase is also used here. Thus, the poet "links the coming disarmed society to the oldest hope of Israel" (Brueggemann 1981:193).

Extraction of Surplus

The systematic extraction of agricultural surplus was accomplished through a careful system of taxation. Two things are critical to the success of the taxation system. First, the highly organized nature of the operations of ruling aristocracy gives them an advantage even though they are a minority. Second, the ruling class can accomplish what it wants because they have the military power, which gives them the political clout.

Amos 5:11–12

11 Therefore, because you make tenants out of the poor
    and take exactions of wheat from them,
    you have built houses of fine stone,
    but you shall not dwell in them;

> You have planted choicest vineyards,
> but you shall not drink their wine.
> 12 I know the magnitude of your crimes,
> and the multiplicity of your wrongs–
> you who are hostile to the innocent,
> who accept bribe(s) and turn away the needy in the gate.

The scholarly consensus converges on an eighth-century dating for this passage. It is generally considered to belong to the collection of Amos's oracles (Coote 1981:13; Jeremias 1998:82; Mays 1969a:5, 90; Paul 1991:171; Ward 1969:74; Wolff 1977: 23). Verse 11 describes the process of latifundialization in specific reference to the shift in the system of land tenure. The key to this interpretation is the phrase "exactions." The text has often been emended to mean "to trample down or tread." Harry Torczyner proposed that a much rarer root word could be the Hebrew equivalent of an Akkadian term for collecting rent from fields (Torczyner 1936:6–7). Torczyner proposed the connotation of levying tax or rent. Shalom Paul makes it even more specific to refer to "straw tax" on the basis of the Akkadian cognate (1991:172–73; see also Ellis 1974). Fundamentally, the text is referring to a tax/exaction of some kind on the agricultural products.

The translation, "because you make tenants out of the poor" (Lang 1982:56; Mays 1969a:90), shifts the focus onto the drastic result of the taxation. It brings to light the shift in the system of land tenure. The peasants who once freely held small plots have now become landless day laborers or tenants in the large estates belonging to the rich. The peasants have lost easy and secure access to arable land. With the growth of the market economy, rent capitalism came into existence, whereby the factors of production became segmented with monetary value attached to each. For instance, the peasants had to pay rent for the land. Most often the rent was exacted in kind as verse 11a indicates. This was one of the ways the landowner extracted agricultural surplus from the primary producers. The undue exactions by the propertied class were burdensome to the peasants, ultimately leading to the loss of access to arable land. Amos speaks against the upper class for driving the peasantry into a condition of impoverishment and slavery. From a religious point of view, such loss of access to land meant the extinction of egalitarian values under Yahweh's sovereignty.

While verse 11a lists the accusation, verse 11b spells out the judgment, echoing the futility curses in Deuteronomy 28:30, 39. It is significant that the judgment spells out what the landlords had done with the extorted surplus. They had built houses of fine stone and planted vineyards. The text refers to houses of stones whose surfaces and edges were trimmed and dressed (Shiloh 1979:61). The royal quarters in Samaria were enclosed by walls built with hewn stones (King 1988:65). The art of ashlar stone masonry was of Phoenician origin. Skilled workers were probably brought to build these structures (King 1988:67). It was a sign of luxury to be able to afford these type of structures. The penchant for elaborate architectural achievements was characteristic of the lifestyle of the elite. The effects of carrying out these projects on the economy and the labor of the peasants need not be belabored again. The planting of vineyards was with a view to cater to the local consumptive needs and also for export. Wine figured prominently in the consumption of the upper class. (See more on this later in the chapter.)

Even though Amos's statement is cryptic, it raises many reverberations concerning the process of latifundialization witnessed in eighth-century Israel. The judgment is offered in terms of a reversal of the situation. The rich will be deprived of the very things of which they had deprived the peasants: the houses and fields they had acquired at the expense and misery of the peasants. In this sense, the judgment comes full circle: the deprivers will be deprived.

Thus, the self-contained nature of this small unit supports the contention that verse 11b originally belonged with verse 11a and not, as Coote places it, after verse 12b (1981:13). Verse 12 picks up the theme of corrupt judicial practices. This time the accusation appears with two more additional dimensions: being hostile to the poor and taking bribes. Because of the overwhelming domination of the aristocracy, the courts had become instruments of promoting their interests. The innocent felt threatened at the prospects of getting their fate sealed. There was no other authority to which to go. The ruling elite through bribery secured the complicity of the judicial officials. It is also conceivable that hostility was meted out to the peasants to dissuade them from taking matters to the courts. (See below on Role of the Judicial Courts.) Thus the odds against the peasants were overwhelming.

Amos 7:1

This is what my Lord Yahweh showed me:
Lo, he was creating locusts

when the latter growth began to sprout
(It was the latter growth after the king's mowing).

The most pertinent information for the purposes of this study is
tucked away in the parenthesis. This appears to be an editorial note
to situate and explain what has preceded—namely, the latter growth.
The crucial phrase is the "king's mowing." Even though the reference
is cryptic and appears almost as an afterthought in the text, in the
context of an agrarian society it speaks volumes. The term *gzz* in
Hebrew means to shear or mow. John Hayes takes it to mean "after
the king's sheep shearing" on the basis of other occurrences in
Genesis 31:19, 38:12, and 2 Samuel 13:23 (1988:202). Being a sheep
breeder himself, Amos could have been thinking about sheep
shearing. It would imply that the shorn wool belonged to the king, not
the sheep breeders themselves. Several others (Andersen and
Freedman 1989:xxxvii; Jeremias 1998:123; Paul 1991:226; Stuart
1987:320) have "king's mowings." Alberto Soggin's rendering "royal
reaping" is right on target (1987:117). Mowing or reaping is the
preferred reading for a variety of reasons. The context of the locusts
swarming poses a threat for the crops. Soggin points out that the
sheep shearing took place at the beginning of summer whereas the
"latter growth" or late-sown crops belong to the early spring period
(Paul 1991:227; Soggin 1987:113). Most likely, these were subsistence
crops such as vegetables and onions (Paul 1991:227). The agricultural
context heightens the drastic nature of the scenario. The prime share
of the agricultural produce has already gone to the king. And now,
locusts threaten the late-sown subsistence crops, which would be
disastrous for the peasant population. Two observations pertaining to
the locust symbolically evoke a tantalizing possibility. First, the term
for locust is used synonymously with "a king of locust or grasshopper"
to describe the princes or court officials in general and the scribes
(King 1988:136). Second, a Hebrew seal with the carved picture of a
locust and an inscription offers interesting information (Avigad
1966:52; King 1988:136). The inscription reads: "Belonging to
Azaryaw [son of] *hgbh.*" Avigad suggests that the locust is used here as
a symbol for the Haggobeh/Haggebah family (1966:52). Following
this, is Amos (7:1) cleverly suggesting that after the king had taken his
share, the second tier of the ruling elite is coming to finish off what
little is left for the common peasants?

Whether one reads it as shorn wool or agricultural reaping, the
king has extracted the prime share of the surplus. And now the

peasants are in the danger of losing what little is left from that. This is an all too familiar scenario in an agrarian context.

Hosea 9:1–3

> 1 Do not rejoice, O Israel!
>> Do not exult like the peoples,
>> for you have gone astray from your God.
>> You love shares on every threshing floor of grain.
> 2 Threshing floor and wine vats shall not benefit them,
>> and the new wine shall fail them.
> 3 They shall not sit in possession in the land of Yahweh;
>> but they shall return to Egypt,
>> and in Assyria they shall eat unclean food.

Some scholars assign this passage to the eighth century (Harper 1905:clx; Mays 1969b:5, 125; Wolff 1974:xxxi, 153). The context of this passage is the autumn festival of Succoth celebrated at the time of harvest (Mays 1969b:125; Wolff 1974:153). The second (v. 1) and third persons (vv. 2–3) designate the same group. The addressees of this oracle are not the entire population, as many commentators would suggest, but a segment of the population–that is, the landowners. Which group will exult in the prospects of a harvest? The practice of exacting the harvest proceeds from the primary producers was the source of happiness and wealth for the rich landowners. The harvest time was the ideal time to shortchange the peasants, because the prices were the lowest at that time. The landowners' practices of exploitation took them away from the principles of Yahweh. In this context, the phrase "gone astray" should be understood in a more general sense of being unfaithful. The motif of harlotry is readily discerned in the book of Hosea by commentators in an effort to play up the sin of religious syncretism. Such enthusiasm, while justifiable in some measures, has tended to obscure one aspect of Hosea's message.

Chaney puts forth an intriguing possibility that Hosea uses promiscuity as a metaphor for agricultural intensification (1993:1). As such, Gomer (the wife of promiscuity) is not a figure for all Israel but only the male elites who are castigated for their "promiscuous pursuit of agricultural intensification" (1993:2).

Hosea's words call for a cessation of all exultation. The reason for the command is given in verse 1b. They have forsaken Yahweh's commands and principles and have loved shares. The term for "shares" is read in most translations as the fee of the harlot. This again is the result of imposing the theme of harlotry with a vengeance. However, it should be translated in its more basic sense of something that is given. In the context of a harvest, it might be fitting to read it as the share of agricultural produce given to the landowners as rent in kind. According to this passage, the landowners loved to exact shares from every threshing floor.

The prophet announces the judgment in verses 2–3. The landlords will not benefit from the threshing floors or the wine vats. In other words, the very thing they exacted from the peasants will no longer be available to them. The judgment predicts the lack of the very items that were keenly sought by the landowning rich. Verse 3 takes the punishment one step further. It is predicted that they would not sit in possession of the land in the land of Yahweh. Here, *yashav* is to be taken in a more specific sense of possessing land. (For a discussion of this nuance, see Isaiah 5:8–10 at the beginning of this chapter.) The phrase "the land of Yahweh" is unique to Hosea. As Wolff points, out it corresponds to the expression "the land is mine" in Leviticus 25:23 (Wolff 1974:155). Leviticus 25:23 is one of the key passages in the Hebrew scriptures that reflects the two basic principles in the land tenure system of ancient Israel, namely Yahweh's ownership of land and, hence, the inalienability of land. The prophet's allusion to the ancient values of the land tenure system brings into sharper focus the context of this passage. The rich landowners are guilty of violating the sacred principles associated with the tenure of land. Hence, they will return to Egypt. Instead of inheriting Yahweh's land, Israel will return to Egypt. Egypt serves as the "antonym" of Yahweh's land (Landy 1995:110). There is a word play here involving *yashav*. Egypt symbolizes a life of bondage. The oppressors will become the oppressed. They will be carried off into exile.

Lifestyle of the Upper Class

The extracted agricultural surplus went to support a life of leisure and luxury for the elite. Leisure is the nonproductive use of time. This comes from a disdain of physical work and a sense of vanity in being able to afford an idle life (Veblen 1912:43). Luxury is written all over their lifestyle. It applies to where they live, what they consume, what they wear, and what they do in their leisure. One common feature of their leisure and luxury is the element of waste. But from the point of view of the elite, these elements constitute symbols of prestige and power. First, the erection of palatial mansions and expensive furnishings was one of the ways the economic surplus was used. From an agricultural point of view, these undertakings were not only nonproductive but also a drain on the royal coffers. Second, the ruling class used the local agricultural specialties (commercial crops) for their conspicuous consumption. The ability to afford a life of decadent consumption became a way of displaying one's wealth. In addition to local consumption, these agricultural specialties were also prominent items in the export-import transactions. They were exported to neighboring territories, often in exchange for military and luxury items. The acquisition of military items is a critical piece in ensuring and perpetuating political dominance and control. Third, in keeping with the elite's flair for pomp and glory, personal adornments such as fine clothing, jewelry, perfume, and footwear became a way of exhibiting their wealth and power. Besides, the long hours spent in self-adornment was in character with their life of leisure. Fourth, the favorite pastime of the upper class consisted of engaging in activities such as war, sports, music, and partying. Large agricultural surpluses enabled a leisurely and luxurious living.

Amos 3:15

I will smash the winter house along with the summer house;
and the houses of ivory shall perish,
and the large estates shall cease to exist. Oracle of Yahweh.

This verse concludes the oracle in verses 13–15. The eighth-century dating of this verse is generally accepted (Hayes 1988:136–37; Jeremias 1998:59; Mays 1969a:12–14; Paul 1991:123; Soggin 1987:65–66; Wolff 1977:107, 201–2). But the relationship of this verse to the rest of the oracle is disputed. The verse is a condemnation of the self-indulgent, privileged life of the upper class. It draws attention, in particular, to the elaborate private dwellings and large landholdings of the elite. A difference of opinion still persists with regard to the interpretation of the "winter house" and the "summer house." It could mean different sections/portions of the same house. This interpretation is not totally unfounded because archaeological excavations have uncovered houses with two floors. The phrases are also taken to mean two separate buildings/houses: one for use in summer and another in winter. In support of this, the building inscription of Barrakab/kib of Sam'al is often cited. This inscription, from the later part of the eighth century B.C.E., was meant to be dedicatory when Barrakab/kib built an additional palace. According to the inscription, his ancestors had only one palace at Kilamuwa, which they used as both summer and winter residence (Pritchard 1969:655). Paul has enumerated some more references from some cuneiform documents. He argues that the specific mention of "winter house" implies the existence of "summer house" (Paul 1978:358–59). It must be pointed out here that in the ninth century, Ahab of Israel owned a palace in Jezreel (1 Kings 21:1) that climatically was warmer, and another one in Samarian hills (1 Kings 21:18). It is likely that the king, as well as members of the upper class, indulged in the luxury of two mansions. That these houses were furnished with ivory inlays is reflected in the phrase "houses of ivory." Even though the many fragments of ivory found in Samaria, both in the ninth- and eighth-century levels, were located in the royal palace, it is quite conceivable that they were used in the private dwellings of the upper class as well. These ivory carvings and furnishings were imported from Phoenicia. The ruling class's flair for pompous structures was one of the ways the economic surplus was used. These huge structures became status symbols.

Another crucial phrase in this verse is "large estates," which some scholars interpret to be an invective against the general population (Jeremias 1998:56; Soggin 1987:64). On the contrary, Amos directs it against a specific group of people, namely the elite. Others translate the phrase as "great houses/mansions" (Paul 1991:123; Stuart 1987:327). The word ebony has also been read in order to parallel ivory, but this reading is textually unwarranted and, in fact, not necessary. The use of "great houses" is intentional in this context as in Isaiah 5: 8–10. (For a detailed discussion of this phrase, see discussion of Isa. 5:8–10 above.) The Akkadian term *bitu* was used in a variety of ways, to refer to house, house and land, or just land. Hence, the meaning of *bitu* and its Hebrew equivalent *bayit* cannot be restricted to just "house." It is significant that the standard formula containing houses and fields occurs precisely in the context of the condemnation of land accumulation in Micah 2:2 and Isaiah 5:8. From this background, it becomes clear that Amos is using "great houses" to refer to large estates (Paul 1991:127). This reading is further reinforced by the occurrence of the same phrase in Isaiah 5:9. The use of "great houses"conjures up, to use Wolff's words, "the amassing of real estate and land holdings in the hands of the small upper class, a phenomenon which thus dissolved the ancient Israelite system of property laws" (1977:202).

Amos 6:4–7

4 Woe to those who stretch out on beds with inlaid ivory,
  and lie sprawling upon their couches;
  who eat lambs from the flock
  and calves from the midst of the stall;
5 who improvise to the sound of the harp,
  (like David) compose for themselves on musical
      instruments;
6 who drink bowls of wine
  and anoint themselves with the best of oils,
  but are not worried over the shattering of Joseph.
7 Therefore, soon they will go into exile at the head of the
      exiles,
  and the *marzeah* celebration of the sprawlers shall vanish.

Most scholars treat verses 1–7 as a unit. But here, verses 4–7 are taken alone for two reasons. First, verses 4–7 form a self-contained unit because of the content. Second, the content of verses 1–3 is more general, whereas that of verses 4–7 is more specific and descriptive and relates to the drunken revelry of the celebration. Scholars generally agree that this passage is authentic to Amos (Andersen and Freedman 1989:559; Coote 1981:14, 37–39; Driver 1915:119; Jeremias 1998:109; Mays 1969a:12–14, 114; Paul 1991:200; Soggin 1987:104–5; Ward 1969:82; Wolff 1977:107). As Coote rightly identified, we have here a detailed description of the extravagant indulgence associated with the *marzeah* feast (1981:37–39). Amos portrays the life of extravagance epitomized in the *marzeah* celebration with concreteness and vividness. Plush furniture, indolent leisure, epicurean food, free-flowing wine, perfumed oil, and the sound of music are the hallmarks of this festivity. The consumptive pattern conveyed through the *marzeah* celebration could only be characterized as voluptuous or conspicuous. The source of such opulence was the labor and toil of the peasantry. The quality of the lifestyles of the peasantry and the upper class were inversely proportional to each other: the more extravagant and affluent the lifestyle of the rich was, the more desperate the life of the peasantry became. The eighth-century oracles of the prophets repeatedly contrast these aspects: the affluence of the rich and the relative deprivation of the peasantry. The rich invested the labor and available resources in procuring commodities for their own enjoyment. These commodities were not only beyond the reach of the peasantry, but drastically left the staples in short supply.

Even though the etymology of the word *marzeah* is uncertain, the existence of the feast is not (Jeremias 1998:111; King 1988:137; Paul 1991:211 n. 104). The *marzeah* was a celebration held in honor of the dead. It was an occasion to comfort the bereaved by offering food and drink. These celebrations continued for many days marked by heavy drinking and eating (King 1988:137). Several texts from Ugarit have contributed a great deal to our understanding of the *marzeah*. (See chapter 3.) Of particular interest is the nature of the group associated with the *marzeah.* One might see here the trappings of a private club. As an association, the members owned houses and vineyards (Ras Shamra 15.70; 15.88; 18.01). The Ras Shamra fragment 18.01 mentions the joint ownership of a vineyard by two groups. Particularly relevant to our present discussion is the mythological text relating to the banquet offered by El (Ras Shamra 24.258). The picture of drunken revelry comes through clearly in this text. El gets drunk to the point of becoming delirious and wallows in his own excrement and urine. Where did they derive the model for describing the world of the gods? This vivid picture of merrymaking is nothing but a projection of the life of the elite into the world of the gods. The Hebrew term *marzeah* occurs only in Amos 6:7 and Jeremiah 16:5.

The major portion of the passage is devoted to the enumeration of the details of the *marzeah* celebration. The reference to beds raises important issues. Earlier in Amos 3:15, we saw the reference to "houses of ivory." Ivory, a luxury item, was not available from local sources. In all likelihood, it came from outside, probably Africa or Asia or Syria (King 1988:139). Excavations at Samaria yielded by far the largest quantity of ivories in the area. Also, among the discoveries at Megiddo was a ten-inch long ivory plaque containing, interestingly, elements associated with the *marzeah* such as the lyre, the cup, and the bowl (King 1988:142–43). The closest example of an ivory bed comes from a tomb in Salamis in Cyprus dating back to the eighth century B.C.E. (King 1988:147–48). The headboard contained three panels of ivory decorated with Phoenician art. The meat for the feasts came from the stall-fattened calves (King 1988:149). Conspicuous consumption of wine accompanied the epicurean food. The bowl (*mizraq*) mentioned in this passage seems to be a vessel of significant capacity (King 1988:158). The finest oil (also called the virgin oil) used for the ceremonial anointing came from the initial crushing before the pressing process (King 1988:161). All these aspects accentuate the affluence and luxury of their lifestyle. Then comes the punch line. The prophet does not proceed without pointing to the consequences of such life. The indifference of the elite comes into focus in verse 6c. The rich do not seem to have the slightest concern over "the shattering of Joseph," that is, Israel. "The shattering of Joseph" draws attention to the plight of the suffering majority. Through this, the prophet contrasts once again the luxury of the few with the oppression and suffering of the many. And then comes the judgment. "With tragic irony Amos lets them be the first to taste the bitter end" (Mays 1969a:117). The judgment calls for a total reversal of the situation: the mirth and revelry will pass away, and the ruling class will be the first to taste the hardships of the exile.

Amos 4:1–3

1 Hear this word, O cows of Bashan
　　who are in the Mount of Samaria,
　　who extort the poor; who crush the needy,
　　who say to their lords, "Bring, that we may drink."
2 The Lord Yahweh has sworn by His holiness,
　　days against you are imminent;
　　you will be carried in butcher's hooks, even the last one
　　of you in fishing harpoons.
You will slip through the breaches one in front of the
　　other that you may be cast out.

This oracle is addressed to the women of Samaria's elite group, probably wives of the court officials, wealthy large estate owners, and merchants (Wolff 1977:205). The eighth-century dating of this oracle is not disputed (Andersen and Freedman 1989:38, 412–13; Coote 1981:12; Jeremias 1998:56; Mays 1969a:5, 9–12; Paul 1991:128; Wolff 1977:205–206). The passage aims at two things. First, it seeks to condemn the indulgence in drinking that is characteristic of the consumption of the upper class. Second, the passage clearly spells out that the affluent lifestyle of the elite was built on the suffering of the poor and the needy from whom the agricultural surplus was extracted. The steady flow of surplus made the elite's easy living possible.

In the passage, the economic opulence of the rich is graphically brought to mind by the reference to Bashan. As noted earlier, Bashan was the most productive part of the Transjordanian plateau. It was famous for its grain, forests, pastures, and fine cattle. According to 2 Kings 14:25, Jeroboam's control extended from Hamath down to the sea of 'Arabah. This would place the Transjordanian territory under his control. Thus, Israel would have benefited from the richness of Bashan. In the passage, the mention of Samaria is also significant. Samaria, being the capital of the Northern Kingdom, was the haven of the upper class. The large agricultural periphery supported the agriculturally nonproductive aristocratic population and its ways of life. This pattern of exploitation led to the impoverishment of the primary producers. In fact, the elaborate lifestyle of the ruling aristocracy was at the expense of the common peasants. Amos would not let that dimension go by unobserved ("who extort the poor; who crush the needy"). The judgment on the upper class women is just as graphic as the description of their lifestyle. The Hebrew word *tsinnot,* translated here as "butcher's hooks," is appropriate to the context. The threat of being carried away by butcher's hooks corresponds to the imagery of the "cows of Bashan." The meaning of "fishing harpoons" is differently understood. Some interpret it to mean fish pots (Coote 1981:12; Paul 1991:134; Snaith 1958:70). Following Wolff (1977:204), it is rendered here as harpoons or sharp spears used in catching large fish.

Hosea 7:3–7

3 With their wickedness they gladden a king
    and with their lies the officials;
4 all of them are adulterers like a burning oven.
    The baker stops stirring the fire,
    from the kneading of the dough until it is leavened.
5 The officials begin the day of their king with the heat of
        wine;
    he joins hands with scorners.
6 For they are kindled like an oven;
    their hearts burn within them.
    All night long their desire lies dormant;
    in the morning it burns like flaming fire.

7 All of them are hot like an oven,
   they devour their judges.
All their kings fall; and none of them calls to me.

The historical background of this passage is the instability of the political realm following the death of Jeroboam II (Andersen and Freedman 1980:clx; Mackintosh 1997:256; Mays 1969b:104; Wolff 1974:111). It depicts certain aspects of the court life, especially the claims and machinations of the rival groups to control the political reins. The ruling elite engages in political activity, not only as a pastime, but also as a means of establishing and securing its political strength. This secures them positions to control the population and extract surplus from them. The ruling class goes about this business with calculated manipulations. The ruling class, though a minority, manages to control the majority of the population because of its ability to function as an organized group. In a court setting, rival interests are bound to exist. This gives rise to factions trying to outmaneuver each other.

In verse 4, there is a reference to adultery. This has usually been explained as the violation of Yahweh's principles. There is no strong reason for not interpreting it in a literal sense, referring to the lascivious nature of the group involved. Verse 5 is particularly significant for the lifestyle of the ruling elite. They begin their day with wine. The mention of wine underlines the part it played in the lifestyle of the elite. (For a discussion of the conspicuous consumption of the upper class, see Am. 6:4–7 above.) The imagery of the oven, which plays a key role in this passage, was probably drawn from commercial and royal installations (Mays 1969a:105). This shows that ovens and the art of baking were in vogue at this time. This corresponds with Silver's observation that, in the eighth century B.C.E., the consumption of finer bread became more common. In verse 4, Silver sees a connection between the search for material welfare and the baking of finer bread, the use of which was considered as a sign of affluence (Silver 1983:95–96).

Isaiah 5:11–13

11 Woe to those early risers,
      they are after strong drink; who are late-nighters,
      wine kindles them.
12 They have lyre, harp, timbrel, and flute,

and wine at their feasts.
But they do not regard the deeds of Yahweh
nor see the work of his hands.
13 Therefore, my people will go into exile for want of
knowledge,
and their wealthy are drained out with hunger,
and their group parched with thirst.

This is the second one in a series of woe oracles in Isaiah 5, including verses 11–17 in the MT. The oracle seems to come to a logical conclusion in verse 13 with the pronouncement of judgment. Verses 14–17 expand on some key motifs from the preceding verses. The imagery of Sheol's swallowing the people recalls the drunken elite swallowing wine. Also, even as the unrighteousness and injustice of the elite would bring them to the depths of Sheol, the justice and righteousness of Yahweh will be exalted (Sweeney 1996:125).

Verses 11–13 speak against the rich and their lifestyle. More specifically, the drunken revelry of the elite is the focus. Wine was an important item in the conspicuous consumption of the ruling elite. It was conspicuous in the sense that consumption was a way of life. This level of affluence was made possible by the large economic surpluses that were transferred from the primary producers to the ruling class.

Conspicuous consumption became a way of distinguishing or symbolizing the elite's status in the society. The free flow of wine, sumptuous food, and the accompaniment of music were the hallmarks of the banquet of the nobility. (For a fuller discussion of such celebrations as epitomized in the *marzeah* festival, see Am. 6:4–7 above.) From a systemic perspective, this passage reflects the shift in the economic sphere toward a market orientation. The orientation toward producing crops for the market was brought about by the shift in the systems of land tenure. The production of commercial crops became important for gaining maximum economic advantage. In a context like this, viticulture became "a highly prized expertise" (Clements 1980:63), both for the purposes of local consumption and export. Both of these aspects supported the lifestyle of the elite at the expense of the rest of the population. Hence comes the judgment, unfolded in chiastic pattern. The threat of exile for want of knowledge (v. 13a) directly corresponds with their lack of perception into Yahweh's deeds and work (v. 12b). Further, verse 13b reflects the theme of verse 12a. The sumptuous feasts of the wealthy will pass away. They will languish with hunger. The translation here reads that the wealthy will be drained out with hunger, similar to Deuteronomy 32:23–24. It is derived from the root *mzh*, meaning "empty out" or "suck out" (Köhler and Baumgartner 1951:509). An alternative reading "are dying" is also possible. A third parallel is that their drinking bouts (v. 11) will give way to parched throats (v. 13c). Thus, the judgments correspond to the issues raised in the accusation. In this sense, verses 11–13 form a self-contained unit.

Isaiah 5:22–23

> 22 Woe to the nobility for drinking wine,
>   and persons of means for drinking strong drinks;
> 23 who declare the guilty innocent for a bribe
>   and thereby deprive the innocent of their right.

The sixth woe oracle in Isaiah 5 continues the themes of the consumption of wine and distortion of justice in the judicial courts. These charges could have been addressed to two different groups of people. It is also possible that they were meant for one group of people. The Hebrew term *gibborim* is usually translated as "warriors" or "strong persons." Wildberger suggests that it might refer to royal bodyguards or influential landowners (1991:209). Another nuance of the term is brought out by its usage in 2 Kings 15:20, the reference being Menahem's levy of taxes on all the *gibbore hahayyil* (wealthy nobles) for paying tribute to the Assyrians. In our present context, the term does not mean warriors of strength but people of means. Moreover, in Isaiah 5:22, *'anshe hayyil* (men of strength, or wealthy people) occurs as a parallel to the wealthy and powerful landowners. There is reason to assume that the judges were the drunkards. At a systemic level, there is a link between their lifestyle and the duties they performed. Their extravagance was sustained by the subsidiary income derived from bribes. In other words, the need to maintain an extravagant lifestyle forced them to augment their income by bribes. This factor made them obligated to the whims of the ruling elite. Thus, bribery provided an excellent way for the elite to manipulate the legal system. The judges acquitted the guilty because they had taken bribes to do so. (See below for more on the Role of the Judicial Courts.) In the process of acquitting the guilty, the judges wrongfully victimized the innocent. One question that arises in relation to the passages dealing with the legal system is whether there was some form of a central court of appeal. We do not have any information regarding this. But if, in fact, there did exist a central court of appeal, it could have drawn its members from the upper classes. And, as Clements points out, since the courts were comprised of officials from the upper classes, and "since all judicial rights were probably related to ownership of land, the scope for corruption of law was certainly considerable" (1980:65). In the brief span of two verses, the prophet addresses three aspects associated with the process of latifundialization: the extravagant lifestyle of the upper class and its effect for the rest of the poorer sections of the population; the miscarriage of justice in the legal courts; and the venality of the ruling elite who used power and authority to accomplish their wicked plans. The legal tradition preserved in Exodus 23:6–8 speaks to this very situation:

> 6 You shall not pervert the justice due your poor in his [her] suit.
> 7 Keep away from a false charge, and do not slay the innocent and the guiltless,
>   for I will not acquit the guilty.
> 8 You shall not receive bribe, for it blinds the clear-sighted and subverts the cause of those who are in the right.

Isaiah 28:1–4, 7–8

> 1 Woe to the eminent crown of the drunkards of Ephraim,
>   and the drooping flower of glorious beauty,
>   which is upon the top of the fertile valley of those smitten with wine.
> 2 The Lord has one, strong and mighty,
>   like a hailstorm, a storm of destruction,
>   like a storm of mighty torrential waters
>   it will bear down upon the earth with power.
> 3 The eminent crown of the drunkards of Ephraim
>   shall be trampled under foot;
> 4 the drooping flower of glorious beauty
>   which is upon the top of the fertile valley
>   shall become like the first-ripe fruit before harvest:
>   when a person sees it, he [/she] swallows it as soon as it is in his [/her] hand.

7 Even these stagger with wine and swerve with strong drink,
    the priest and the prophet wobble with strong drink;
    they are engulfed with wine;
    they stagger with strong drink;
    their vision is blurred;
    they stumble in giving judgment.
8 All the tables are full of vomit,
    there is no place without excrement.

Although the Isaianic origin of these verses is generally accepted, the difficulty in explaining the inclusion of verses 1–4, an oracle concerning Samaria, is raised by some (Clements 1980:225–26; Fohrer 1960-61:17; Wildberger 1978:1046; Willis 1980:286). The oracle against the drunkenness of the Samarian elite is included here to illustrate that the leaders of Judah are as sinful as the leaders of Israel. The inclusion of Ephraim followed by Judah may be with a view to give an indictment of all Israel (Clements 1980:224). The Samarian elite are characterized as drunkards. It summarizes their lifestyle. The very fact that the prophet chose to characterize them as drunkards indicates how typical drinking was of their lifestyle. Ephraim was the area where the richest and the most advanced sector of the population lived in the Northern Kingdom (Baron 1958:65). In this connection, the information obtained from the Samaria ostraca is illuminating. Aharoni traced the clan names in the ostraca as belonging mostly to the tribe of Manasseh (1979a:367). More significantly, all the places mentioned in the ostraca are located in the northern part of Mount Ephraim in the ancient territory of Manasseh.

The description of verse 1 has a dual reference. On the one hand, it is a description of the fertile vine-covered hills of Samaria. On the other hand, it is a metaphorical representation of the rich section of the population. These characterizations are repeated in verses 3–4. The oracle predicts a sudden and violent destruction. It is fitting that the judgment also draws upon imagery from the wine industry. The destruction will be as sudden as a person picking and swallowing a first-ripe fruit. This brings to mind the process of tasting the first-ripe fruit before the harvest. Further, the end will be violent in that they will be trodden under foot. This, again, is clearly derived from the process of crushing grapes in wine industry.

Verses 7–8 describe the drunkenness of the priests and the prophets. The connection between this unit and verses 1–4 is established by the phrase "even these." Verses 5–6 seem to be a later addition. This section contains a message of hope and, hence, does not relate to the present context. It is striking how the words for wine and getting drunk are used as many as eleven times in this short section. In a cryptic two-verse span, the prophet manages to convey the different aspects of drunkenness. The drunkards stagger, wobble, and swerve. They are engulfed in wine. Their vision is blurred, and they stumble in speech. The picture closes with tables full of vomit and excrement everywhere. This picture is clearly reminiscent of the banquet hosted by El (as discussed in Chapter 3 above).

Here we might have a description of the *marzeah* as in Amos 6:4–7 (see above). It seems likely that this sodality also included members from the priestly and prophetic circles. They probably belonged to the circles of the court or those associated with it. The top officials of Jerusalem were following the lead of their Samarian counterparts. Without belaboring the point, this extravagance had a devastating effect on the lives of the common population.

Isaiah 24:7–13

7 The wine dries up; the vine withers;
  all the merry-hearted groan.
8 The flourish of timbrels is ceased;
  the clamor of the rejoicers has stopped;
  the sound of the lyre is ended.
9 No longer do they drink wine with singing,
  strong drink is bitter to those who drink it.
10 The empty city has been shattered;
  every house is shut, preventing entrance.
11 There is an outcry on the streets concerning (lack of)
  wine; all joy is disappearing; the happiness of the earth
  has been removed.
12 Desolation is left in the city;
  the gate is crushed into ruin;
13 for thus it shall be in the midst of the earth, in the midst of
    the peoples;
  like the shaking of olives, like the gleaning when the
    harvest is complete.

Isaiah 24–27 has been characterized as the "Apocalypse of Isaiah." Whether it is to be reckoned as full-blown apocalyptic literature is doubtful. The purpose of these chapters as a whole is to show the place of Israel in the coming age. Several scholars take it to originate in the postexilic period (Clements 1980:197; Fohrer 1960-61:22; Gray 1912:401; Kaiser 1974:173; Sweeney 1996:317; Wildberger 1991:445).

In Isaiah 24:1–13, we have a picture of the impending catastrophe. Within this section, there are two distinct units. Verses 1–3 form one unit and verses 4–13 another. In the first unit, the focus is on the effect of the catastrophe on the people. Here, the universality of punishment is stressed. No class of people will escape the punishment. This oracle does not allude to the process of land accumulation per se. Of particular interest are the groups of people mentioned. Among those listed are priests and people, slaves and masters, maids and mistresses, buyers and sellers, creditors and debtors, and lenders and borrowers. The opposite ends of a spectrum of each socioeconomic category are paired. It is intriguing that the buyers/sellers and creditors/debtors are picked out for special mention. Is it because they played a key role in the economy?

Verses 4–13 describe the effects of the coming judgment on the lifestyle of the people, while the previous section portrays the effects on kinds of groups. The life of the people will be radically altered. It is contended that the members of the upper class are being addressed here. There are two indications of that. First, in this section, variants of the term *yoshevim*, referring to the landed elite, occurs three times (once in v. 5 and twice in v. 6). It could not possibly refer to the whole population. It is inconceivable that the prophet would condemn all the inhabitants for the "pollution of the earth." The ruling elite have violated all the statutes, transgressed all the laws, and broken the contractual obligations. This includes violation of all norms of justice and fairness in dealing with the less privileged. Through oppressive measures, they have afflicted the poor. Verse 6 refers to the "guilt" of those who dwell in the land (*yoshve 'erets*). That the addressees of this oracle are the ruling elite is further supported by the nature of lifestyle described in this passage. It is noteworthy that wine is mentioned three times: verses 7, 9, and 11. Verse 7 predicts the drying up of wine and the groaning of the merry-hearted. Verse 9 also refers to wine consumption. This time, it occurs in conjunction with singing. In verse 8, we have the silenced timbrels, lyres, and those who are jubilant. Verse 11 repeats the theme of wine. Is it accidental that verse 13 talks about the gathering of olives and the end of vintage? While reading these verses, one cannot help but ask: Why is there such an emphasis on the consumption of wine? Why is the punishment seen in terms of lack of wine? Which particular group was given to such conspicuous consumption?

A systemic approach would put the matter in perspective. Wine figured prominently in the consumption of the upper class. Here we are dealing with drinking wine as a way of life. The elite controlled the distribution of items such as wine and oil in such a way that most of it went to underwrite their heavy consumption and for the purposes of export. The drunken revelry of the rich often constituted the target of the prophets' tirade. (See earlier discussion of Am. 6:4–7 and Isa. 28:7–8.) The extravagant lifestyle of the rich is condemned precisely because of its drastic results for the rest of the population. The more extravagant the life of the elite was, the more miserable the lives of the peasants became. The opulent lifestyle of the rich was made possible by the surplus extracted from the poor peasants. The pervasiveness of the imagery of revelry and wine drinking and music clearly fits the lifestyle of the rich class. To assume such a luxurious life for all "inhabitants" (*yoshevim*) is absurd. It also belies the reality of agrarian societies. One further piece of detail in support of the reference to the elite is the occurrence of "city" in verses 10 and 12. The target of the impending destruction, according to the pronouncement, would be the city. The city, as we have seen in connection with numerous other passages, played a key role in preindustrial society. It was important for its political, economic, and religious functions. But it survived, even thrived, at the cost of the rural periphery. Hence, the city figures so often in the prophetic oracles.

Isaiah 3:16–24

16 And Yahweh said: Because the daughters of Zion are
            haughty
      and walk with outstretched necks, and ogling eyes,
      tiptoeing along as they walk and jingling with their feet;
17 the Lord will make the heads of the daughters of Zion scabby,
      and lay bare their foreheads.
18 On that day the Lord will remove the anklet ornaments,
      the headbands and the crescents;
19 the earrings and the veils;

20 the headdresses, the anklets, and the bands; the scarves
and the shells;
21 the rings and the nose rings;
22 the extra fine robes, the tunics, the gowns and the purses;
23 the pocket mirrors, the shawls, the headgear and the
upper garment.
24 Instead of perfume, foul smell;
instead of the girdle, a rope;
and in place of fancy hairdo, baldness;
and in place of an embroidered robe, a girding of sack
cloth; instead of beauty...

A variety of opinions are expressed with regard to the dating of this passage. Many consider verses 18–23 as an interpolation. Duhm was the first one to posit this. The phrase "on that day," according to Duhm, gives away the redactor's hand (1922:50). Wildberger follows Duhm's suggestion (1991:147). In G. B. Gray's view, there is very little in the passage to determine the date. The careful attention to minute details of articles of clothing and ornaments, according to Gray, is uncharacteristic of Isaiah (1912:71). Clements considers this section to be an addition of uncertain date and origin. However, he does entertain the possibility of the period between 733–727 B.C.E. as the most appropriate background for this passage (1980:50). Among those who defend the authenticity of this passage are Willis (1980:119–23), G. A. Smith (1908:28), Fohrer (1960-61:9), and Kaiser (1972). In Kaiser's opinion, since this prophetic saying "assumes a period of undisturbed economic prosperity and outward security, this passage must have been composed before the war between Syria and Ephraim" (1972:47). The argument that the enumeration of details is uncharacteristic of Isaiah is not convincing. It is quite possible that Isaiah has taken the effort to illustrate his point with detailed enumeration. Since the oracle is addressed against the wealthy women of Judah, a detailed description of their ways and possessions is not out of place, particularly if the prophet wants to impress upon the readers the nature of the lifestyle of the wealthy women. This aspect is related to the lifestyle of the elite as a whole. Gideon Sjoberg's discussion of the lifestyle of the ruling elite in the preindustrial society throws light on Isaiah's purpose in including the list of the personal items of wealthy women:

Sociologists have viewed women as the carriers of status in social systems, an observation that is best dramatized in the world of the pre-industrial city elite. Here, women, utilizing elaborate dress, make-up, coiffures and/or display of jewelry, reflect, indeed advertise to other women of the elite, the family's socioeconomic position, their own exemption from physical labor and their ability to spend long hours in self-adornment. (1960:166)

Three observations stand out in Sjoberg's comment. First, a display of personal adornments becomes a way of exhibiting the family's socioeconomic position. Second, the long hours spent in self-adornment are in keeping with the elite's life of leisure. Third, their nonengagement in physical labor is also characteristic of their lifestyle. The judgment on the wealthy women is rendered in terms of depriving them of the very things they have enjoyed and esteemed. The passage offers a contrast between the present state of beauty and wanton behavior, and the coming disfiguration and total deprivation. Why should Isaiah go to such lengths to condemn the women of the elite group? One can see from the list of the personal items that only the rich could afford these. This relates to their penchant for luxury items. These items were obtained mostly through imports. The economic consequences of the export-import trade for the local economy were enormous. The special local items such as wine, oil, and grain were exported in exchange for these luxury items. The common people had no access to these items. Worse yet, they were affected severely, because the dynamics of the export-import trade left the staples in short supply. It is this lack of justice and denial of a basic decent living to the peasants that led the prophets to speak out against the situation and those who were responsible for it.

Trade and Commerce

One other area with significant impact at many levels is the growth of trade and commerce. This comes with the expansion of the market network. In agrarian monarchies, trade and commerce were initiated, maintained, and monopolized by the royal group. Hence, the beneficiaries of this enterprise were also the same group of people. In fact, interregional or international trade was geared toward procuring items that were of value and interest to this group. In this connection, the systematic development and control of trade routes were vital for the movement of goods, as well as for generating revenues from trading caravans.

Isaiah 2:6–7

> 6 You have rejected your people, the house of Jacob,
>   for they are abundant from before,
>   and of soothsayers like the Philistines,
>   and they negotiate business with foreigners.
> 7 Their land is filled with silver and gold;
>   there is no end to their storehouses.
>   Their land is filled with horses;
>   and there is no end to their chariots.

This oracle reflects the conditions prevalent in Judah during the earlier part of the eighth century B.C.E. or, at the latest, the eve of the Syro-Ephraimite war (Clements 1980:43; Gray 1915:51; Fohrer 1960-61:9; Kaiser 1972:35; Watts 1985:34; Wildberger 1991:104). Some place it on the eve of Sennacherib's invasion during Hezekiah's reign (Sweeney 1996:104). The overall condemnation by the prophet is aimed at the accumulation of riches through efforts of trade and commerce and also the proliferation of military items.

The meaning of verse 6b is not clear. Many commentators add *qosemim*, "diviners" to the text to read: "they are full of diviners from the east." This is taken as a parallel to the characterization of the Philistines in the following line. This addition, however, is not warranted by the text. Retaining the MT reading, it can be read "they are abundant from before," meaning that they have been enjoying the abundance for a long time. The characterization of the Philistines as diviners or soothsayers does not fit with what we know of the Philistines. There is no indication that they were experts in the art of divination. On the other hand, we do know that they were expert traders. What follows in verse 6c definitely refers to the business negotiations between traders. This literally means "clasping hands" or "shaking hands." We probably have here an allusion to a custom in trade negotiations. Verse 7 clearly indicates that the context of the oracle is the accumulation of wealth and military items. These two were the results of active trade relations with other countries.

One of the indicators of the growth of the economy was the development of trade and commerce. Extensive trade was possible through the expansion of the market. The enormous increase in the wealth of the country could be attributed to two factors. First, there was an increase in the commercial activity. Second, the control of trade routes brought wealth by way of tolls and transit trade. As hypothesized in the previous chapter, the eighth century B.C.E. was a period of economic prosperity in Israel and Judah. This is attested by the specialized production and extensive trade operations. The colonization activity under the royal directive of Israel and Judah enabled them to control the trade routes that crossed their lands. The two kingdoms must have benefited enormously from the commercial activity that passed through the Via Maris, the King's Highway, and other routes in the Negev. In the words of John Skinner, "This passage reflects the wealth of the country, which had increased enormously through the commercial activity and the control of the Red Sea traffic [2 Kings 14: 22] in the reigns of Uzziah and Jotham" (1915:20).

With regard to trade in the eighth century B.C.E., two general observations should be made. First, the crown monopolized the trade. Even though we could conceivably speak of a merchant class engaged in trade, it was probably under the royal control. Second, the beneficiaries of the commercial enterprises were the royal court and the immediate circles associated with it. In fact, the whole commercial activity was geared to providing for the royal household and the ruling elite. The main items of import were luxury articles and strategic military items. In return, wheat, oil, and wine were exported.

It is significant that verse 7 mentions countless "storehouses." This points to the availability of storage facilities for the agricultural surpluses. Increased storage facilities played a key role in preserving the commodities for a longer period of time. This enabled the ruling class to control the supply of the goods in accordance with the market conditions. Further, an improved network of roads facilitated the movement of goods from place to place. The storage of commodities such as wine and oil also ensured a year-round supply for the conspicuous consumption of the ruling elite.

The reference to their land being "filled with horses" is interpreted in two ways. Clements argues that it "scarcely points to the military use of the horse but must rather indicate the presence of numbers of trading caravans passing through Judah" (1980:44). The question is whether horses were used for caravan purposes. The use of horses in the military for chariots is a better possibility. Even though the source of horse trade is debated, it is clear that horses were imported into Palestine.

Commenting on this section, Brueggemann draws attention to the triad of "fullness" that has altered the identity of the community (1998:28–29). First, their land is full of wealth. Second, their land is full of strategic military items: horses and chariots. Third, their land is full of idols–false centers of devotion. These things have created a false sense of security and identity based on their own might. Their identity as "people of Yahweh" has been lost. The proliferation of material resources (gold, silver, and stores) and equipment of war (horses and chariots) had been the result of the long and successful reigns of Jeroboam II in the north and Uzziah in the south. If this produced prosperity and economic growth, why did the prophets condemn? They did so because only a small group of people benefited from the material welfare. The lucrative trade, which was initiated and monopolized by the crown, benefited only the royal court and those who were close to it.

Isaiah 23:1–3, 8–9, 17–18

1 An utterance concerning Tyre.
> Wail, O Tarshish ships!
> For it [Tyre] is devastated without house or access.
> From the land of the Cypriotes
> it is revealed to them.
2 Be still, O rulers of the coast, O traders of Sidon;
> those who traverse the sea fill you
3 and over many waters;
> the grain of Sihor, the harvest of Nile is your revenue;
> you were the trader among the nations.

8 Who has planned this concerning Tyre,
> the crowning city whose merchants were nobles,
> and whose traders were the honored of the earth?
9 Yahweh of hosts has planned this,
> to undo the pride, to slight all glory
> of all those who are honored of the earth.

17 And it shall be at the end of seventy years, Yahweh will visit Tyre, and she will return to her hire, and play the harlot with all the kingdoms of the world upon the face of the earth. 18 Her merchandise and her profit will become sacred to Yahweh; it will not be stored nor hoarded, for her merchandise will supply abundant food and splendid clothing to those who live before Yahweh.

Even though three small segments are chosen for treatment here, the chapter as a whole is relevant. It is an oracle against the Phoenicians. Scholars have debated whether this is a prophecy of the future or a prophecy lamenting the fate that befell Tyre and Sidon. There are at least four possible dates suggested for its origin. The political developments involving Assyria and other nations during 709–701 B.C.E. are suggested as a possible context (Skinner 1915:186; Hayes and Irvine 1987:288–89; Sweeney 1996:307–308). A second suggestion is the campaign of Esarhaddon against Phoenicia around 679–671 B.C.E. (Clements 1980:192; Wildberger 1991:419). A third suggestion pertains to the capture of Sidon around 343 B.C.E. by Artaxerxes III (Kaiser 1974:162–68). Yet another possibility is the capture of Tyre by Alexander the Great in 332 B.C.E. (Fohrer 1960-61:22).

Isaiah 23 forms part of a larger corpus consisting of oracles against foreign nations. The oracles against foreign nations are complex to assess in terms of dating. They cannot be automatically treated as late. There are some older materials present in the corpus. Part of the difficulty in assigning a certain date is because older materials seem to have been used at a later time. Fohrer's point is well taken, that the oracles against foreign nations "existed at one time independently. Before its inclusion in the book of Isaiah it was dismantled and merged with numerous other sayings" (1960-61:8). Many scholars have noted the stylistic differences between this poem and the rest of Isaiah (Kaiser 1974:162; Smith 1908:295; Wildberger 1991:415–16).

Whether one accepts Isaianic authorship or not, the reality that the poem conveys is the supremacy of the Phoenicians in maritime trade. The Phoenicians' mastery of the sea did not develop overnight. It has a long history. The Phoenician commerce had its heyday in the eighth century B.C.E. The economic prosperity enjoyed by Israel and Judah benefited the Phoenician commerce. Like any other maritime society, mercantile interests primarily motivated the Phoenicians. The colorfast dye produced by the Phoenicians was much in demand. The textile industries at places like Tell en-Nasbeh, Lachish, and Tell Beit Mirsim depended on the purple dye of the Phoenicians. The Phoenician export trade depended on cedar and fir forests for providing wood for the neighboring countries (Oded 1979a:228; Silver 1983:57; Moscati 1968:83). The hewn-stone technique in architecture is attributed to the Phoenicians (Katzenstein 1973:199;

Moscati 1968:83). Close trade relations with Phoenicia can explain the spread of this technique in Israel. Textiles were another industry of the Phoenicians. They also had a notable glass industry. They seemed to have developed the art of producing transparent glasses (Moscati 1968:84). That the Phoenicians had trained experts to work in metal, ivory, stone, and wood is attested to in 2 Chronicles 2:14. This gives us a picture of the Phoenician economy as a mercantile economy based on the exploitation of local resources and other technical expertise. In addition to this, because of their expertise in navigation, the Phoenicians facilitated the movement of goods in international trade, thereby benefiting from the transit trade.

The nature and extent of Phoenicia's commercial activity was very diverse and over distant lands as Ezekiel 27 describes. This chapter is of immense importance since it describes in great detail the commercial activity of the Phoenicians with other nations. From the descriptions in this chapter, it is clear that Tyre (and Phoenicia) was at the center of the then-known global network of economic centers (Brueggemann 1998:183). The identification of the specific localities, and sometimes the merchandise, may be doubtful. But the overall picture is most impressive and reflects the abundance and intensity of Phoenician trade. Why did the prophet Isaiah proclaim judgment against the Phoenicians? The prophet had ample reasons for doing so. Israel and Judah were involved in the international trade scene. It is the nature and effects of such involvement that drew the prophet's criticism. First, foreign trade was initiated and monopolized by the state/crown. Second, the beneficiaries of such enterprises were the crown and those close to the royal circles. Third, the international trade was geared to procuring luxury and strategic military items for the upper class. Fourth, the imports were obtained in exchange for the local export items. This meant that the agricultural surplus was transferred from the primary producers to provide for the aristocracy. The production of commercial crops for the international market affected the production of staples. This situation forced the peasants into the market system with which they were unfamiliar, and there they were cheated by the merchants with false measures and crooked scales.

The Phoenicians are referred to as "rulers of the coast"(*yoshve 'i*). It is significant that *yoshev* occurs as a parallel to "merchants." The usual translation of *yoshev* as "inhabitants" does not bring out the force of its usage here. The emphasis here is the undisputed control of the coastline by the Phoenicians. Their hegemony over the sea resulted from their expertise in navigation and sea trade. They crossed many seas (v. 2). The description of the Phoenician merchants (v. 8) fits with what we know of the status of merchants in the maritime societies. Since commerce was the main source of economic surplus, in the political and distributive spheres merchants occupied a prominent position in the maritime societies (Lenski 1966:192). In other words, the merchants were a dominant class.

Besides profiting from direct trade exchange, Tyre and Sidon also earned gains through transit trade. This is reflected in the corn trade of Egypt passing through Sidon as in verse 3 (Kaiser 1974:165). The use of "revenue" suggests transit trade. The reference to Tyre's being forgotten for seventy years is not to be taken literally. It probably is a way of indicating how completely the city will be forgotten (Clements 1980:195). According to the proclamation, at the end of seventy years Tyre and Sidon will return to their former trade and prosperity, but this time under the patronage of Yahweh. Their merchandise and gains will be brought to Yahweh. It is significant that the prophet sees the regeneration of the economy, not for the sake of storing or hoarding, but for distributing food and clothing–the essentials of life to those who dwell before Yahweh. They will partake of Yahweh's inheritance.

Market Conditions

This refers to the abuses/corrupt practices in the market situation. With the advent of a wider market orientation, drastic changes occur in the area of production. The demands of the market forces promote the cultivation of cash crops, which can gain maximum economic advantage. This means that more and more lands are converted to producing commercial crops, leaving the staples in short supply. The peasants need these for their survival. Consequently, they are forced to go to the market to buy the staples that they once produced themselves. The merchants can take advantage of their unfamiliarity with the market conditions and shortchange them through unscrupulous tampering and deceit in the transactions.

Amos 8:4–6

4 Hear this, you who drag the needy,
    to destroy the impoverished of the land,

5 saying, "When will the New Moon be over that we may
      sell grain,
  and the Sabbath that we may offer wheat for sale;
  to use a reduced dry measure,
  to [shortchange] with heavier weight,
  to defraud with rigged scales;
6 to buy the poor for the silver,
  and the needy for a pair of sandals;
  and even sell the refuse of the wheat?"

There are no serious questions about the eighth-century dating of this oracle (Andersen and Freedman 1989:801; Coote 1981:14; Mays 1969a:12, 142; Paul 1991:256–57; Stuart 1987:383; Wolff 1977:327–28). Verses 4–6 belong together as a unit. Even though the eighth-century context of this unit remains unquestioned, its placement in this passage is not. The editorial shaping of verses 4–14 may come from a later period (Jeremias 1998:145). From a structural point of view, verse 6 offers a good parallel to verses 4–5a. The opening lines focus on the "needy," the "impoverished," and "grain/wheat," which is balanced by references to "poor," the "needy," and "grain/wheat" in verse 6.

This section focuses on another dimension in the process of latifundialization, namely, the plight of the peasantry in unfamiliar market conditions. In the market economy, production was aimed for the market. This brought about a change from mixed subsistence farming to cash crop farming. With the growth of the large estates, more and more peasants were evicted from their land. As they were forced to sell their labor due to poverty, their dependence on markets for staples became essential. The staples that they once produced themselves had to be bought in the market. This forced them into the market with which they were unfamiliar. The merchants capitalized on this several ways. They sold the grain at a higher price. By stockpiling and creating an artificial scarcity, they could further raise the prices. Using false measures, weights, and rigged scales, they cheated the peasants in the sale transaction.

In this oracle, Amos isolates the cheating methods of the merchants. The merchants grudgingly observed the holidays, because these took them away from business. The New Moon was observed as a religious occasion in the biblical period: for instance, Numbers 10:10; 28:11–15; 1 Samuel 20:5; 2 Kings 4:23; and Isaiah 1:13–14

(Paul 1991:257). The celebrations of the New Moon once every four weeks and the Sabbath every seventh day were observed as days of rest in which shops were closed and no transaction was possible. The merchants were so greedy in their fraudulent practices that they could not wait to open their shops for business after the holiday. They not only sold the commodities at a high price but also shortchanged the peasants with tampered measurements.

A further nuance to the use of false measures is the practice of keeping two sets of measures and weights, one for selling and another one for buying (Deut. 25:13–16). The merchants shortchanged the primary producers by using one set of measures when they bought or exacted the agricultural produce to gain maximum advantage. When they sold the commodities in retail, they sold it in smaller measures to reduce the quantity. The "selling of the refuse of the wheat" reflects the practice of adulterating the grain with chaff and refusal to increase the quantity/weight. In both the wholesale and retail transactions, the peasants were victims.

It is doubtful whether verse 6a originally belonged in this context. It was probably added later to emphasize the fact that the merchants not only dealt in the trade of goods but also of human beings. From a systemic perspective, it is not hard to see the connection between the corrupt practices in the market affecting the peasantry and eventual debt slavery and foreclosures. The definite article in front of "money/silver" *(kesef)* seems to be intentional because something specific is intended. As Mays points out, it might indicate "a particular sum as debt" (1969a:45). It could refer either to the whole amount in debt or more specifically to the interest on loans. In ancient Hebrew laws, loans of money are referred to as "money," literally "silver" *(kesef)*: Exodus 22:25; Leviticus 25:35–37; Deuteronomy 23:19–20. In all these passages, *neshek* is used for "interest." The provision in Exodus and Leviticus is related to the economic status of the borrower. In other words, interest is not to be taken from an impoverished Hebrew borrower. But in Deuteronomy, loans at interest are prohibited irrespective of the economic status. In other words, it prohibits loans at interest to any Hebrew resident. The common feature of all the three laws is the disapproval of taking interest. The prohibition of taking interest was meant to protect the poor and the needy from plunging into debt (Neufeld 1955). Amos 2:6b indicates that there was not only a practice of taking interest, but that it did, in fact, become a means of driving the peasantry into debt slavery. (For further comments on this aspect, see the discussion on Am. 2:6–8, below.)

Hosea 12:7–9 [Heb. 12:8–10]

7 A merchant in whose hands are rigged scales,
   he loves to extort.
8 Ephraim says: "I have become rich, I have made myself a
   fortune.
   All my gains that are sinful earn me no punishment."
9 "I am Yahweh your God from the land of Egypt;
   I will again make you dwell in tents as in the days of the
   tabernacle."

Scholars favor the reign of Hoshea or the aftermath of Jeroboam's death in general as the possible background for this passage (Andersen and Freedman 1980:37; Mackintosh 1997:497; Mays 1969b:16; Wolff 1974:xxxi). The particular aspect described in this passage is the fraud in the market. The full import of this can be realized only from a systemic perspective. The present text makes no secret of the fact that the merchants grew rich out of their fraudulent practices. In fact, the text has them boasting about their riches, oblivious to the fact that they were ill-gotten at the expense of the peasantry.

The word *Canaan* has a double entendre. Originally, it referred to Phoenicia, signifying its export of the red purple dye. Because of their reputation as traveling merchants, *Canaanites* (the gentilic form of the word) came to mean a trader or merchant (Köhler and Baumgartner 1951:444), irrespective of the ethnic background. In our present passage this image of a merchant is used in a derogatory sense for Israel, because of their corrupt and deceitful behavior in the market.

The judgment of Yahweh in this context is also significant. The references to "the land of Egypt," and "tabernacle" have important associations. The judgment calls for a radical reversal of the present situation to that of premonarchic Israel. The socioeconomic egalitarianism ushered in by the premonarchic Israelite movement serves as an ideal in this context. The judgment ensures that the economic differences will be leveled and that those who are enjoying or, in fact, boasting about their ill-gotten wealth will be made to dwell in the tents. This means that they, too, would be like any other member of the premonarchic Israelite group. In other words, retributive justice will take the shape of equalizing the socioeconomic differences.

Debt Slavery

Many factors drove the peasants into debt. First, the exactions in agricultural produce were heavy, sometimes more than half of the total produce. Prices tend to be the lowest at the time of the harvest. Illegal business practices on the part of the landowners further cut into the returns. Second, the common peasants bore the brunt of much of the taxation to support the programs of the state. The energies of the peasants were expended between fulfilling their agricultural and corvée obligations. Participation in one did not earn them a reprieve in the other. But, their performance and productivity suffered in both. Third, when the peasants were dependent primarily upon rain for agriculture, there were serious consequences if rains failed. They were forced to borrow to feed the family. If the rains failed for subsequent seasons, the peasants went into deeper debt. Often, the peasants offered either the piece of land they owned or an article of value or a member of the family as collateral. Failure to repay mounting loans resulted in the foreclosure of land and/or being sold into debt slavery. Accumulation of land through debt instruments became a way of creating large estates.

Amos 2:6b–8

> 6b Because they sell the innocent for the money,
>   and the needy for a pair of sandals;
> 7 those who drag the head of the poor in the dust of the earth,
>   and thrust aside the just claim of the impoverished;
>   a man and his father go to the maid
>   in order to profane my holy name;
> 8 upon confiscated pledge garments, they stretch out
>   (beside every altar)
>   and drink the wine of those whom they exact by defraud
>   (in the house of their God).

These verses are part of Amos's judgment oracle against Israel in 2:6–16. Verses 9–12 seem to be editorial expansions and, hence, clearly do not belong in this context. The dating of this passage is generally agreed to be eighth century B.C.E. (Andersen and Freedman 1989:307–308; Coote 1980:11, 34–35; Jeremias 1998:32, 35; Mays 1969a:12–13; McKeating 1971:22–23; Paul 1991:76–77; Wolff 1977:141). Based on the content, there are four sets of couplets dealing with some aspects of the process of latifundialization. The first couplet describes the role of debt instrument. The word *innocent* renders the Hebrew word *tsadiq* that the prophets used with legal connotation: the *righteous* is one who is declared *innocent* from the legal point of view. The counterpart of that is the *wicked* one, who has been found *guilty* in the legal process. The eighth-century prophets often use the combination poor/innocent/righteous interchangeably over against rich/guilty/wicked. The use of "money/silver" in v. 6b indicates interest and possible debt slavery, as in Amos 8:4–6, as discussed above.

This grim reality corresponds with what has been hypothesized about the particulars of latifundialization in the eighth century B.C.E. in the previous chapter. The vicissitudes of rain agriculture, repeated failure of crops due to drought and pestilence, loans at high interest rates, and inability to repay the loans pushed the peasants into debt. The interest rates on the loans were probably so high that the total interest accrued alone was a huge amount to repay. In this sense, it is appropriate to interpret "the money" as the interest on loans. Debt slavery is not unusual in Israel, as the story of the widow and her two sons in 2 Kings 4:1–7 shows. In the story, the creditor threatens to take the sons as his slaves for failure to repay debts. Selling one's own self and/or one's own household was one of the consequences of nonpayment of loans.

Another consequence for nonpayment of loans was foreclosure of landed property. This is referred to in the latter part of Amos 2:6b (selling the needy for a pair of sandals). The pair of sandals stands here symbolic of a legal process. One of the common ways to interpret this has been that the poor could be enslaved for such a trifle thing as a pair of shoes. This is wide of the mark. The clue for a different interpretation comes from two passages. Ruth 4:7 attests to a practice of giving one's sandal as a sign of confirming a transaction. According to Deuteronomy 25:9, the removal of sandals from a man's feet signified his inability to perform his levirate obligation. In both cases, the pair of sandals functions as a legal symbol, an act of confirmation. The same principle seems to be at work in Amos 2:6b and 8:6. Here, sandals are a sign of confirming the foreclosure of land. Other scholars corroborate this interpretation (Andersen and Freedman 1989:312; Mays 1969a:45). The ruling class used their control of the courts to exercise every legal right, foreclosing on the honest persons who have gotten into debt because of circumstances beyond their control (Snaith 1958:36). The phrase "a pair of sandals" is used as a symbol for the legal transaction. In this instance, it is for the transfer of land. Without the transfer of the pair of sandals, the party would have been guilty of an illegal practice. What is witnessed here is a clever manipulation of the legal system to validate or rubberstamp an unjust practice. This points to the way the legal courts were controlled and/or manipulated by the ruling elite. The courts, instead of protecting the interests of the peasants, have, in fact, become instruments of defrauding them. Paul reads "hidden gift or payoff" instead of "a pair of sandals," based on a much rarer Hebrew word meaning "to hide" (1991:78).

The second couplet in Amos 2:7a is also a condemnation of the corrupt judicial system. Most commentators read in the text a much rarer root meaning "crush, trample, shuffle, or drag." The line "those who drag the head of the poor in the dust of the earth" may be a metaphorical and a more graphic way of illustrating the drastic effects of wrongful sentences on the lives of the peasantry. Similar expressions occur in Micah 3:1–3. The second half of the couplet "and thrust aside the just claim of the impoverished," is more specific. It again refers to the manipulation of the legal system to deprive peasants of what legally belongs to them. The word translated as "just claim" is *derek* ("way, manner, or custom"), which in this context refers to the "common law of relief, remission and just standards that the peasantry appeal to in grievance procedures against their overlords" (Coote 1981:33). But the ruling class did not hesitate to violate such common norms and just standards by using their political and economic influence. It is possible that the court officials themselves belonged to the ruling class or were puppets in the hands of the elite. Thus the judicial courts, because of the successful venal practices of the elite, became instruments of oppression instead of upholding the just claims of the peasantry. (See below on the Role of the Judicial Courts.)

The meaning of the third couplet in Amos 2:7b is not clear. Most commentators take it to mean sexual involvement of the father and the son with the same woman. Many see here Amos protecting the rights of the young woman from sexual abuse. Two observations go against such a reading. The Hebrew word *halak* (used here) means "to go to" and not "go into." For sexual connotation, one would expect *bo'* instead of *halak*. Does the combination of *halak 'el* (walk/go to) have an idiomatic connotation as Paul argues on the basis of an Akkadian cognate (1991:82)? Far from settling the argument, Paul's treatment raises further questions. He points out that *halak* "can also signify having dealings with someone" (1991:82). Both of the passages he cites in support of this meaning—Numbers 22:13 and Proverbs 1:11—have nothing to do with sexual behavior. Further, conjecturing on why Amos might have used *halak* here, Paul points out that the reason might be to establish a connection to 2:4 (1991:82). Again, as Paul himself acknowledges, the connection is only verbal, not contextual (1991:82). There is nothing in the context of 2:4 that has sexual connotation. Furthermore, no biblical law prohibits the sexual involvement of the father and son with "the young woman" (Paul 1991:81). The often cited passages (Ex. 21:9; Lev. 18:8, 15, 17; 20:11, 12, 14; Deut. 22:30 [Heb. 23:1]; 27:20) all speak about prohibited sexual relations within a familial context. It is also critical to note that the text has "a man and his father," not father and son as one would expect it. This might mean in a generic sense that everybody is "going to the girl," that it is a common practice. Andersen and Freedman suggest that "man" is used here in a distributive sense meaning "each" (1989:318). Further, the Hebrew text does not have the word "same" (Coote 1981:35). Most translators supply the word "same" on the assumption that the text is talking about sexual encounter. Coote sees here, with caution however, a probable allusion to the institution of alewife or barmaid serving as brokers. The barmaid offered drinks on credit in exchange for grain. Persistent excessive drinking could bring a person into debt (Coote 1981:35–36). It is also interesting how scholars make the assumption that since the text says "to profane my holy name," this must refer to sexual behavior. Why couldn't other types of activities, such taking advantage of the peasants, be taken as profaning God's name? Coote's suggestion concerning the institution of alewife or barmaid is reasonable, but, unfortunately, it is not attested in Israel.

The fourth accusation in Amos 2:8 describes two practices. In verse 8a, the practice of taking garments as collateral for obtaining a loan is mentioned. Here, this implies a sense of coercion, because the poor peasant would not have wanted to part with the few garments he or she had. The creditor probably forced the peasant to leave behind the garment as a security. It is also possible that the garments could have been confiscated for failure to repay a debt. Ancient Hebrew laws in Exodus 22:23–26 and Deuteronomy 24:10–13 lay down stipulations concerning the pledge. Particularly relevant is the clause in Deuteronomy 24:12: "And if [the debtor] is a poor person, you shall not sleep in his/her pledge." Both the Exodus and Deuteronomy passages stress the fact that the pledged garment should be restored before sundown. The debtors in Amos's case may have been tenants who sought loans to meet the basic needs of their families. The creditors were either moneylenders or landlords. In this connection, the information contained in the Metsad Hashavyahu letter from Yavneh Yam is illuminating. The letter is the complaint of a poor man whose garment has been seized for not fulfilling a certain obligation. He asks that his garment be returned. The nature of the obligation is not clear. Some interpret it as the obligation of a corvée worker (Pardee 1978:33–66). Cross's suggestion that it refers to the claims of a creditor from a tenant farmer makes better sense (1962:46). The document is usually dated to the seventh century, based on the assumption that the military establishments mentioned in the document belong to the time of Josiah. Such military fortresses adjoining farming communities were also common in the eighth century under Uzziah. (See chapter 3, the section on the Judean expansion in the Negev.) There is no compelling reason not to attribute this letter to the eighth century B.C.E.

The second half of Amos 2:8 refers to another dimension of the economic oppression to which the peasants were subjected. This line could be read in several ways. The exaction mentioned in this line could refer to payments in kind required of the debtor-tenant. It could also refer, as Coote points out, to the proceeds from latifundialized estates (which were once small plots) by way of interest and fines (1981:32). What is certain is that this line mirrors the plight of the peasantry who were subject to undue exactions. The indebted peasant was forced to turn over the proceeds of the land to the landowner or moneylender. The more obligated the peasants became, the more the landowners got by way of economic surplus. Such impoverishment of the peasantry eventually led to the loss of secure access to arable land.

Role of the Creditors

The creditors and moneylenders played a critical role in the impoverishment of the peasantry. It is conceivable that the creditors and moneylenders were the landed elite themselves or a separate class within that group who specialized in that operation. There is no doubt, whatsoever, about the drastic result of their operation on the condition of the peasantry.

Isaiah 3:12–15

12 My people: moneylenders extort them,
  and creditors rule them.
  O, my people, those who should be fair to you deceive you,
  and swallow up the course of your welfare.
13 Yahweh has taken a stand for disputation,
  and is standing to arbitrate.
14 Yahweh comes in judgment
  against the heads of his people and their officials:
  "It is you who have devoured the vineyard,
  and what is taken forcefully from the poor is now part of
    your estate.
15 Why do you crush my people,
  and grind the face of the poor?"
  Oracle of the Lord God of Hosts.

The Isaianic origin of this passage is not questioned (Clements 1980:49; Fohrer 1960–61:9; Kaiser 1972:44–45; Sweeney 1996:110; Wildberger 1991:138, 141; Willis 1980:117). There is no question that the oracle is directed against the upper class. But how one renders some key words and phrases remain crucial. Several English translations, following MT, have read verse 12a something like this:

My people–children are their oppressors
and women rule over them.

The *New English Bible* was one of the first ones to translate it correctly:

Moneylenders strip my people bare,
and usurers lord it over them.

The MT reading does not fit the context, let alone convey sense. A slight rearrangement of the consonants and repointing a few vowels would throw a different light on the passage. This verse focuses on the infamous role of the moneylenders and creditors in impoverishing peasantry. One of the key words in this verse means "to exact or extort" (Brown, S. R. Driver, and Briggs 1978:620; see also G. R. Driver 1937:38). The Septuagint has *praktores*, which refers to "tax collectors." It is also significant that the word for the office building of the tax collector, *praktoreion*, had the connotation of the debtor's prison (Liddell and Scott 1940:1458). The use of the related verb in Deuteronomy 15:2 is relevant to our discussion. The context is the creditors' writing off loans. At the end of every seven years, the creditors were required to release what they had loaned their neighbors. The creditors could not exact of their neighbors. In another instance, the verb is used in the context of Jehoiachin's exacting silver and gold to pay tribute to Pharaoh Neco (2 Kings 23:35).

The word translated as "children" is also problematic (Gray 1912: 67). Following Samuel Driver's suggestion (1937:38), the proper meaning is to "deviate from justice, impose burden upon, exact more than just or exceed bounds." Wildberger suggests, "fleece people" (1991:137). The third person plural verbal suffix could have been dropped due to haplography. Thus, this offers a parallel to "rule" in the second half of the verse. There seems to be a connection between 3:12 and 3:4. The reference to "babes" in 3:4 could have influenced the reading in 3:12. However, in verse 4 the translation "babes" is questionable. The word in question has the connotation of "arbitrary power" (Köhler and Baumgartner 1951:1036). If it is to be assumed that "babes" refers to the rulers, neither Jotham nor Ahaz were really young when they became rulers. The reference to "women" could have come about due to the influence of the oracle against the wealthy women in the following verses (16–24). The term "women" could be emended to "creditors/usurers." The Septuagint and the Targum support this reading.

Verse 12b/c addresses civil and court officials. The occurrence of *derek* in verse 12c, as in Amos 2:7, has the connotation of manner or custom and hence, in the case of the peasants, just claims. That verse 12e is an accusation against the judicial court officials is further strengthened by the reference to Yahweh as the judge in verse 13. The distorted human institution of justice is placed under the judgment of Yahweh, who is the ultimate judge. In verses 14–15, we have an invective against the ruling elite. Verse 14 specifies the nature of the offense. The elite are accused of forcefully grabbing the inheritance of the peasants. This has particular reference to the growth of large estates. The lawful inheritance of the peasants has now been foreclosed through debt instruments. In this connection, the legal courts have served as means of legitimizing corrupt practices. This refers to what has been forcefully taken away from the poor. Rainey suggests that it could refer to the exactions taken in kind from the peasants (1982:61). In this context it probably refers to the confiscated small landed property of the peasants, now part of the large estates. (See "great houses," discussed above in Am. 3:15.)

Role of the Judicial Courts

Judicial institutions played a critical role in sealing the fate of the peasantry. The only court of appeal for the peasants to seek redress of a situation or arbitration was the juridical institution. But the chances of getting a fair trial were dim, because the ruling class controlled the courts and its officials. Again, the judicial officials were either part of the upper class or puppets in the hands of the ruling elite. The venality of the ruling class is in its calculated and concerted effort to manipulate the system to render an air of legality to their evil machinations.

Amos 5:7, 10

7 [Woe to] Those who change judgment into wormwood
    and abandon justice to the earth;

10 They hate the one who arbitrates justly,
    and abhor the one who speaks with integrity.

The thought pattern logically follows from verse 7 into verse 10. Verses 8–9 seem to be an intrusion, probably from a later hand. Most scholars take verses 7 and 10 to be authentic to Amos (Andersen and Freedman 1989:484; Driver 1915:119; Jeremias 1998:82; Mays 1969a:5, 13, 90; Paul 1991:166–67; Soggin 1987:88–89; Wolff 1977:233). Part of the difficulty here is the mixed nature of the material in Amos 5:7, 10–13. Coote's point about a later editor (B stage) mixing and editing the older material is well taken (1981:74–77). However, the charges leveled in these verses represent the systemic reality of eighth-century Israelite society. Amos points to the corruption rampant in the judicial courts. In verse 7, the distortion of justice in the courts is described. The willful perversion of justice and skillful illegal manipulation of laws by the officials of the court were done under the influence and command of the ruling elite. The corrupt practices had become so pervasive that any official who dared to dispense justice and act with integrity was scorned and despised. The conscientious officials incurred the wrath and hatred of both their colleagues and the members of the aristocracy.

The place for dispensing justice was the gate. Any legal dispute was brought before the legal assembly convened at the city gate (Köhler 1956:152–53). The multichambered gate area seems to have been used for legal business (King 1988:75–76; Stuart 1987:348). The establishment of *mishpat* ("justice") meant the process of establishing what was right and who was in the right. The "just one" *(tsadiq)* was vindicated as innocent by virtue of being in the right. The "wicked one" *(rasha')* was declared guilty for being in the wrong. The legal assembly had the crucial task of helping the innocent party by establishing justice and protecting the social order by locating the wrong and rectifying it. The vulnerable members of the society, with no power or influence, could not protect themselves in the social order. They needed the help of the court (Mays 1969a:92). But the irony of the situation was that the very courts meant to promote and maintain justice have, in fact, become the instruments of distorting and subverting justice.

Isaiah 5:20

> Woe to those who call evil good and good evil;
> who put darkness for light and light for darkness;
> who set bitter for sweet and sweet for bitter.

This woe oracle, along with the other woe oracles in this chapter, is placed in the early years of Isaiah's prophetic ministry. It is a judgment on the legal court officials for their perversion of justice. In reaching legal decisions, the judges willfully distorted truth, "disregarding all the accepted standards of public and civil conduct in their policies" (Clements 1980:65). The ruling elite manipulated the judicial system for achieving their own ends. From a systemic perspective, this points to the way the legal courts functioned as instruments for legitimizing corrupt and unjust practices. The illegal claims of the elite were upheld, whereas the legal claims of the peasants were struck down. Their warped sense of morality and justice made them declare good as evil and evil as good. The officials employed their skill and legal knowledge to make a case for abuses. The very institutions that were meant to preserve and protect the claims of the common people became means of legally approving corrupt practices. (On the role of the legal courts in the process of latifundialization, see also the discussion of Am. 2:6–8 and 5:7, 10 above.)

Isaiah 10:1–4a

1 Woe to those who proclaim baneful verdicts,
  and to the writers who keep rubberstamping oppression;
2 to turn aside the needy from justice,
  and to wrest away the right from the poor of my people,
  making widows their spoil and plundering the orphans.
3 What will you do on the day of punishment,
  and the devastation to come from afar?
  To whom will you flee for help?
  And where will you abandon your wealth?
4 Nothing remains but to crouch among the prisoners
  or fall among the slain.

This oracle is seen as part of the woe oracle collection in Isaiah 5:8–24 because this collection has only six oracles, one short of the wholesome number seven. Moreover, there is similarity of content between Isaiah 5 and 10:1–4a. The oracle is authentic to Isaiah, originating in the period preceding the Syro-Ephraimite crisis, probably in the time of Jotham.

Isaiah 10:1–4a draws attention to the role of the legal system in underwriting oppression. The administrators of law failed to carry out their responsibility. The venality of the ruling class was responsible for their baneful verdicts. The just claims of the poor litigants were ignored. The prophet conveys the disastrous effects of the legal procedures on the peasant population. The verdicts were baneful in the sense that they put a seal on the foreclosure procedure. The term "verdict" in Hebrew refers to statute, law, or decree. In the present context, it could possibly refer to the new laws created for the benefit of members of the ruling class. As Brueggemann points out, such "'lawmaking' is the privilege of the powerful, most often done to their own advantage" (1998:90). The official with power could make such regulations at will, as, for example, in 1 Samuel 30:25 (Wildberger 1991:213). "Verdict" could also refer to the verdict rendered in a legal case. In a more specific way, verse 1b might reflect some kind of documentation process in the proceedings of the court. The Hebrew reads literally thus: "And writers keep writing oppression/misfortune." This might reflect a process whereby the legal proceedings were finalized in the court. In other words, the oppression had been fully legitimized. Hence, the translation "rubberstamping oppression" has been preferred to convey the sense of officially validating a corrupt practice.

Verse 2a further reinforces the accusation against the partisan judicial officials. The just claims of the needy were turned down. The phrase *ligzol mishpat* has been rendered as "wrest away the right." Exodus 23:6 warns: "You shall not pervert the *mishpat* due your poor in his [her] suit." *Mishpat* (justice) has a legal connotation. It refers to the judicial process of establishing what is right and who is in the right and rendering the judgment accordingly (Mays 1969a:92). The function of the judge, according to Deuteronomy 25:1, was to acquit the innocent and condemn the guilty. When the court achieved this purpose, *mishpat* was established.

The occurrence of *gzl* in the passage is noteworthy. It is significant that the various forms of *gzl* appear in the context of seizing immovable property (Isa. 3:14; Mic. 2:2 and 3:2, in addition to our present passage). Other similar occurrences outside the eighth-century prophets are Ezekiel 18:12, 16, 18; 22:29; Jeremiah 21:12; 22:3; and Job 20:19; 24:2. Since most of the disputes probably related to landed property, it is possible that in Isaiah 10:2a, the wresting away of the right could have reference to the foreclosures legitimated by legal process. By seizing the plot of land from the small farmer, the officials in fact deprived them of their just claim.

Verse 2b brings in another dimension to our discussion. This has to do with the special responsibility towards the underprivileged in the society. In the Hebrew Bible, this concern is demonstrated in two sections: in the legal traditions—the Book of the Covenant (Ex. 20:22–23:33), the Deuteronomic Code (Deut. 12–26), and the Code of Holiness (Lev. 17–26)—and in the preexilic prophets. The prophets' emphasis seems to presuppose the legal traditions. Some relevant passages are:

> You shall not afflict any widow or orphan. (Ex. 22:22 [Heb 22:21])

> You shall not pervert the justice due your poor in his [her] suit. (Ex. 23:6)

> You shall not deprive the justice due to the sojourners and orphan and you shall not confiscate the widow's garment in pledge. (Deut. 24:17)

Sojourners, orphans, and widows needed special protection because of their unfortunate position of being outside their kinship or community groups. As long as one was part of the community, one could enjoy security and protection (von Waldow 1970:186). The widow lost the ties of her own family after her marriage and, then, the ties of her husband's family after the death of her husband. Even though she could possibly return to her family, she was very vulnerable to exclusion. The children derived their kinship rights through their father. If, after the father's death, the widow decided to return to her family, the children would have been considered as "outsiders as their kinship was different" (von Waldow 1970:187). Hence, they needed special protection. The depravity of the officials is seen in their willingness to victimize the very groups that they were supposed to protect. It is noteworthy that verse 3b refers to the wealth they have acquired through their venality. The prophet proclaims that they will not escape the curse of punishment.

Micah 3:1–4, 9–12

1 And I said, Hear, O leaders of Jacob
   and judges of the house of Israel!
   Is it not for you to know justice?
2 You who hate good and love wickedness,
   who tear away their skin from upon them,
   and their flesh from upon their bones;
3 and who devour the flesh of my people,
   and strip their skin from upon them,
   and break their bones,
   and spread them in a pot like flesh in a cauldron.
4 Then they will cry to Yahweh,
   but he will not answer them;
   he will hide his face from them at that time,
   because they have made their deeds wicked.

9 Hear this, you heads of the house of Jacob
   and judges of the house of Israel,
   who detest justice and pervert every thing that is right;
10 who build Zion with blood
   and Jerusalem with violence.

11 Its leaders give judgment for a bribe
and its priests teach for a price,
its prophets practice divination for money;
yet they lean on Yahweh saying:
"Is not Yahweh in our midst?
Evil shall not befall us."
12 Therefore, on account of you Zion shall be plowed into a field,
and Jerusalem shall become a planting ground,
and the mountain of the house, woodland for cattle.

Micah 3:1–4 and 9–12 are taken together because of the similarity of content. This passage unquestionably comes from Micah (Fohrer 1968:444; Hillers 1984:42–48; Kaiser 1975:228; Lescow 1972:50–52; Mays 1976:21; Stansell 1988:101ff; Wolff 1990:95–97). Both the oracles begin with the same formula. They are addressed to the leaders ("heads") of Jacob and judges of the house of Israel. The category of people addressed here is public officials. The king appointed these officials (Mays 1976:78). The word translated as judge appears in the premonarchic Israelite setting for military leaders (Josh. 10:24; Judg. 11:6, 11). In the eighth century, Isaiah (1:10; 3:6, 7; 22:3) and Micah (3:1, 9) used it to refer to officials in Jerusalem. The precise nature of their office is not known. References to dispensation of justice in both the passages indicate that the targets of Micah's attack are the judicial officials.

Micah juxtaposes the responsibility of the judges and their actual conduct. The judges' responsibility was to be knowledgeable in the norms of justice and to enforce them. But, in reality, their conduct did not reflect an awareness of that responsibility. Bribery and the resultant partiality led them to "hate good and love wickedness." They upheld the claims of the oppressors, that is, the landed elite. Consequently, the just claims of the powerless peasants fell by the wayside. Under the coercive influence of the rich, the judges became instruments of oppression and injustice.

Micah 3:1–4 and 9–12 clearly focus on the role of the judicial courts in the foreclosure of the peasants' lands. The primary concern is with establishing justice (*mishpat*) evident from the repeated references to justice in verses 1b and 9b (Stansell 1988:104–5). The perversion of justice that Micah condemns is the court officials' practice of upholding the illegal claims of the elite by taking away the land from the peasants. The courts were the places where the important issues relating to land were decided. But, because of the venality of the rich, the judges have become instruments of legitimizing corrupt practices. The deprivation of the peasantry by the rich landlords is portrayed through gruesome cannibalistic metaphors. The intensity of the suffering inflicted upon the poor is felt from the skin down to the bones. The imagery starts with the tearing off of the skin, then the flesh is devoured, and the butchery finally ends with the breaking of the bones. Interestingly, in verse 2b, the verb used for tearing away the skin (*gzl*) appears in some key passages where the object is the land (Wolff 1990:99). The metaphors used in this section seek to expose the economic and legal oppression of the powerless peasants. The basic thrust of the description is to convey that these economic and legal injustices struck at the very existence of the peasants. The confiscation of their land was as good as devouring them physically, because it took away the source of sustenance, livelihood, and residence from the peasants. No other eighth-century prophet speaks with such passion and vehemence.

Verse 4 announces the punishment. In an ironic fashion, Micah reverses the situation so that the guilty will be the sufferers crying to Yahweh in anguish. As is often the case with the announcement of punishment, the description of the punishment corresponds to the crime. Since Yahweh will not listen to their cries, "those who prey upon the helplessness of others will themselves know the terror of being helpless" (Mays 1976:80).

Micah 3:9–12 continues the theme of perversion of justice. As in the case of 3:1–4, first the general nature of the crime is stated, followed by a description of the specific deeds. This time the accusations are directed, not just against the judges, but also against the priests and prophets. The crime of the leaders was the rejection of *mishpat*, that is, the established values and norms safeguarding the rights and interests of the innocent in the legal context. The officials willfully deviated from the established norms of justice.

The inhumanity and severity of the oppression are described by references to bloodshed and violence. Could it be that Micah is referring to the pattern of building large estates as witnessed in the story of Naboth's vineyard in 1 Kings 21 (Mays 1976:88)? In a more general sense, these verses reflect the adverse effects of the growth of the urban centers at the expense of the agricultural periphery. The agricultural surplus was the major source of revenue for the urban centers. In a more specific sense, the building of Jerusalem might have reference to vast building projects and other fortification systems under the royal directive. The peasants supplied the labor force for these royal undertakings. In this sense, the city was built with the sweat and blood of the peasants.

In verse 11, Micah specifies some of the charges. He lists three groups of people for accusation: the judges, the priests, and the prophets. The commonality of the charges is that they have become manipulable through monetary incentives in their respective offices. The prediction of punishment is given in verse 12. Here, "therefore" marks the transition. The source or agent of punishment is not specified. But, the nature of the punishment is spelled out. It envisions a situation when there will no longer be a city on Zion. The trappings of urban life will disappear. In its place, the land will revert to agriculture. This is conveyed in three images. The first image is in terms of plowing a field. The second one is usually translated that Jerusalem shall become a "heap of ruins," but this interpretation does not seem likely. The same word occurs in Micah 1:6 with a different meaning. There, it is mentioned that Samaria will be made into a place for planting vineyards. It could, then, refer to places designated for growing vines. It is clear that the change is envisioned in terms of conversion to agriculture for a place that flourished as an urban center. The third image evokes the picture of pastoral economy. "The mountain of the house [of Yahweh shall become a] woodland for cattle," reading *behemot* instead of *bamot*. This is analogous to the occurrence of the same combination in Micah 5:8 [Heb. 5:7]. The punishment is predicted in terms of a radical liquidation of the urban characteristics and the installation of a rural setting in its place.

Isaiah 5:21

> Woe to those who are shrewd in their own eyes,
> and smart in their own estimation.

Along with the other five woe oracles in Isaiah 5, this one also comes from Isaiah. It is not explicit what group of people is addressed here. There are two possibilities. It could be the leaders in general. Interestingly, the combination of "wise/shrewd" and "discerning/smart" also occurs in Deuteronomy 1:13, 15 in the context of specifying what kind of people to choose as leaders. In a more specific sense, it could refer to the officials of the legal courts. The placement of this verse between two oracles (vv. 20 and 22–23) that clearly deal with the crimes of the judiciary officials suggests this possibility.

The cleverness and skill of the leaders could be seen in their ability to manipulate the legal system to their own ends. They probably took pride in their smartness in outwitting the common people and the system. Their smartness lay, not just in outwitting the peasants, but also in making the whole process look legal. They were shrewd in the sense that they knew ways to accomplish things that benefited them. But the prophet condemns this kind of smartness and shrewdness, because it brought misery to many.

Isaiah 29:20–21

20 The terrorizing one will cease to be,
    and the prattler will be finished;
    and all those who are watchful to do evil shall be cut off:
21 those who bring people into condemnation by word,
    and lure the one, who judges in the gate,
    and thrust aside the one who is in the right, with
    fabricated argument.

Isaiah 29:17–24 form a unit. This unit stands in sharp contrast to the threats in verses 1–16. Verses 17–24 project a picture of assurance and hope associated here with the age to come. The presence of apocalyptic motifs has led many scholars to reject the Isaianic origin of this section (Clements 1980:241; Kaiser 1974:279; Skinner 1915:236; Wildberger 1978:1137–38). It is not unequivocally clear that the passage comes from a later time, as it is normally assumed. The presence of a message of hope does not of necessity point to a late origin. The proclamation of regeneration and redress could be taken as integral to prophetic judgment. In fact, the drawbacks, inadequacies, and problems give rise to a picture of fulfillment and completion. The ideals of fulfillment represent the sum total of what is lacking in society and what needs to be set right.

In verse 20, the process of regeneration is seen in terms of the annihilation of the corrupt and evil leaders. The following verse expands on the nature of the offenses committed by these leaders. All three offenses mentioned in verse 21 relate to the wholesale suborning of the courts. Brueggemann's rendering—"those who cause a person to lose a lawsuit" (v. 21a)—gives specificity to the reference to condemnation by word (1998:237). Those who arbitrate "in the gate" are trapped with "lures," meaning bribes (v. 21b). The situation indicated here reflects the processes by which the legal system was manipulated for legitimizing the foreclosures of land. Debt instrument was a major means of foreclosing upon the lands of the small peasants. The ruthless landed elite brought the common folk under condemnation by the influence of their word. This was accomplished by alluring the judges with bribery. The judges, thus obligated to the elite, lent legal sanction to the illegal practices. With the judges under their thumb, the ruling elite managed to deprive the peasants of their rights with groundless argument. The key word in verse 21c should be translated as "groundless argument" (Köhler and Baumgartner 1951:1019). In other words, the whole case was fabricated against the peasants to victimize them.

Micah 7:2–3

2 The loyal ones have perished from the earth,
    and there is none among humans;
    all of them lie in wait for blood,
    and each one hunts for one's own kinsperson with a
        dragnet.
3 In doing evil their hands perform well;
    the official asks for the judgment with a bribe,
    and the rich one speaks his wish,
    and [thus] they fabricate/weave it.

A majority of scholars assign an exilic or postexilic dating for this oracle (Fohrer 1968:446; Kaiser 1975:253; Lescow 1972:205; Mays 1969b:150–52; Wolff 1990:204). Customarily, 7:1–6 is taken as a unit. Some leave open the possibility of Micah's authorship for 6:9–16 and 7:1–6 (Hillers 1984:85; Smith 1929:308; Smith, Ward, and Bewer 1911:15). The Mican authorship has also found some advocates (Marsh 1956:123–24; Wolfe 1956:899–900). Those who reject the authenticity of this passage often do so on the assumption that authentic Mican oracles are to be found only in the first three chapters. (This question has been addressed above in connection with Mic. 5:10–11.) Recognizing the limitation of this presupposition puts the question of dating in a different light. In the absence of clear pointers for dating, helpful clues may be sought in the content: Who is being addressed? What is the subject matter? What kind of systemic reality does the passage reflect? It is not assumed that these questions will provide the ultimate answers, but the responses may suggest one more avenue of approach into the past.

Earlier scholarship has not focused on verses 2–3. The systemic reality reflected here corresponds to that of the eighth century B.C.E. hypothesized in chapter 3 and tested against numerous oracles belonging to the eighth century in the earlier part of this chapter. The situation mentioned here matches the ruthless and unscrupulous acts of the members of the upper echelons against the peasant population. The officials design to take advantage of the poor. Verse 3 draws attention to the role of the ruling elite in perverting justice by buying out the judges with bribes. The elites have become adept at doing this. They ask for a favorable verdict with a bribe. The Masoretic text as it stands is difficult to interpret. Verse 3 is emended to read: "the official asks for the judgment [i.e., the judgment that will suit their purpose] with a bribe." The combination of *sh'l mishpat* ("ask for judgment") is attested elsewhere in Numbers 27:21 where Eleazer's function is described as inquiring *(sh'l)* for Joshua the verdict *(mishpat)* of Urim. This is contrasted to the monetary benefit offered to the judge for rendering a favorable verdict. *Haggadol* here stands for the rich. Second Kings 4:8 and 10:6 offer examples of similar usage. *Haggadol* stands as a parallel to the officials. Both clauses serve to reinforce the idea that the members of the ruling class sought to carry out their desire. They managed to fabricate their case against the poor. On the basis of this, it is possible to argue that the text describes deliberate tampering with the legal system by the upper class for the purpose of executing their covetous desires. Without belaboring the point, it must be observed that the legal courts have become instruments in the hands of the elite to lend a touch of legitimacy to their oppressive measures. This has reference to the suborning of the courts to legitimize land foreclosures resulting from debt.

5

Conclusion

What is the relevance and significance of the eighth-century prophetic message for our times? How can the message of the eighth-century prophets, spoken in an agrarian context, be relevant to our computer generation? What can we possibly learn from their ministry and message? Even though the questions seem formidable, there are meaningful ways of addressing them.

First, the growth of large estates, which forms a key concern in the eighth-century prophets, is not such a strange phenomenon. The disappearance of small family farms in the U.S.A. in the 1930s offers an interesting parallel. The large-scale mechanization of the farms and the cost involved drove many small family-owned operations out of business.

Second, the more fundamental issue raised by the prophets is this: Who has access to the economic base? The basic concern that prompted the prophets to address the question of land ownership and distribution was the realization that not everyone had just and equitable access to the economic base. This is a question that can be raised in any society, irrespective of time and place. Who has access to the economic base? For the ancient Israelites, land constituted the primary economic base. For our society (or societies), the primary economic base may be something else. Not only is it important to ascertain what the primary economic base is, but, also, who has access to that. Better yet, does everyone in a society have just and equitable access to the economic base? This is a justice question. The eighth-century prophets' assessment of their societies clearly showed them there was no justice in the situation. They readily recognized the lopsided nature of the situation.

In this connection, it is relevant to take note of the discussion revolving around the concept of the peasantry. Just as one might question the relevance of the prophetic message from an agrarian context for our time and society, the usefulness of the concept of peasantry itself has been challenged within the field of social sciences. The lack of precision, the persistence of opposing models, and the changing reality of our times have led some to question the wisdom of continuing to use the concept of peasantry. The persistence of opposing models alone cannot warrant abandoning the concept. On the contrary, opposing views and proposals can lead to more realistic and sophisticated analysis. Peasantry represents a reality that is complex and has important historical connotations (Shanin 1987:473). It is by no means extinct. Turning away from the study of peasants is tantamount to closing our eyes to oppression, injustice, and inequality. The analysis of peasants has a broader symbolic significance. The concept of peasantry serves to witness to a particular configuration of social relations (Shanin 1987:474). In the struggle to better the human condition, the chances of change for the better depend on our commitment to discern and define the dimensions of oppression of humans by other humans. The study of peasantry has opened our eyes to these realities. It will continue to do so.

Third, one thing we learn from the prophets is that poverty or injustice is no accident. They knew exactly what the causes were and who was responsible for it. They did not speak in abstraction. They knew what the oppression/injustice was, and who the oppressors and oppressed were.

Fourth, just as modern formulations may be helpful in the analysis of the ancient societies, so also the understanding of the structures of the less complex societies may, in a reciprocal way, aid in clarifying the basic dynamics in modern situations.

Fifth, the systemic sociological analysis of the eighth-century social reality and the reflections of it in the prophetic literature retrieve for us an arena for encountering people, our predecessors, who embodied certain values and faith. This encounter allows us to discern from their accounts what is meaningful for our own existence.

Sixth, the prophets called for a liberated life, which was interpreted in relation to the socioeconomic, political, and cultural conditions of their time. In our own struggles for a fully liberated existence amidst our own circumstances, the prophetic call becomes central. The crucial factor here is the realization of the operational ties between our religious symbol system and the current forms of social struggle (Gottwald 1979:705). Any form of religious faith that fails to grasp this link is doomed to become an exercise in irrelevance. Forms of religious faith capable of grasping and acting on that link have something to contribute in the long struggle for human liberation. And in commitment to that purpose, we will always have something to learn and relearn from the message and ministry of the eighth-century prophets.

Finally, the relevance of the prophetic message is very much linked to the unique function of prophetic imagination. Prophetic imagination/vision is an area of critical importance to a community of faith. One of the least trodden paths in the study of the prophets in the Hebrew Bible is examination of the nature and function of prophetic vision. The only work to address this issue with sustained effort and immediacy is by Brueggemann (1978). My comments here seek to further that investigation by focusing on the nature of prophetic visions and the way they function in society. This can be fruitful both for understanding the prophets in the Hebrew Bible and for contemporary theological thinking. Part of the problem in relation to the secondary literature pertaining to the prophets is the undue emphasis on the ethical dimension. The Hebrew prophets as "moralists" and "champions of ethical conduct" are some of the common characterizations with which readers in prophetic studies are all too familiar. Some of these earlier characterizations have had a lasting impact on later scholarship. This does not do justice to the richness and complexity of the nature and function of prophetic vision. One needs to become alert to the nuances and subtleties of the prophetic vision. A better appreciation is possible only through an understanding of the nature of visions.

In essence, vision can be defined as the ability to see things that are invisible. Even though the present study will not confine itself to a single-criterion definition, the description mentioned above is a good starting point. A more useful approach will be to explore the nature of visions in its multiple facets. The nature of visions will be explored using the following aspects:

1. Diagnostic
2. Prospective
3. Individual and Collective
4. Integrative

Diagnostic

Visions are diagnostic in the sense that they reveal the contradictions between what is and what ought to be. Fantasies try to escape contradictions, disjunctions, and disorientations in life. Visions do not. In fact, visions arise out of a full awareness of the contradictions that disorient life. They are born out of the painful experience of seeing disorientation and contradiction. That is a judgment on reality/history. Visions embody the ideal set of norms and relations that act as the basis of this critique. If visions perceive the gulf between "what is" and "what ought to be," the basis for that judgment is the awareness of the disorientation, which in turn sets forth the ideal. The ideal, in turn, begins to impinge on the current reality. Many examples can be cited from the oracles of the Hebrew prophets. A major portion of the prophetic utterances from the preexilic period are diagnostic in character. They clearly laid out the maladies that afflicted their society. But the basis of their critique was the vision of what things ought to be, which in turn was drawn from the values and norms of the premonarchic society. The premonarchic society becomes so central because of some bold and radical experiments undertaken by that community. A full-length discussion of this important period is beyond the scope of this work. For a detailed and systematic treatment of this subject the reader is directed to the works of Gottwald (1979) and Chaney (1983). The prophets may not offer a blueprint for the better society to come. But they certainly have a vision of how things ought to be.

In a sense, visions provide the basis for the alternative, the "ought-to-be." Sometimes, visions may be dismissed as utopian. The truth is visions are utopian. Even as the term suggests, *u-topia* means "no-place/nowhere." Obviously, it is not here. This u-topia or no-place puts our system at a distance. A vision removes us from our cultural system to a distance from where we can see our systems critically. It enables us to distance ourselves from reality so that we can begin to perceive alternative ways of living. The world of possibilities is opened up. Alternatives to the present system and orderings are unfolded. These alternatives would be at odds with the current form of living. Visions, thus, preserve the contradiction between what is and what ought to be. Those who dismiss visions as utopian often do so on the grounds that visions are not realizable. Clearly, this viewpoint arises out of a misunderstanding of the nature and function of visions. The most essential characteristic of vision is not its realizable potential but its preservation of opposition.

The preservation of opposition in the form of alternatives is necessary for various reasons. First of all, by perceiving self and society in alternative ways, the impermanent and mutable character of the present reality is exposed. Nothing remains forever. The present order cannot be taken as immutable and beyond reproach. Second, the preservation of opposition is absolutely essential for fighting the psychological battle with regard to change. The first and most important battle to be won is overcoming the psychological resistance to change. If changes have to be effected, breaches have to be made in the incrustations of fear, inertia, indifference, ignorance, or despair that insulate the psyche of the people and prevent them from responding to change. These incrustations have been built up over a period of time and have become like fossils. This psychological colonization of the people is where the battle begins first. Visions initiate this process.

Prospective

The prophetic vision, by exposing the structure of what is, suggests in subtle ways what is to come. These are tentative suggestions at best. One cannot expect to find blueprints for programs and action. Given the nature of visions, only hints are possible. The ability to see breakthroughs is the function of imagination. It is the imagining of "something else" or "elsewhere." We are loosened from our current systems and perceptions. We are forced out of the narrow confines of our cultural systems, orders, and mindsets to look toward a beyond. There is power in visions. Through visions, alternative ways of perceiving and living are created. When we are caught up in the maze of intricate realities of life, it is hard to perceive clearly. We become creatures of habit. Creative imagination can disconnect us from this stupor. It can break the vicious cycle. It can provide the necessary jolt "to snap out of it."

Individual and Collective

There is both an individual and a collective dimension to vision. Visions are basically conceived in an individual's mind. They are essentially the products of an individual's imagination. But these individuals' visions have their roots in common experience, inherited concepts, images, language, belief systems, and world. At the experiential level, visions share in the collective experience of crisis, disjunction, and discontinuity. Not that experience is perceived alike by everybody collectively (although this factor will be important for the success of the movement toward transformation), but the individual sees the crisis as widespread and pervasive. The outward reality of disjunction and brokenness begins to impinge on the individual psyche so strongly that he/she begins to seek ways of resolving the crisis. The contradictions become so pronounced that the individual is driven in search of wholeness. The quest for individual wholeness leads invariably to a social vision. The bottom line is that if we do not let contradictions and brokenness vex us or bother us or affect us deeply, there can never be visions. In a fundamental way, "vision is the embodied nexus of the particular human being and his [sic] social matrix" (Wilner 1975:2). Visions arise in response to the experience of dislocation and disjunction.

In another sense, visions are collective and individual. First, it is the collective experience of dissonance that is perceived and addressed by the individual. Second, the tools of perception are collective in nature as well. At the level of both perception and articulation, an individual has to use conceptual and linguistic categories that are, in fact, drawn from collective heritage. The stimulus for the vision comes out of the experience of contradictions perceived as affecting larger entities. But the tools of perception have their origin in images, categories, language, values, and belief systems collectively inherited and shared. There is no such thing as "raw" experience. Even in order to perceive an experience as "experience," one needs these inherited tools. Strangely, these tools themselves may become the means for the breakthrough. This is yet another way the collective impinges on the individual. Third, visions are conceived in an individual's mind. But for transformation to take place, they will have to be embraced by the larger community. The feeling of crisis and dislocation and the search for wholeness that have prompted the visions will have to become pervasive. They will have to become widespread. The larger community will have to embrace this feeling collectively. Visions, for their part, are intended to liberate the suppressed feelings–to cut through layers of numbness to expose the nerve endings to feel the pain readily. Herein may lie a crucial distinction of being a prophet. If only a few individuals articulate the experience of dislocation, they may be characterized as "visionaries," or worse, "crazy ones." But if the feeling that the present reality is oppressive and disoriented is made widespread, the visionary assumes the mantle of the prophet (Wilner 1975:8). One may wonder, how can the vision of one person move many people in their depths? The answer to that is in the charisma of the prophet, in its fundamental sense. As Weston LaBarre explains, "charisma is only the shared unconscious wishes and symbiotic thought-paradigms in leader and communicants" (LaBarre 1970:48). In other words, like a magnet, the prophet draws out forces and feelings felt before but not expressed. The dislocated people, a people without a center, find in the prophet's vision a new center (a relocation) that gathers around it the individual members of the community in an unbroken circle of belief (Wilner 1975:38). Individuals dream dreams and see visions, but, in the final analysis, it is the response of the collective that defines the prophet.

Integrative

One other aspect of visionary imagination is its integrative capacity. The human mind seems to be capable of tremendous synthesizing power with its ability to combine and recombine experience, perceptions, and images into new patterns and new paradigms. In this way, the mind does not simply reflect or repeat what it perceives in reality as experience. It can produce new combinations and syntheses. Therein lies the power of the human imagination to create alternatives. A situation may appear hopeless and conflicts irreconcilable. But the power of the human mind can generate new visions and syntheses. In fact, visions are produced out of situations of deep crisis. Not every change produces such a response but only changes that affect in such a way that the center cannot hold together. Experiences of dis-location, dis-orientation, and dis-junction threaten human existence in a fundamental way because there is no center/location–no point of focus, no point of cohesion– that can hold things together. Under such circumstances, it seems as if the automatic mechanism of the human mind produces the response of an integrative function. The deeper and more acute the crisis, the bolder the visions. Some of the boldest visions have come precisely amidst conditions of seemingly utter hopelessness. Classic examples are in abundance in the prophecies of Second Isaiah. More than the content or style of these prophecies, what is even more impressive is the very context in which they were spoken. The exuberant oracles of redemption were spoken to a mixed audience, a majority of whom were either utterly hopeless about the situation of exile, or were those who had found their niche in foreign culture and therefore could not care less. Sometimes even good news is hard to preach. But this did not deter the poetic vision of Second Isaiah. Instead, public resistence intensified the poetry of prophecy. The deeper the crisis, the bolder the vision. The life-affirming force within the human psyche seems greater than we realize. Not every mind responds the same way. Otherwise we might have countless visionaries competing for attention. In all societies, there are certain types of people for whom the experiences of disunity, dislocation, and disorientation are very painful and who, therefore, need to struggle through them to new forms of synthesis. This "po(e)tential" is probably in everyone but is more acute in some than in others (Wilner 1975:140). The quest for individual wholeness leads to a vision that has consequences for the collective. Thus, visions may be embraced by the larger community even though they are the products of an individual mind. However, in the very act of being embraced, visions can be altered as well. That is the constant challenge. Visions never settle for the "given." They always prompt us to see things in a new configuration, or a new combination of relationships, or new patterns of alignments. Out of this process emerge new possibilities, possibilities we thought never existed before—the invisible.

Bibliography

Aharoni, Yohanan
—— 1958 "The Negev of Judah." *Israel Exploration Journal* 8:26–38.
—— 1967 "Forerunners of the Limes: Iron Age Fortresses in the Negev." *Israel Exploration Journal* 17:1–17.
—— 1972 "The Stratification of Israelite Megiddo." *Journal of Near Eastern Studies* 31:302–11.
—— 1973 *Beer-Sheba I. Excavations at Tell Beer-Sheba 1969–1971.* Tel Aviv: Tel Aviv University, Institute of Archaeology.
—— 1975 *Investigations at Lachish: The Sanctuary and the Residency (Lachish V).* Publications of the Institute of Archaeology, no. 4. Tel Aviv: Gateway.
—— 1979a *The Land of the Bible: A Historical Geography.* 2d ed. Translated by A. F. Rainey. Philadelphia: Westminster Press.
—— 1979b "The Negev and the Southern Borders," in *The Age of Monarchies: Political History.* Edited by A. Malamat. Vol. 4:1, 290–307, of *The World History of the Jewish People,* edited by B. Mazar. Jerusalem: Masada Press.
—— 1982 *The Archaeology of the Land of Israel.* Translated by A. F. Rainey. Philadelphia: Westminster Press.
Aharoni, Yohanan, and Ruth Amiran
—— 1964 "Excavations at Tell Arad." *Israel Exploration Journal* 14:131–47.
Aharoni, Yohanan, and Michael Avi-Yonah
—— 1981 *The Macmillan Bible Atlas.* Revised ed. New York: Macmillan.
Aharoni, Yohanan, M. Evenari, L. Shanan, and N. H. Tadmor
—— 1960 "The Ancient Desert Agriculture of the Negev. An Agricultural Settlement at Ramat Matred." *Israel Exploration Journal* 10:23–35, 97–111.
Ahlström, Gösta W.
—— 1978 "Wine Presses and Cup-Marks of the Jenin-Megiddo Survey." *Bulletin of the American Schools of Oriental Research* 231:19–49.
—— 1993 *The History of Ancient Palestine from the Paleolithic Period to Alexander's Conquest.* JSOT Supplement, no. 146; Sheffield: Sheffield Academic Press.
Alavi, Hamza
—— 1965 "Peasants and Revolution," in *The Socialist Register.* Edited by Ralph Miliband and John Saville. London: Merlin Press.

Albright, William F.

—— 1925 "The Administrative Divisions of Israel and Judah." *Journal of Palestine Oriental Society* 5:17–54.

—— 1935 "Archaeology and the Date of the Hebrew Conquest of Palestine." *Bulletin of the American Schools of Oriental Research* 58:10–18.

—— 1939 "The Israelite Conquest of Canaan in the Light of Archaeology." *Bulletin of the American Schools of Oriental Research* 74:11–23.

—— 1943 *The Excavation of Tell Beit Mirsim. Vol. 3: The Iron Age. Annual of the American Schools of Oriental Research* 21–22. New Haven: American Schools of Oriental Research.

—— 1957 *From Stone Age to Christianity.* 2d ed. Baltimore: Johns Hopkins Press.

—— 1960 *The Archaeology of Palestine.* Revised ed. Baltimore: Penguin.

—— 1963 *The Biblical Period from Abraham to Ezra: A Historical Survey.* New York: Harper & Row.

Alt, Albrecht

—— 1953 "Meros," in *Kleine Schriften zur Geschichte des Volkes Israel,* Vol. 1, 274–277. Munich: C. H. Beck'sche.

—— 1959 "Micha 2,1–5," in *Kleine Schriften zur Geschichte des Volkes Israel,* Vol. 3, 373–381. Munich: C. H. Beck'sche. First published 1955 in *Interpretationes ad Vetus Testamentum pertinentes Sigmundo Mowinckel septuagenario missae.* Ed. Nils Alstrup Dahl and Arvid Schou Kapelrud. 13–23. Oslo: Forlaget Land og Kirke.

—— 1966 "The Settlement of the Israelites in Palestine," in *Essays in Old Testament History and Religion.* Translated by R. A. Wilson. 135–69. Oxford: Blackwell.

Andersen, Francis I., and David Noel Freedman

—— 1980 *Hosea: A New Translation with an Introduction and Commentary. The Anchor Bible,* vol. 24. Garden City, N.Y.: Doubleday.

—— 1989 *Amos: A New Translation with an Introduction and Commentary. The Anchor Bible,* vol. 24A. New York: Doubleday.

Andreason, Niels E.

—— 1981 "Town and Country in the Old Testament." *Encounter* 42:259–75.

Ap-Thomas, Daffyd R.

—— 1970 "All the King's Horses?" in *Proclamation and Presence: Old Testament Essays in Honor of G. H. Davies.* Edited by J. I. Durham and J. R. Porter. 135–51. Richmond, Va.: John Knox Press.

Archer, Gleason L.

—— 1970 "Old Testament History and Recent Archaeology from Solomon to Zedekiah." *Bibliotheca Sacra* 127:195–211.

Arieti, James A.
—— 1974 "The Vocabulary of Septuagint Amos." *Journal of Biblical Literature* 93:338–47.
Astour, Michael C.
—— 1971 "841 BC: The First Assyrian Invasion of Israel." *Journal of American Oriental Society* 91:383–89.
—— 1979 "The Arena of Tiglath-Pileser III's Campaign against Sarduri II (743 BC)." *Assur* 2:69–71.
Auld, A. Graeme
—— 1980 "Poetry, Prophecy, Hermeneutic: Recent Studies in Isaiah." *Scottish Journal of Theology* 33:567–81.
—— 1986 *Amos*. Sheffield: JSOT Press.
Avigad, Nahman
—— 1961 "The Jotham Seal from Elath." *Bulletin of the American Schools of Oriental Research* 163:18–22.
—— 1966 "A Hebrew Seal with a Family Emblem." *Israel Exploration Journal* 16:50–53.
—— 1979 "The Hebrew Epigraphic Sources," in *The Age of Monarchies: Political History*. Edited by A. Malamat. Vol. 4:1, 20–43, of *The World History of Jewish People*, edited by B. Mazar. Jerusalem: Masada Press.
—— 1982 "A Hebrew Seal Depicting a Sailing Ship." *Bulletin of the American Schools of Oriental Research* 246:59–61.
Avi-Yonah, Michael, and Ephraim Stern, eds.
—— 1975 *Encyclopedia of Archaeological Excavations in the Holy Land*. Vols. 1–4. Jerusalem: Israel Exploration Society and Masada Press.
Bagnall, Roger
—— 1976 *Administration of the Ptolemaic Possessions outside Egypt*. Columbia Studies in the Classical Tradition, vol. 4. Leiden: Brill.
Baly, Dennis
—— 1963 *Geographical Companion to the Bible*. London: Lutterworth.
—— 1974 *The Geography of the Bible*. 2d. ed. New York: Harper & Row.
Barag, Dan
—— 1963 "Survey Pottery Recovered from the Sea off the Coast of Israel." *Israel Exploration Journal* 13:13–19.
Bardtke, Hans
—— 1971 "Die Latifundien in Juda während der zweiten Hälfte des acten Jahrhunderts v. Chr. (Zum Verständnis von Jes. 5, 8–10)," in *Hommages à André Dupont-Sommer* 235–54. Paris: Adrien-Maisonneuve.
Barkay, Gabriel
—— 1992 "The Iron Age II–III," in *The Archaeology of Ancient Israel*. Edited by Amnon Ben-Tor. 302–73. New Haven: Yale University Press.

Baron, Salo
—— 1958 *A Social and Religious History of the Jews*. Vol. 1. New York: Columbia University Press.
—— 1972 *Ancient and Medieval Jewish History*. New Brunswick, N.J.: Rutgers.
Barré, Michael L.
—— 1978 "New Light on the Interpretation of Hosea VI: 2." *Vetus Testamentum* 28:129–41.
Barth, Hermann
—— 1977 *Die Jesaja-Worte in der Josiazeit*. Wissenschaftliche Monographien zum Alten und Neuen Testament, no. 48. Neukirchen-Vluyn: Neukirchner Verlag.
Barton, John
—— 1995 *Isaiah 1–39*. Sheffield: Sheffield Academic Press.
Bates, Daniel G., and Amal Rassam
—— 1983 *Peoples and Cultures of the Middle East*. Englewood Cliffs, N.J.: Prentice-Hall.
Bee, Ronald E.
—— 1979 "An Empirical Dating Procedure for Old Testament Prophecy." *Journal for the Study of Old Testament* 11:23–35.
Behrens, E. K.
—— 1983 "...Like those who remove the landmark (Hosea 5:10a)." *Studia Biblica et Theologia* 1:1–5.
Ben-Barak, Zafrira
—— 1981 "Meribaal and the System of Land Grants in Ancient Israel." *Biblica* 62:73–91.
Ben-Tor, Amnon
—— 1974 "Tell Qiri: A Look at Village Life." *Biblical Archaeologist* 42:105–13.
Berger, Peter L.
—— 1963 "Charisma and Religious Innovation: The Social Location of Israelite Prophecy." *American Sociological Review* 28:940–50.
Bergheim, Samuel
—— 1894 "Land Tenure in Palestine." *Palestine Exploration Quarterly* 26:191–99.
Bergmann, Theodor
—— 1977 "Agrarian Movements and their Context." *Sociologia Ruralis* 17:167–90.
Bess, Stephen
—— 1963 "System of Land Tenure in Ancient Israel." Ph.D. dissertation. University of Michigan.
Birch, Bruce
—— 1997 *Hosea, Joel and Amos*. Westminster Bible Companion. Louisville, Ky.: Westminster John Knox Press.

Blenkinsopp, Joseph
—— 1976 *Prophecy and Canon.* Notre Dame: University of Notre Dame Press.
—— 1981 "Fragments of ancient exegesis in an Isaian Poem (2:6–22)." *Zeitschrift für die Alttestamentliche Wissenschaft* 93:51–62.
—— 1996 *A History of Prophecy in Israel.* Revised ed. Louisville, Ky.: Westminster John Knox Press.
Bloch-Smith, Elizabeth
—— 1992 *Judahite Burial Practices and Beliefs about the Dead.* JSOT Supplement, no. 123. JSOT/ASOR Monograph, no. 7. Sheffield: JSOT Press.
Blum, Jerome
—— 1961 *Lord and Peasant in Russia from the Ninth to the Nineteenth Century.* Princeton: Princeton University Press.
Bobek, H.
—— 1962 "The Main Stages in Socioeconomic Evolution from a Geographical Point of View," in *Readings in Cultural Geography.* Edited by Philip L. Wagner and Marvin N. Mikesell. 218–47. Chicago: University of Chicago Press.
Bonte, Pierre
—— 1979 "Pastoral Production, Territorial Organization and Kinship in Segmentary Societies," in *Social and Ecological Systems.* Edited by P. C. Burnham and R. F. Ellen. 203–34. New York: Academic Press.
Borowski, Oded
—— 1979 "Agriculture in Iron Age Israel." Ph.D. diss., University of Michigan.
Bottomore, T. B.
—— 1975 *Sociology as Social Criticism.* New York: Pantheon Books.
Bright, John
—— 1981 *A History of Israel.* 3d ed. Philadelphia: Westminster Press.
Broshi, Magen
—— 1974 "The Expansion of Jerusalem in the Reigns of Hezekiah and Manasseh." *Israel Exploration Journal* 24:21–26.
Broshi, Magen, and Israel Finkelstein
—— 1992 "The Population of Palestine in Iron Age II." *Bulletin of the American Schools of Oriental Research* 287:47–60.
Brown, F., S. R. Driver, and C. A. Briggs
—— 1978 *A Hebrew and English Lexicon of the Old Testament.* Reprint of 1953 edition. Oxford: Clarendon Press.
Brueggemann, Walter
—— 1968 *Tradition for Crisis: A Study in Hosea.* Richmond, Va.: John Knox Press.
—— 1978 *The Prophetic Imagination.* Philadelphia: Fortress Press.

—— 1979 "Trajectories in Old Testament Literature and the Sociology of Ancient Israel." *Journal of Biblical Literature* 98:161–85.

—— 1980 "On Land-losing and Land-receiving." *Crux* 19:166–73.

—— 1981 "Vine and Fig Tree: A Case study in Imagination and Criticism." *Catholic Biblical Quarterly* 43:188–204.

—— 1998 *Isaiah*. Vol. 1. Louisville, Ky.: Westminster John Knox Press.

Bryant, David J.

—— 1978 "Micah 4:14–5:14: An Exegesis." *Restoration Quarterly* 21:210–30.

Buheiry, Marwan R.

—— 1981 "The Agricultural Exports of Southern Palestine." *Journal of Palestine Studies* 10:61–81.

Bürlow, S., and R. A. Mitchell

—— 1961 "An Iron Age II Fortress in Tell Nagila." *Israel Exploration Journal* 11:101–10.

Chaney, Marvin L.

—— 1973 "You shall not covet your neighbor's house." *Pacific Theological Review* 15:3–13.

—— 1983 "Ancient Palestinian Peasant Movements and the Formation of Premonarchic Israel," in *Palestine in Transition: The Emergence of Ancient Israel*. Edited by D. N. Freedman and D. F. Graf. 39–90. Social World of Biblical Antiquity Series, no. 2. Sheffield: Almond Press.

—— 1986 "Systemic Study of the Israelite Monarchy." *Semeia* 37:53–76.

—— 1989 "Bitter Bounty: The Dynamics of Political Economy Critiqued by the Eighth-century Prophets," in *Reformed Faith and Economics*. Edited by Robert L. Stivers. 15–30. Lanham, Md.: University Press of America.

—— 1993 "Agricultural Intensification as Promiscuity in the Book of Hosea." Paper presented at the Annual Meeting of the Society of Biblical Literature, Washington, D.C., 20–23 November.

Childe, V. Gordon

—— 1951 *Man Makes Himself*. New York: New American History.

—— 1964 *What Happened in History*. Baltimore: Penguin Books.

Childs, Brevard S.

—— 1967 *Isaiah and the Assyrian Crisis*. Naperville, Ill.: Alec R. Allenson.

Clements, Ronald E.

—— 1975 *Prophecy and Tradition*. Atlanta: John Knox Press.

—— 1980 *Isaiah 1–39*. New Century Bible Commentary. Grand Rapids, Mich.: William B. Eerdmans.

Cogan, Mordechai (Morton)

—— 1974 *Imperialism and Religion: Assyria, Judah and Israel in the Eighth and Seventh Centuries BC*. Society of Biblical Literature Dissertation Series, no. 19. Missoula, Mont.: Scholars Press.

Cohen, S.
—— 1962 "Transjordan," in *Interpreter's Dictionary of the Bible*. Edited by G. A. Buttrick. Vol. 4, 687–88. Nashville: Abingdon Press.
Coote, Robert B.
—— 1971 "Hosea XII." *Vetus Testamentum* 21:389–482.
—— 1974 "Hosea 14:8: They who are filled with grain shall live." *Journal of Biblical Literature* 93:161–73.
—— 1981 *Amos among the Prophets: Composition and Theology*. Philadelphia: Fortress.
Coote, Robert B., and Keith W. Whitelam
—— 1987 *The Emergence of Early Israel in Historical Perspective*. The Social World of Biblical Antiquity Series, no. 5. Sheffield: Almond Press.
Cross, Frank M.
—— 1962 "Epigraphic Notes on Hebrew Documents of the Eighth–Sixth Centuries BC. The Murabb'at Papyrus and the Letter found at Yabneh-Yam." *Bulletin of the American Schools of Oriental Research* 165:34–46.
—— 1964 "Judean Stamps." *Eretz Israel* 9:9–20.
—— 1975 "A Reconstruction of the Judean Restoration." *Journal of Biblical Literature* 94:4–18.
Cross, Frank M., and Joséf T. Milik
—— 1956 "Explorations in the Judean Buei'ah." *Bulletin of the American Schools of Oriental Research* 142:5–17.
Curwen, E. Cecil, and Gudmund Hatt, eds.
—— 1961 *Plough and Pasture: The Early History of Farming*. New York: Collier Books.
Dahood, Mitchell J.
—— 1971 "Additional Notes on the *Mrzh* Text," in *The Claremont Ras Shamra Tablets*. Edited by Loren Fisher. 51–54. Rome: Pontifical Biblical Institute.
Dalman, Gustaf
—— 1964 *Arbeit und Sitte in Palästina*. Vol. 5. Darmstadt: G. Olms.
Dalton, George
—— 1972 "Peasantries in Anthropology and History." *Current Anthropology* 13:385–415.
Davies, Eryl W.
—— 1981 "Inheritance Rights and the Hebrew Levirate Marriage." *Vetus Testamentum* 31:138–44.
Davies, Graham I.
—— 1993 *Hosea*. Old Testament Guides. Sheffield: JSOT Press.
Davies, Philip R.
—— 1995 *In Search of "Ancient Israel."* JSOT Supplement Series, no. 148. Sheffield: Sheffield Academic Press.

Dearman, John A.
—— 1988 *Property Rights in the Eighth Century Prophets: The Conflict and Its Background.* Society of Biblical Literature Dissertation Series, no. 106. Atlanta: Scholars Press.

Dever, William G.
—— 1995 "Social Structure in Palestine in the Iron II Period on the Eve of Destruction," in *The Archaeology of Society in the Holy Land.* Edited by Thomas E. Levy. 416–30. New York: Facts on File Books.

Diakonoff, Igor M.
—— 1973 *Ancient Mesopotamia: Socio-Economic History.* Wiesbaden: Martin Sändig oHG.
—— 1975 "The Rural Community in the Ancient Near East." *Journal of the Economic and Social History of the Orient* 17:121–33.

Diaz, May N.
—— 1967 "Economic Relations in Peasant Society," in *Peasant Society: A Reader.* Edited by Jack M. Potter, May N. Diaz, and George M. Foster. 50–56. Boston: Little Brown & Co.

Diringer, D.
—— 1949 "The Royal Jar-handle Stamps of Ancient Judah." *Biblical Archaeologist* 12:70–86.

Donner, Herbert
—— 1977 "Separate States of Israel and Judah," in *Israelite and Judean History.* Edited by J.H. Hayes and J. M. Miller. 281–421. Philadelphia: Westminster Press.

Dorner, Peter
—— 1971 *Institutions in Agricultural Development.* Ames, Iowa: Iowa State University Press.

Dothan, Moshe
—— 1959 "Tell Mor (Tell Kheidar)." *Israel Exploration Journal* 9:271–72.
—— 1965 "The Fortress at Kadesh-Barnea." *Israel Exploration Journal* 15:134–51.
—— 1967 "Ashdod: A City of the Philistine Pentapolis." *Archaeology* 20:178–86.

Dothan, Trude
—— 1982 *The Philistines and Their Material Culture.* Jerusalem: Israel Exploration Society.

Driver, Godfrey R.
—— 1937 "Linguistic and Textual Problems: Isaiah I–XXXIX." *Journal of Theological Studies* 38:36–50.
—— 1938 "Linguistic and Textual Problems: Minor Prophets." *Journal of Theological Studies* 39:154–66, 260–73, 393–405.
—— 1956 *Canaanite Myths and Legends.* Edinburgh: T & T Clark.

Driver, Samuel R.
—— 1915 *The Books of Joel and Amos.* The Cambridge Bible. 2d ed. London: Cambridge University Press.

Duhm, Bernhard
—— 1911 "Anmerkungen zu den zwölf kleinen Propheten." *Zeitschrift für die Alttestamentliche Wissenschaft* 31:1–43, 81–110.
—— 1922 *Das Buch Jesaja.* Handkommentar zum AltenTestament. Göttingen: Vandenhoeck & Ruprecht.
Dybdahl, John L.
—— 1981 "Israelite Village Land Tenure: Settlement to Exile." Ph.D. diss., Fuller Theological Seminary.
Edelstein, Gershon, and Mordecai Kislev
—— 1981 "Mevasseret Yerushalayim: The Ancient Settlement and its Agricultural Terraces." *Biblical Archaeologist* 44:53–56.
Eisenstadt, Shmuel N.
—— 1969 *The Political Systems of Empires: The Rise and Fall of the Bureaucratic Empires.* New York: Free Press.
Eitam, David
—— 1979 "Olive Presses of the Israelite Period." *Tel Aviv* 6:146–55.
Elat, Moshe
—— 1978 "The Economic Relations of the Neo-Assyrian Empire with Egypt." *Journal of American Oriental Society* 98:20–34.
—— 1979a "Trade and Commerce," in *The Age of Monarchies: Culture and Society.* Edited by Abraham Malamat. Vol. 4:2, 173–86, of *The World History of the Jewish People*, edited by B. Mazar. Jerusalem: Masada Press.
—— 1979b "The Monarchy and the Development of Trade in Ancient Israel," in *State and Temple Economy in the Ancient Israel.* Edited by Edward Lipinski. Vol. 2, 528–46. Leuven: Departement Oriëntalistiesk.
Ellis, Maria DeJong
—— 1974 "Taxation in Ancient Mesopotamia: The History of the Term *Miksu.*" *Journal of Cuneiform Studies* 26:211–50.
Emerton, John A.
—— 1980 "Notes on the Text and Translation of Is. 22:8–11 and 65:5." *Vetus Testamentum* 30:437–51.
Erlandsson, Seth
—— 1970 *The Burden of Babylon. A Study of Isaiah 13:2–14.* Coniectanea Biblica, Old Testament Series, no. 4. Lund: Gleerup.
Evenari, Michael, Yohanan Aharoni, Leslie Shanan, and Naphtali Tadmor
—— 1958 "The Ancient Desert Agriculture of the Negev. III, Early Beginnings." *Israel Exploration Journal* 8:231–68.
Fallers, Lloyd A.
—— 1961 "Are African Cultivators to Be Called 'Peasants'?" *Current Anthropology* 2:108–10. Repr. 1967 in *Peasant Society: A Reader.* Edited by Jack M. Potter, May N. Diaz, and George M. Foster, 50–56. Boston: Little Brown & Co.

Feder, Ernest
—— 1971 *The Rape of the Peasantry: Latin America's Landholding System.* New York: Anchor Books, Doubleday.
Fenton, J.
—— 1877 "The Primitive Hebrew Land Tenure." *London Theological Review* 14:489–503.
Finley, Moses I.
—— 1974 *Studies in Ancient Society.* New York: Routledge.
—— 1980 *Ancient Slavery and Modern Ideology.* London: Chatto & Windus.
—— 1985 *The Ancient Economy.* London: Chatto & Windus.
Flanagan, James W.
—— 1981 "Chiefs in Israel." *Journal for the Study of Old Testament* 20:47–73.
Fohrer, Georg
—— 1960–61 "The Origin, Composition and Tradition of Isaiah I–XXXIX." *Annual of the Leeds University Oriental Society* 3:3–38.
—— 1968 *Introduction to the Old Testament.* Translated by David E. Green. Nashville: Abingdon Press.
Forbes, Robert J.
—— 1964 *Studies in Ancient Technology.* Vol. VIII. Leiden: Brill.
—— 1972 *Studies in Ancient Technology.* Vol. IX. 2d ed. Leiden: Brill.
Forde, C. Daryll, and M. Douglas
—— 1967 "Primitive Economies," in *Tribal and Peasant Economies.* Edited by G. Dalton. 13–28. New York: The Natural History Press.
Forman, Shepard
—— 1975 *The Brazilian Peasantry.* New York: Columbia University Press.
Foster, George M.
—— 1967 "Introduction: What is a Peasant?" in *Peasant Society: A Reader.* Edited by Jack M. Potter, May N. Diaz, and George M. Foster. 2–14. Boston: Little Brown & Co.
Frank, Harry T.
—— 1972 *An Archaeological Companion to the Bible.* London: SCM Press.
Frankel, Rafael
—— 1999 *Wine and Oil Production in Antiquity in Israel and Other Mediterranean Countries.* JSOT/ASOR Monograph Series, no. 10. Sheffield: Sheffield Academic Press.
Free, Joseph P.
—— 1958 "The Fifth Season at Dothan." *Bulletin of the American Schools of Oriental Research* 152:10–18.
—— 1959 "The Sixth Season at Dothan." *Bulletin of the American Schools of Oriental Research* 156:22–29.
—— 1960 "The Seventh Season at Dothan." *Bulletin of the American Schools of Oriental Research* 160:6–15.

Frick, Frank S.
—— 1977 *The City in Ancient Israel.* Chico, Ca.: Scholars Press.
—— 1985 *The Formation of the State in Ancient Israel.* Social World of Biblical Antiquity Series, no. 4; Sheffield: Almond Press.
Fried, Morton
—— 1967 *The Evolution of Political Society.* New York: Random House.
Friedman, Richard
—— 1979/80 "The *Mrzh* Tablet from Ugarit." *Maarav* 2/2:187–206.
Fritz, Volkmar
—— 1996 "Monarchy and Re-urbanization," in *The Origins of the Ancient Israelite States.* Edited by V. Fritz and P. R. Davies. JSOT Supplement, no. 228. 187–95. Sheffield: Sheffield Academic Press.
Gelb, Ignace
—— 1967 "Approaches to the Study of Ancient Society." *Bulletin of the American Schools of Oriental Research* 87:1–8.
Gesenius, Friedrich H., and E. Kautzsch
—— 1910 *Gesenius' Hebrew Grammar.* 2d ed. Oxford: Clarendon Press.
Geus, C. H. J. de
—— 1975 "The Importance of the Archaeological Research into the Palestinian Agricultural Terraces with an Excursus on the Hebrew word *gbi.*" *Palestine Exploration Quarterly* 107:65–74.
Ginzberg, Eli
—— 1932 *Studies in the Economics of the Bible.* Philadelphia: Jewish Publication Society of America.
Gitay, Yehoshua
—— 1991 *Isaiah and His Audience: The Structure and Meaning of Isaiah 1–12.* Assen: Van Gorcum.
Glueck, Nelson
—— 1938 "The First Campaign at Tell el-Kheleifeh (Ezion-Geber)." *Bulletin of the American Schools of Oriental Research* 71:3–18.
—— 1959 *Rivers in the Desert.* New York: Farrar, Straus & Cudahy.
—— 1965 "Ezion-Geber." *Biblical Archaeologist* 28:70–87.
Good, Edwin M.
—— 1966 "Hosea 5:8–6:6: An Alternative to Alt." *Journal of Biblical Literature* 85:273–86.
Gottwald, Norman K.
—— 1999 *The Tribes of Yahweh. A Sociology of the Religion of Liberated Israel, 1250–1050 B.C.E.* Reprint with new preface. Sheffield: Sheffield Academic Press.
—— 1983 "Early Israel and the Canaanite Socioeconomic System," in *Palestine in Transition: The Emergence of Ancient Israel.* Edited by D. N. Freedman and D. F. Graf. The Social World of Biblical Antiquity Series, no. 2. Sheffield: Almond Press.

Grant, Elihu
—— 1939 *'Ain Shems Excavations.* Biblical and Kindred Studies, no. 8. Haverford, Pa.: Haverford College.
Gray, George B.
—— 1912 *A Critical and Exegetical Commentary on Isaiah I–XXXIX.* International Critical Commentary Series. London: Edinburgh.
—— 1913 *A Critical Introduction to the Old Testament.* New York: Charles Scribner's Sons.
Gray, John
—— 1970 *I & II Kings.* 2d ed. Philadelphia: Westminster Press.
Grayson, Albert K.
—— 1972 *Assyrian Royal Inscriptions.* Vol. 1; Vol. 2 (1976). Wiesbaden: Harrassowitz.
—— 1975 *Assyrian and Babylonian Chronicles. Texts from Cuneiform Sources.* Locust Valley, N.Y.: J. J. Augustin.
—— 1976 "Studies in Neo-Assyrian History." *Bibliotheca Orientalis* 33:134–45.
Hadley, Judith
—— 1987 "The Khirbet el-Qom Inscription." *Vetus Testamentum* 37:5–62.
—— 1993 "Kuntillet 'Ajrud: Religious Center or Desert Way Station?" *Palestine Exploration Quarterly* 125:115–24.
Hallo, William W.
—— 1964 "From Qarqar to Carchemish: Assyria and Israel in the Light of New Discoveries," in *Biblical Archaeologist Reader 2.* Edited by Edward F. Campbell, Jr., and David Noel Freedman. 152–88. Garden City, N.Y.: Doubleday.
—— 1977 "New Moons and Sabbaths. A Case Study in the Contrastive Approach." *Hebrew Union College Annual* 48:1–17.
Hallo, William W., and William K. Simpson
—— 1998 *The Ancient Near East: A History.* 2d ed. New York: Harcourt, Brace & Jovanovich.
Halpern, Baruch
—— 1979/80 "A Landlord-Tenant Dispute at Ugarit." *Maarav* 2/1:121–40.
Haran, Menahem
—— 1967 "The Rise and Decline of the Empire of Jeroboam ben Joash." *Vetus Testamentum* 17:266–97.
—— 1968 "Observations on the Historical Background of Amos 1:2–2:6." *Israel Exploration Journal* 18:201–12.
Harper, William R.
—— 1905 *A Critical and Exegetical Commentary on Amos and Hosea.* International Critical Commentary Series. New York: Charles Scribner.

Harris, Marvin
—— 1968 *The Rise of Anthropological Theory: A History of Theories of Culture.* New York: Crowell.
—— 1979 *Cultural Materialism: The Struggle for a Science of Culture.* New York: Random House.
Hauer, Christian E.
—— 1981 "The Economics of National Security in Solomonic Israel." *Journal for the Study of Old Testament* 18:63–73.
Hayes, John H.
—— 1988 *Amos: The Eighth Century Prophet: His Time and His Preaching.* Nashville: Abingdon Press.
Hayes, John H., and Stuart Irvine
—— 1987 *Isaiah: The Eighth Century Prophet: His Time and His Preaching.* Nashville: Abingdon Press.
Hayes, John H., and J. Maxwell Miller, eds.
—— 1977 *Israelite and Judean History.* Philadelphia: Westminster Press.
Heaton, E. W.
—— 1968 *The Hebrew Kingdoms.* London: Oxford University Press.
Heilbroner, Robert L., and Lester C. Thurow
—— 1978 *The Economic Problem.* 5th ed. Englewood Cliffs, N.J.: Prentice-Hall.
Heltzer, Michael
—— 1976 *The Rural Community in Ancient Ugarit.* Wiesbaden: Reichert.
Henrey, K. H.
—— 1954 "Land Tenure in the Old Testament." *Palestine Exploration Quarterly* 86:5–15.
Hermann, Sigfried
—— 1975 *A History of Israel in Old Testament Times.* 2d ed. Philadelphia: Fortress Press.
Hillers, Delbert R.
—— 1984 *Micah: A Commentary on the Book of the Prophet Micah.* Hermeneia Series. Philadelphia: Fortress Press.
Hobsbawm, Eric. J., ed.
—— 1981 *Peasants in History: Essays in Honor of Daniel Thorner.* London: Oxford University Press.
Hoenig, Sidney, B.
—— 1979 "Tarshish." *Jewish Quarterly Review* 69:181–82.
Holladay, John S., Jr.
—— 1995 "The Kingdoms of Israel and Judah: Political and Economic Centralization in the Iron IIA-B (ca. 1000–750 BCE)," in *The Archaeology of Society in the Holy Land.* Edited by Thomas E. Levy. 368–98. New York: Facts on File Books.

Holladay, William. L.
—— 1987 *Isaiah: Scroll of a Prophetic Heritage*. Reprint of 1978. New York: Pilgrim Press.
Hopkins, David C.
—— 1985 *The Highlands of Canaan*. The Social World of Biblical Antiquity Series, no. 3. Sheffield: Almond Press.
—— 1996 "Bare Bones: Putting Flesh on the Economics of Ancient Israel," in *The Origins of the Ancient Israelite States*. Edited by V. Fritz and P. R. Davies. 121–39. JSOT Supplement Series, no. 228. Sheffield: Sheffield Academic Press.
Ikeda, Yutaka
—— 1982 "Solomon's Trade in Horses and Chariots in International Setting," in *Studies in the Period of David and Solomon and Other Essays*. Edited by T. Ishida. 215–38. Winona Lake, Ind.: Eisenbrauns.
Irwin, William H.
—— 1977 *Isaiah 28–33. Translation with Philological Notes*. Biblica et Orientalia 30. Rome: Pontifical Biblical Institute Press.
Ishida, Tomoo
—— 1977 *The Royal Dynasties in Ancient Israel*. Berlin: W. deGruyter.
Jaher, Frederic C., ed.
—— 1973 *The Rich, the Well-Born and the Powerful. Elites and Upper Classes in History*. Urbana: University of Illinois Press.
James, Frances W.
—— 1966 *The Iron Age at Beth-Shan*. Philadelphia: University of Pennsylvania.
Jensen, Joseph
—— 1981 "Weal and Woe in Isaiah: Consistency and Continuity." *Catholic Biblical Quarterly* 43:167–87.
Jeppesen, Knud
—— 1978 "New Aspects of Micah Research." *Journal for the Study of Old Testament* 8:3–32.
—— 1979 "How the Book of Micah Lost its Integrity: Outline of the History of Criticism of the Book of Micah with Emphasis on the Nineteenth Century." *Studia Theologica* 33:101–31.
Jeremias, Jörg
—— 1998 *Book of Amos: A Commentary*. Old Testament Library. Louisville, Ky.: Westminster John Knox Press.
Johnstone, William
—— 1969 "Old Testament Expressions in Property Holding." *Ugaritica* 6:308–17.
Kaiser, Otto
—— 1972 *Isaiah*. Vol. 1. *Isaiah 1–12*. Old Testament Library. Philadelphia: Westminster Press.

—— 1974 *Isaiah.* Vol. 2. *Isaiah 13–39.* Old Testament Library. Philadelphia: Westminster Press.

—— 1975 *Introduction to the Old Testament.* Translated by John Sturdy. Minneapolis: Augsburg.

Kapelrud, Arvid S.

—— 1961 "Eschatology in the Book of Micah." *Vetus Testamentum* 11:392–405.

Katzenstein, H. Jacob

—— 1973 *The History of Tyre, from the Beginning of the Second Millennium BCE until the fall of the Neo-Babylonian Empire in 538 BCE.* Jerusalem: The Schoecken Institute for Jewish Research, Jewish Theological Seminary of America.

Kelso, James L., and John P. Thorley

—— 1943 "The Potter's Technique at Tell Beit Mirsim," in *The Excavation of Tell Beit Mirsim.* Vol. 3. *The Iron Age.* 86–142. *Annual of the American Schools of Oriental Research,* vols. 21–22. New Haven: American Schools of Oriental Research.

Kenyon, Kathleen M.

—— 1971 *Royal Cities of the Old Testament.* London: Barrie & Jenkins.

—— 1978 *The Bible and Recent Archaeology.* Atlanta: John Knox Press.

—— 1979 *Archaeology of the Holy Land.* 4th ed. New York: W. W. Norton.

Kimbrough, S. T.

—— 1978 *Israelite Religion in Sociological Perspective: The Work of Antonin Causse.* Studies in Oriental Religions, no. 4. Wiesbaden: Harrossowitz.

King, Philip J.

—— 1988 *Amos, Hosea, Micah: An Archaeological Commentary.* Philadelphia: Westminster Press.

Kitchen, Kenneth A.

—— 1973 *The Third Intermediate Period in Egypt (1100–650 BC).* Warminster: Aris & Phillips.

Klat, Paul J.

—— 1957 "*Musha'a* Holdings and Land Fragmentation in Syria." *Middle East Economic Papers,* vol. 4, 12–23. Lebanon: Economic Research Institute, The American University of Beirut.

Klein, Ralph W.

—— 1969 "Jeroboam's Rise to Power." *Journal of Biblical Literature* 89:217–18.

Knight, George A. F.

—— 1960 *Hosea. Introduction and Commentary.* London: SCM Press.

Koch, Klaus

—— 1982 *The Prophets.* Vol. 1. *The Assyrian Period.* Translated by M. Kohl. Philadelphia: Fortress Press.

Köhler, Ludwig
——— 1956 *The Hebrew Man*. London: SCM Press.
Köhler, Ludwig, and Walter Baumgartner
——— 1951 *Lexicon in Veteris Testamenti Libros*. Leiden: E.J. Brill.
LaBarre, Weston
——— 1970 *Ghost Dance; Origins of Religion*. 1st ed. Garden City, N.Y.: Doubleday.
LaBianca, Øystein S., and Randall W. Younker
——— 1995 "The Kingdoms of Ammon, Moab and Edom: The Archaeology of Society in Late Bronze/Iron Age Transjordan (Ca. 1400–500 BCE)," in *The Archaeology of Society in the Holy Land*. Edited by Thomas E. Levy. 399–415. New York: Facts on File Books.
Lambton, Ann K. S.
——— 1953 *Landlord and Peasant in Persia: A Study of Land Tenure and Land Revenue Administration*. London: Oxford University Press.
Lamon, Robert S., and Geoffrey M. Shipton
——— 1939 *Megiddo I. Seasons of 1925–1934*. Oriental Institute Publications, no. 42. Chicago: University of Chicago Press.
Lance, H. Darrell
——— 1971 "The Royal Stamps and the Kingdom of Josiah." *Harvard Theological Review* 64:315–32.
Landsberger, Henry A.
——— 1974 *Rural Protest: Peasant Movements and Social Change*. London: Macmillan.
Landy, Francis
——— 1995 *Hosea*. Readings, A New Biblical Commentary. Sheffield: Sheffield Academic Books.
Lang, Bernhard
——— 1982 "The Social Organization of Peasant Poverty in Biblical Israel." *Journal for the Study of Old Testament* 24:47–63.
Lapp, Paul
——— 1960 "Late Royal Seals from Judah." *Bulletin of the American Schools of Oriental Research* 158:11–22.
——— 1967 "The Conquest of Palestine in the Light of Archaeology." *Concordia Theological Monthly* 38:283–300.
Lemche, N. Peter
——— 1985 *Early Israel: Anthropological and Historical Studies on the Israelite Society*. Leiden: Brill.
Lenski, Gerhard E.
——— 1966 *Power and Privilege: A Theory of Social Stratification*. New York: McGraw-Hill.
——— 1976 "History and Social Change." *American Journal of Sociology* 82:548–64.

Lenski, Gerhard E., and Jean Lenski
—— 1974 *Human Societies: An Introduction to Macrosociology*. 2d ed. New York: McGraw-Hill.

Lescow, Theodor
—— 1972 "Redaktionsgeschichteliche Analyse von Micha 1–7." *Zeitschrift für die Alttestamentliche Wissenschaft* 85:315–31.

Liddell, Henry G. and Robert Scott
—— 1940 *A Greek-English Lexicon.* Oxford: Clarendon Press.

Limburg, James
—— 1988 *Hosea–Micah*. Interpretation, A Bible Commentary for Teaching and Preaching. Atlanta: John Knox Press.

Lindblom, Johannes
—— 1962 *Prophecy in Ancient Israel*. Philadelphia: Fortress Press.

Lohfink, Norbert
—— 1981 "Hosea 9:5 als Bezugstext von Dtn. 17:16." *Vetus Testamentum* 31:226–28.

Lundblom, Jack
—— 1979 "Poetic Structure and Prophetic Rhetoric in Hosea." *Vetus Testamentum* 29:300–308.

Mackintosh, A. A.
—— 1997 *A Critical and Exegetical Commentary on Hosea*. The New International Critical Commentary. Edinburgh: T & T Clark.

Maddin, Robert, James D. Muhly, and Thomas S. Wheeler
—— 1978 "How the Iron Age Began." *Scientific American* 237:122–31.

Maisler (Mazar), Benjamin
—— 1950/51a "The Excavations at Tell Qasileh." *Israel Exploration Journal* 1/No.2:61–76.
—— 1950/51b "The Excavations at Tell Qasileh." *Israel Exploration Journal* 1/No.4:194–218.

Malchow, Bruce
—— 1980 "The Rural Prophet: Micah." *Currents in Theology and Mission* 7:48–52.

Malina, Bruce
—— 1982 "The Social Sciences and Biblical Interpretation." *Interpretation* 37:229–42.

Marfoe, Leon
—— 1978 "Between Qadesh and Kumidi: A History of Frontier Settlement and Land Use in the Biqa' Lebanon." Ph.D. diss., University of Chicago.

Margalit, Baruch
—— 1979/80 "The Ugaritic Feast of the Drunken Gods: Another Look at Ras Shamra 24.258 (KTU 1.114)." *Maarav* 2/1:65–120.

Marmorstein, Emile
—— 1953 "The Origins of Agricultural Feudalism in the Holy Land."
Palestine Exploration Quarterly 85:111–17.
Marsh, John
—— 1959 Amos and Micah: *Introduction and Commentary*. London:
SCM Press.
Mays, James L.
—— 1969a *Amos: A Commentary*. Old Testament Library. Philadelphia:
Westminster Press.
—— 1969b *Hosea: A Commentary*. Old Testament Library. Philadelphia:
Westminster Press.
—— 1976 *Micah: A Commentary*. Old Testament Library. Philadelphia:
Westminster Press.
Mazar, Benjamin
—— 1964 "The Aramean Empire and the Relation with Israel," in *The
Biblical Archaeologist Reader 2*. Edited by Edward F. Campbell, Jr.,
and David Noel Freedman. 127–51. Garden City, N.Y.: Doubleday.
Mazar, Benjamin, Avraham Biran, Trude Dothan, and I. Dunayevsky
—— 1964 "'Ein-Gev." *Israel Exploration Journal* 14:1–49.
Mazar, Benjamin, Trude Dothan, and I. Dunayevsky
—— 1966 "En-Gedi: The First and Second Seasons of Excavations
1961–62." *'Atiqot* 5:1–100.
McClellan, Thomas L.
—— 1978 "Towns to Fortresses: The Transformation of Urban Life in
Judah from the Eighth Century to Seventh Century BCE." *Society of
Biblical Literature Seminar Papers* 13:277–86.
McCown, Chester C.
—— 1947 *Tell en-Nasbeh*. Excavations under the direction of William
Badè. Vol. 1. Berkeley/New Haven: The Palestine Institute of the
Pacific School of Religion and the American Schools of Oriental
Research.
McKeating, Henry
—— 1971 *The Books of Amos, Hosea and Micah*. The Cambridge Bible
Commentary. London: Cambridge University Press.
McNutt, Paula M.
—— 1999 *Reconstructing the Society of Ancient Israel*. Library of Ancient
Israel. London/Louisville, Ky.: SPCK/Westminster John Knox
Press.
Melugin, Roy F.
—— 1978 "The Formation of Amos: an Analysis of Exegetical
Method." *Society of Biblical Studies Seminar Papers* 13:369–91.
Mendenhall, George E.
—— 1962 "The Hebrew Conquest of Palestine." *Biblical Archaeologist*
25:66–87.

Meshel, Zeev
—— 1978 *Kuntillet 'Ajrud. A Religious Center from the Time of the Judean Monarchy on the Border of Sinai.* The Israel Museum Catalog, no. 175. Jerusalem: Israel Museum.
—— 1992 "Kuntillet 'Ajrud," in *Anchor Bible Dictionary.* Edited by David Noel Freedman. Vol. 4, 103–9. New York: Doubleday.

Milgrom, Jacob
—— 1964 "Did Isaiah prophesy during the reign of Uzziah?" *Vetus Testamentum* 14:164–82

Miller, Patrick D.
—— 1971 "The *Mrzh* Text," in *The Claremont Ras Shamra Tablets.* Edited by Loren Fisher, 37–50. Rome: Pontifical Biblical Institute.

Moore, Barrington
—— 1966 *Social Origins of Dictatorship and Democracy. Lord and Peasant in the Making of the Modern World.* Boston: Beacon Press.

Moran, William
—— 1967 "The Conclusion of the Decalogue (Ex 20:17–Dt 5:21)." *Catholic Biblical Quarterly* 29:543–54.

Moscati, Sabatino
—— 1968 *The World of the Phoenicians.* Translated by A. Hamilton. London: Weidenfeld & Nicolson.

Na'aman, Nadav
—— 1979 "Sennacherib's Campaign to Judah and the Date of the *lmlk* Stamps." *Vetus Testamentum* 29:61–86.

Nash, Manning
—— 1967 "The Organization of Economic Life," in *Tribal and Peasant Economies.* Edited by G. Dalton. 3–11. New York: The Natural History Press.

Neufeld, Edward
—— 1955 "The Prohibitions against Loans at Interest in Ancient Hebrew Laws." *Hebrew Union College Annual* 26:355–412.
—— 1960 "The Emergence of a Royal-Urban Society in Ancient Israel." *Hebrew Union College Annual* 31:31–53.
—— 1962 "The Inalienability of Mobile and Immobile Pledges in the Laws of the Bible." *Revue Internationale de Droits de l'Antiquité,* 3d series. 9:33–44.

Niditch, Susan
—— 1980 "The Composition of Isaiah 1." *Biblica* 61:509–29.

North, Christopher R.
—— 1954 *Sociology of Biblical Jubilee.* Rome: Pontifical Biblical Institute.

Noth, Martin
—— 1960 *The History of Israel.* 2d ed. Translated by Peter Ackroyd. New York: Harper & Row.

Oded, Bustanay
—— 1972 "The Historical Background of the Syro-Ephraimite War Reconsidered." *Catholic Biblical Quarterly* 34:153–65.
—— 1979a "Neighbors on the West," in *The Age of Monarchies: Political History*. Edited by A. Malamat. Vol. 4:1, 222–46, of *The World History of the Jewish People*, edited by B. Mazar. Jerusalem: Masada Press.
—— 1979b "Neighbors on the East," in *The Age of Monarchies: Political History*. Edited by A. Malamat. Vol. 4:1, 247–75, of *The World History of the Jewish People*, edited by B. Mazar. Jerusalem: Masada Press.

Offord, J.
—— 1918 "Archaeological Notes on Jewish Antiquities: Land Ownership in Ancient Palestine and Egypt and the Jubilee Year." *Palestine Exploration Quarterly* 50:37–39.

Oppenheim, A. Leo
—— 1957 "A Bird's Eye View of Mesopotamian Economic History," in *Trade and Market in the Early Empires*. Edited by K. Polanyi, C. M. Arsenberg, and H. W. Pearson. 27–37. Glencoe, Ill.: The Free Press.

Paige, Jeffrey M.
—— 1978 *Agrarian Revolution: Social Movements and Export Agriculture in the Underdeveloped World*. New York: The Free Press.

Pardee, Dennis
—— 1978 "The Judicial Plea from Mesad Hashavyahu (Yabneh Yam): A New Philological Study." *Maarav* 1/1:33–66.

Parsons, Kenneth H.
—— 1956 "Land Reform and Agricultural Development," in *Land Tenure*. Proceedings of the International Conference on Land Tenure and Related Problems in World Agriculture, 1951. Edited by K. H. Parsons, R. J. Penn, and P. M. Raup. 3–22. Madison, Wis.: University of Wisconsin Press.

Parsons, Talcott
—— 1977 *The Evolution of Societies*. Edited by J. Toby. Foundations of Modern Sociology Series. Englewood Cliffs: Prentice-Hall.

Paul, Shalom
—— 1978 "Amos 3:15. Winter and Summer Mansions." *Vetus Testamentum* 28:358–60.
—— 1991 *Amos: A Commentary on the Book of Amos*. Hermeneia Series. Philadelphia: Fortress Press.

Paul, Shalom, and William G. Dever
—— 1974 *Biblical Archaeology*. New York: Quadrangle/New York Times Book Co.

Peckham, Brian
—— 1976 "Israel and Phoenicia," In *Magnalia Dei: The Mighty Acts of God. Essays on the Bible and Archaeology in Memory of G. E. Wright.* Edited by F. M. Cross, W. E. Lemke, and P. D. Miller, Jr. 224–48. Garden City, N.Y.: Doubleday.
Pope, Marvin
—— 1972 "A Divine Banquet in Ugarit," in *The Use of the Old Testament in the New and Other Essays.* Edited by James Efird. 170–203. Durham, N.C.: Duke University Press.
—— 1977 "Notes on the *Rephaim* Texts from Ugarit," in *Essays on The Ancient Near East.* Edited by Maria deJong Ellis. 164–66. Memoirs of the Connecticut Academy of Arts and Sciences, vol. 19. Hamden, Conn.: Archon Books.
Pritchard, James B.
—— 1962 *Gibeon: Where the Sun Stood Still.* Princeton: Princeton University Press.
—— 1964 *Winery, Defenses and Soundings at Gibeon.* Philadelphia: University of Pennsylvania.
—— 1969 *Ancient Near Eastern Texts.* 3d ed. Princeton: Princeton University Press.
Rainey, Anson F.
—— 1962 "Administration in Ugarit and the Samaria Ostraca." *Israel Exploration Journal* 12:62–63.
—— 1965 "Royal Weights and Measures." *Bulletin of the American Schools of Oriental Research* 179:34–36.
—— 1967 "The Samaria Ostraca in the Light of Fresh Evidence." *Palestine Exploration Quarterly* 99:32–41.
—— 1979 "The *Sitz im Leben* of the Samaria Ostraca." *Tel Aviv* 6:91–94.
—— 1982 "Wine from Royal Vineyards." *Bulletin of the American Schools of Oriental Research* 245:57–62.
—— 1988 "Toward a Precise Date for the Samaria Ostraca." *Bulletin of the American Schools of Oriental Research* 272:69–74.
Redfield, Robert
—— 1955 *The Little Community and Peasant Society and Culture.* Chicago: University of Chicago Press.
Reisner, George A., Clarence S. Fisher, and David G. Lyon
—— 1924 *Harvard Excavations at Samaria.* Cambridge, Mass.: Harvard University Press.
Renfrew, Colin
—— 1974 "Beyond Subsistence Economy: The Evolution of Social Organization in Prehistoric Europe," in *Reconstructing Complex Societies.* Edited by Charlotte Moore. 69–85. Cambridge, Mass.: American Schools of Oriental Research.

Roberts, J. J. M.
——— 1973 "The Davidic Origin of the Zion Tradition." *Journal of Biblical Literature* 92:329–44.
Rodd, Cyril
——— 1981 "On Applying Sociological Theory to Biblical Studies." *Journal for the Study of Old Testament* 19:95–106.
Rosen, Baruch, and Israel Finkelstein
——— 1992 "Subsistence Patterns, Carrying Capacity and Settlement Oscillations in the Negev." *Palestine Exploration Quarterly* 124:42–58.
Rothenberg, Beno
——— 1962 "Ancient Copper Industries in the Western 'Arabah." *Palestine Exploration Quarterly* 94:5–71.
——— 1975 "Metals and Metallurgy," in *Investigations at Lachish (Lachish V)*. Edited by Y. Aharoni. 72–83. Tel Aviv: Gateway.
Sahlins, Marshall D.
———1968 *Tribesmen*. Foundations of Modern Anthropology Series. Englewood Cliffs: Prentice-Hall.
Ste. Croix, Geoffrey Ernest Maurice de
——— 1981 *Class Struggle in the Ancient Greek World. From the Archaic Age to the Arab Conquests*. Ithaca, N.Y.: Cornell University Press.
Schaeffer, C. F. A., and J. Nougayrol, eds.
——— 1955 *Le Palais Royal d'Ugarit*, Vol. 3. Paris: Impr. nationale.
——— 1956 *Le Palais Royal d'Ugarit*, Vol 4. Paris: Impr. nationale.
Schaeffer, Henry
——— 1922 *The Hebrew Tribal Economy and the Jubilee as Illustrated in the Semitic and Indo-European Village Communities*. New York: G. E. Stechert.
Scott, Robert B. Y.
——— 1970 "Weights and Measures of the Bible," in *The Biblical Archaeologist Reader* 3. Edited by Edward F. Campbell, Jr., and David Noel Freedman. 345–58. Garden City, N.Y.: Doubleday.
Seitz, Christopher R.
——— 1993 *Isaiah 1–39*. Interpretation, A Bible Commentary for Teaching and Preaching. Louisville, Ky.: John Knox Press.
Service, Elman R.
——— 1975 *Origins of the State and Civilization: The Process of Cultural Evolution*. New York: Norton.
Shanin, Teodor
——— 1971 "Peasantry as Political Factor," in *Peasants and Peasant Studies*. Edited by Teodor Shanin. 238–63. New York: Basil Blackwell.
——— 1987a "Introduction," in *Peasants and Peasant Studies*, 2d ed. Edited by Teodor Shanin, 1–11. New York: Basil Blackwell.

—— 1987b "Short Historical Outline of Peasant Studies," in *Peasants and Peasant Studies*. 2d ed. Edited by Teodor Shanin. 467–75. New York: Basil Blackwell.

Shaw, Charles S.
—— 1993 *The Speeches of Micah: A Rhetorical-Historical Analysis*. JSOT Supplement, no. 145. Sheffield: JSOT Press.

Shea, William H.
—— 1977 "The Date and Significance of the Samaria Ostraca." *Israel Exploration Journal* 27:16–27.

Shiloh, Yigal
—— 1979 *The Proto-Aeolic Capital and Israelite Ashlar Masonry*. Qedem Series, no. 11. Jerusalem: Institute of Archaeology, Hebrew University.
—— 1980 "The Population of Iron Age Palestine in the Light of a Sample Analysis of Urban Plans, Areas, and Population Density." *Bulletin of the American Schools of Oriental Research* 239:25–35.

Silver, Morris
—— 1983 *Prophets and Markets*. Boston/The Hague/London: Kluwer-Nijhoff.

Sjoberg, Gideon
—— 1960 *The Pre-Industrial Society: Past and Present*. New York: Free Press.

Skinner, John
—— 1915 *The Book of the Prophet Isaiah I–XXXIX*. Vol. I, Revised ed. London: Cambridge University Press.

Smelser, Neil. J.
—— 1967 "Toward A Theory of Modernization," in *Tribal and Peasant Economies*. Edited by G. Dalton. 29–48. New York: The Natural History Press.

Smilianskaya, I. M.
—— 1966 "From Subsistence to Market Economy," in *The Economic History of the Middle East*. Edited by Charles Issawi. 226–47. Chicago: University of Chicago Press.

Smith, G. A.
—— 1908 *The Book of Isaiah*. 2 vols. New York: A. C. Armstrong & Sons.
—— 1929 *The Book of the Twelve Prophets*. New York: Doubleday.

Smith, John M. P., William H. Ward, and Julius A. Bewer
—— 1911 *A Critical and Exegetical Commentary on Micah, Zephaniah, Nahum, Habakkuk, Obadiah and Joel*. International Critical Commentary Series. New York: Charles Scribner's Sons.

Smith, Ralph L.
—— 1984 *Micah–Malachi*. Word Bible Commentary Series, vol. 32. Waco, Tex.: Word Books.

Snaith, Norman H.
—— 1956 *Amos, Hosea and Micah.* Epworth Preacher's Commentaries. London: Epworth Press.
—— 1958 *The Book of Amos.* London: Epworth Press.
Soggin, Alberto
—— 1987 *The Prophet Amos.* Translated by John Bowden. London: SCM Press.
Speiser, Ephraim A.
—— 1940 "Of Shoes and Sheckels." *Bulletin of the American Schools of Oriental Research* 77:15–20.
Stade, Bernhard
—— 1881 "Bemerkungen über das Buch Micha." *Zeitschrift für die Alttestamentliche Wissenschaft* 1:161–72.
Stager, Lawrence E.
—— 1976 "Farming in the Judean Desert during the Iron Age." *Bulletin of the American Schools of Oriental Research* 221:145–58.
Stansell, Gary
—— 1988 *Micah and Isaiah: A Form and Tradition Historical Comparison.* Atlanta: Scholars Press.
Stavenhagen, Rodolfo
—— 1975 *Social Classes in Agrarian Societies.* Translated by Judy Hellman. New York: Anchor Press.
Stech-Wheeler, T., J. D. Muhly, D. R. Maxwell-Hyslop, and R. Maddin
—— 1981 "Iron at Taanach and Early Iron Metallurgy in the Eastern Mediterranean." *American Journal of Archaeology* 85:245–68.
Stern, Ephraim
—— 1975 "Israel at the Close of the Period of the Monarchy: An Archaeological Survey." *Biblical Archaeologist* 38:26–54.
—— 1979 "Craft and Industry." In *The Age of Monarchies: Culture and Society.* Edited by A. Malamat. Vol. 4:2, 237–64, of *The World History of the Jewish People,* edited by B. Mazar. Jerusalem: Masada Press.
—— 1993 Ed. *The New Encyclopedia of Archaeological Excavations in the Holy Land.* Vols. 1–4. Jerusalem: Israel Exploration Society.
Stuart, Douglas
—— 1987 *Hosea–Jonah.* Word Bible Commentary Series, vol. 31. Waco, Tex.: Word Books.
Sweeney, Marvin
—— 1996 *Isaiah 1–39: With an Introduction to Prophetic Literature.* Grand Rapids, Mich.: William B. Eerdmans.
Tadmor, Hayim
—— 1975 "Assyria and the West: The Ninth Century and Its Aftermath," in *Unity and Diversity.* Edited by H. Goedicke and J. J. M. Roberts. 36–48. Baltimore: Johns Hopkins Press.

Torczyner, Harry
—— 1936 "Presidential Address." *Journal of Palestine Society* 16:6–7.
Tsirkin, Yu B.
—— 1979 "Economy of the Phoenician Settlements in Spain," in *State and Temple Economy in the Ancient Near East.* Edited by Edward Lipinski. Vol. 2, 547–64. Leuven: Departement Oriëntalistiesk.
Tufnell, Olga
—— 1953 *Lachish III (The Iron Age).* London: Oxford University Press.
Ussishkin, David
—— 1976 "Royal Judean Storage Jars and Private Seal Impressions." *Bulletin of the American Schools of Oriental Research* 223:1–13.
—— 1977 "The Destruction of Lachish by Sennacherib and the Dating of the Royal Judean Storage Jars." *Tel Aviv* 4:28–57.
—— 1978 "Excavations at Tel Lachish, 1973–1977." *Tel Aviv* 5:1–97.
—— 1980 "Was the 'Solomonic' city gate at Megiddo built by King Solomon?" *Bulletin of the American Schools of Oriental Research* 239:1–18.
Van Zyl, A. H.
—— 1960 *The Moabites.* Leiden: Brill.
Vaux, Roland de
—— 1956 "The Excavations at Tell el-Farah (North) and the Site of Ancient Tirzah." *Palestine Exploration Quarterly* 88:125–40.
—— 1965 *Ancient Israel. Its Life and Institutions.* Translated by John McHugh. New York: McGraw-Hill.
Veblen, Thorstein
—— 1912 *The Theory of the Leisure Class. An Economic Study of Institutions.* New York: Macmillan.
Virolleaud, Charles
—— 1947 "Six textes de Ras Shamra provenant de la 14me campagne (1950)." *Syria* 28:163–79.
—— 1968 "Les nouveaux textes mythologiques et liturgiques de Ras Shamra." *Ugaritica* 5: 545–51.
Waldow, H. E. von
—— 1970 "Social Responsibility and Social Structure in Early Israel." *Catholic Biblical Quarterly* 32:182–204.
Ward, James M.
—— 1966 *Hosea: A Theological Commentary.* New York: Harper & Row.
—— 1969 *Amos and Isaiah: Prophets of the Word of God.* Nashville: Abingdon Press.
Watts, John D. W.
—— 1985 *Isaiah 1–33.* Word Bible Commentary, vol. 24. Waco, Tex.: Word Books.
Weber, Max
—— 1998 *The Agrarian Sociology of Ancient Civilizations.* Translated by R. I. Frank. Atlantic Highlands, N.J.: Humanities Press.

Weippert, Manfred

—— 1971 *The Settlement of the Israelite Tribes in Palestine: A Critical Survey of Recent Scholarly Debate.* Studies in Biblical Theology, no. 21. Naperville, Ill.: Alec R. Allenson.

Wellhausen, Julius

—— 1963 *Die Kleinen Propheten.* Berlin: W. de Gruyter.

Wildberger, Hans

—— 1978 *Jesaja 13–39.* Biblischer Kommentar Altes Testament. Neukirchen-Vluyn: Neukirchner Verlag.

—— 1991 *Isaiah: A Commentary.* 2 vols. Translated by Thomas H. Trapp. Minneapolis: Fortress Press.

Williams, James G.

—— 1969 "The Social Location of Israelite Prophecy." *Journal of the American Academy of Religion* 37:153–65.

Willis, John T.

—— 1969 "The Structure of Micah 3–5 and the Function of Micah 5:9–14 in the Book." *Zeitschrift für die Alttestamentliche Wissenschaft* 81:191–214.

—— 1980 *Isaiah.* The Living Word Commentary on the Old Testament. Austin, Tex.: Sweet.

Wilner, Eleanor

—— 1975 *Gathering the Winds: Visionary Imagination and Radical Transformation of Self and Society.* Baltimore: Johns Hopkins University Press.

Wilson, Robert R.

—— 1980 *Prophecy and Society in Ancient Israel.* Philadelphia: Fortress Press.

Wolf, Eric R.

—— 1966 *Peasants.* Foundations of Modern Anthropology Series. Englewood Cliffs, N.J.: Prentice-Hall.

—— 1969 *Peasant Wars of the Twentieth Century.* New York: Harper & Row.

Wolfe, Rolland E.

—— 1956 "The Book of Micah. Introduction and Exegesis," in *Interpreter's Bible.* Edited by G. A. Buttrick, Vol. 6, 897–949. Nashville: Abingdon Press.

Wolff, Hans W.

—— 1973 *Amos the Prophet.* Philadelphia: Fortress Press.

—— 1974 *Hosea.* Hermeneia Series. Philadelphia: Fortress Press.

—— 1977 *Joel and Amos.* Hermeneia Series. Philadelphia: Fortress Press.

—— 1981 *Micah the Prophet.* Philadelphia: Fortress Press.

—— 1990 *Micah: A Commentary.* Translated by Gary Stansell. Minneapolis: Augsburg Press.

Wright, G. Ernest
—— 1946 "The Literary and Historical Problem of Joshua 10 and Judges 1." *Journal of Near Eastern Studies* 5:105–14.
—— 1958 "The Provinces of Solomon." *Eretz Israel* 8:58–68.
—— 1962 *Biblical Archaeology.* Revised edition. Philadelphia: Westminster.
—— 1965 *Shechem: The Biography of a Biblical City.* New York: McGraw-Hill.
Yadin, Yigael
—— 1958 "Solomon's City Wall and Gate at Gezer." *Israel Exploration Journal* 8:80–86.
—— 1959 "Recipients or Owners: A Note on the Samaria Ostraca." *Israel Exploration Journal* 9:184–87.
—— 1961 "Ancient Judean Weights and the Date of the Samaria Ostraca." *Scripta Hierosolymitana* 8:9–25.
—— 1962 "A Further Note on the Samaria Ostraca." *Israel Exploration Journal* 12:64–66.
—— 1968 "A Further Note on the *Lamed* in the Samaria Ostraca." *Israel Exploration Journal* 18:50–51.
—— 1969 "The Fifth Season of Excavations at Hazor." *Biblical Archaeologist* 32/3:50–71.
—— 1970 "Megiddo of the Kings of Israel." *Biblical Archaeologist* 33/3:66–96.
—— 1972 *Hazor.* London: Oxford University Press.
Yadin, Yigael., Y. Aharoni, R. Amiran, and I. Dunayevski
—— 1989 *Hazor III.* Jerusalem: Hebrew University and Magna Press.
Yee, Gale E.
—— 1983 "The Form-Critical Study of Is. 5:1–7 as a Song and Juridical Parable." *Catholic Biblical Quarterly* 43:30–40.
Yeivin, Samuel
—— 1979 "The Divided Kingdom: Rehoboam–Ahaz/Jeroboam–Pekah," in *The Age of Monarchies: Political History.* Edited by A. Malamat. Vol. 4:1, 126–78, of *The World History of the Jewish People,* edited by B. Mazar. Jerusalem: Masada Press.
Young, Edward. J.
—— 1965–72 *The Book of Isaiah.* The New International Critical Commentary. Vol. 1: Isaiah 1–18, 1965; Vol. 2: Isaiah 19–39, 1969; Vol. 3: Isaiah 40–66, 1972. Grand Rapids, Mich.: William B. Eerdmans.

Scripture Index

Author Index

Subject Index

T

Trade and commerce 22–23
 eighth century 72–78
 in *Isaiah* 152–58
 under Solomon 33–34
Trade routes
 King's Highway 50–51
 in the Negev 52–56
 Transjordan region 48–51
 Via Maris 46–48

U

Urban centers
 in *Amos* 109–11
 growth of 20–21
 in *Hosea* 122–23
 in *Isaiah* 111–16
 in *Micah* 116–22
 under Solomon 35
Use of surplus
 attire 93
 consumption 91–93
 living quarters 89–91
 pastime 93

W

Wool industry 69–70